MW01092123

Every Hazard and Fatigue

The Siege of Pensacola 1781

Joshua Provan

Helion & Company

Para mi familia, y mi amigos. Yo no Solo.

Helion & Company Limited
Unit 8 Amherst Business Centre
Budbrooke Road
Warwick
CV34 5WE
England
Tel. 01926 499619
Email: info@helion.co.uk
Website: www.helion.co.uk
Twitter: @helionbooks
Visit our blog at http://blog.helion.co.uk/

Published by Helion & Company 2023
Designed and typeset by Mach 3 Solutions (www.mach3solutions.co.uk)
Cover designed by Paul Hewitt, Battlefield Design (www.battlefield-design.co.uk)

Text © Joshua Provan 2023
Cover: Siege of Pensacola, 1781. Original artwork by Christa Hook
(www.christahook.co.uk) © Helion & Company 2023
Illustrations © as individually credited
Maps by George Anderson © Helion & Company 2023

Every reasonable effort has been made to trace copyright holders and to obtain their
permission for the use of copyright material. The author and publisher apologise
for any errors or omissions in this work, and would be grateful if notified of any
corrections that should be incorporated in future reprints or editions of this book.

ISBN 978-1-804513-42-2

British Library Cataloguing-in-Publication Data.
A catalogue record for this book is available from the British Library.

All rights reserved. No part of this publication may be reproduced, stored in a retrieval
system, or transmitted, in any form, or by any means, electronic, mechanical, photocopying,
recording or otherwise, without the express written consent of Helion & Company Limited.

For details of other military history titles published by Helion & Company Limited,
contact the above address, or visit our website: http://www.helion.co.uk

We always welcome receiving book proposals from prospective authors.

Contents

Preface

Standing on the beach on the evening of 9 March 1781, the Governor could see the town in the distance to the northwest, glimpsed across the waters of the bay which had typically taken on their dusk colours against the darkening hues of the land. Behind him and in front of him, the fine white sand of Santa Rosa Island was still luminous beneath his feet. The trace of the tide leaving mirror-like flats of sky on the coral bed, which bled away in shimmering flows of glassy illusion. Here a man might be seen to walk on water, out to where the dark lines of the incoming waves rippled at the join of land and sea. The masts and rigging of a few British warships were the only impediment to the view. The town of Pensacola stood at the verge of the water between two bayous, its long quays stretching far into the *teredo*-worm infested bay, just below a low elevation of ground covered in the furze of tall pine and oak scrubland that dominated the landscape in the coastal regions of West Florida.

Don Bernardo de Gálvez had seen it on maps before, and he had read and re-read the reports of his spies describing it, but this was his first sight of it, low and quite ordinary looking, but the goal of the last two years of organising, marching, arguing and fighting. Above the town on the hill, he could just make out trails of woodsmoke coming from the British fortifications, the town itself with its sandy streets and old defences would fall any time he pleased, but only once the redoubts on the high ground had been taken. Gálvez shifted his gaze from the bay to follow the pale line of the beach to the terminus point of the island, and then across the channel to the pale pink, sandy cliffs, marked on his maps as *Barrancas Coloradas*, that were the principal feature of the western shore. There he could discern the low, dark shape of the enemy earthwork that guarded the entrance to the bay, and though he could not see them, he knew well enough that heavy calibre guns were most certainly pointing in his direction. A light southerly breeze, blowing up from the Gulf of Mexico picked up the British flags from time to time, just to remind him that he had a fight on his hands. The Governor's gaze travelled across the treetops from the cliffs to the spires of the town, he did not care very much for the enemy artillery, the great mass of sails anchored behind him in the lee of the island, filled with troops, some of whom were still disembarking, were ample security, but those dense woods held many dangers. How many warriors were encamped with the British? Hundreds?

Thousands? Of all the dangers in the Americas Bernardo de Gálvez was wary of only two, hurricanes and Indians, and he had good cause to be. Three of the several scars he now carried had been the work of indigenous arrows and spears, and over the course of his arduous but successful campaigns since the war broke out in 1779, his plans had been very much subject to the hand of nature. The Governor looked out to sea, turning his back on the town and its defences, beyond the campfires of the grenadiers and *cazadores*, and beyond the warships from Havana. All was peaceful for now, and he was relieved, for he well knew that no painted war-party in the Americas could do so much damage to his plans as a simple accident of weather.

History is a field that needs constant ploughing. The soil of the American Revolution has been well turned. The repeated blows of the historian's plough have continually cut furrows from which have been raised rich harvests of similar informational crops since the drum beat the parlay over the earthworks of Yorktown almost two and a half centuries ago. These harvests nourish those who are familiar with them and are always fresh to those who have never tasted. Because the ground is so fertile, and because there are dedicated people who are willing to lavish care and toil over it, every now and then a new crop is grown which surprises everyone, but if the field is left to wild, there can be no hope of that fresh seed ever being planted, so it is necessary for new furrows of similar crops to be continually made, even if the crop it raises is not, to use an apt idiom, 'ground-breaking.' Is there any wonder why the subject of scholarly endeavour is called a 'field?'

In large part, this book was written with the intention of keeping the weeds away from the subject of the Spanish in the American Revolution, and though the furrow it creates has been turned before, I trust it has not been so marked in exactly the same way, or indeed, in the in the same place.

Although general histories of the war will mention the Mississippi and the Gulf Coast, many, such as Samuel B. Griffith's, or even excellent popular narrative studies like, Hibbert's, critiques like Bicheno's, and revisions like Harvey's have almost nothing to say about the Spanish and the fighting below Georgia or west of the Alleghenies.[1]

On the other hand, many of the fine works which appeared between the Bicentennial and the Millennium, naturally stress the role of the Spanish, who had been unfairly side-lined in the story of the War of Independence. They hoped to break new ground and reap fresh rewards, but in so doing neglected or gave an overly poor, or for reasons of patriotism, overly exaggerated impression of the British defenders, a trait common in the historiography before the end of the twentieth century. Until recent times, too, it was far from unusual for authors to completely ignore the role of Native American allies or relegate them to the status of footnotes; and worse, the criticisms of contemporaries are sometimes unconditionally accepted as truth.

---

1   See: Samuel B. Griffith II, *The War for American Independence* (Chicago: University of Illinois Press, 2002); Christopher Hibbert, *Rebels and Redcoats: The American Revolution Through British Eyes* (New York: Norton W. W. & Company, 2002); Hugo Bicheno, *Rebels & Redcoats: The American Revolution* (London: Harper Collins, 2003); Robert Harvey, *A Few Bloody Noses: The American Revolutionary War* (London: Constable and Robinson, 2001).

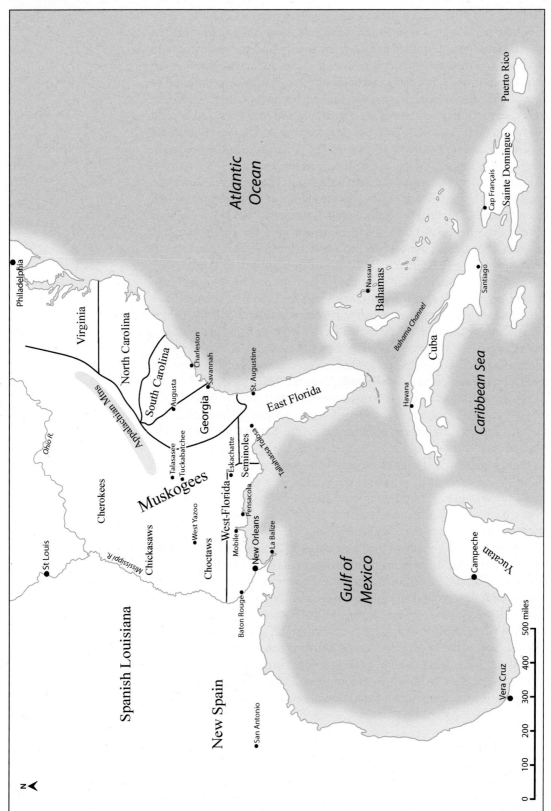

The Gulf and Southern Theatres of the American Revolution.

Since our own world was turned upside down, I have had cause to spend much time with the individuals that fought in Florida, Louisiana, Alabama and Mississippi in 1781, and I humbly direct the reader to the edited collection of Don Hagist, *Waging War in America,* where you will find what might be termed the prologue of the book you know hold in your hand, as the author's chapter covers the Mississippi and Mobile operations and their logistical support in isolation.[2]

---

2   Don, N. Hagist, *Waging War in America, 1775-1783: Operational Challenges of Five Armies* (Warwick: Helion & Company, 2023).

Acknowledgments

Although, due to the challenges of word counts, I did not include my thanks to those who assisted in my last book, the regret I felt in not at least advertising my gratitude to those who have helped me on my way leads me to not repeat the same mistake here.

Family comes first. The support of my family, especially my parents and siblings has been keenly felt throughout this process in the shape of advice, interest and support. *Mi Madre, y mi Hermana* always ensured I kept up with everything and also could be depended on to remind me to relax. *Mi Padre's* enquiries into how the writing was going often allowed me to talk through ideas. *Mi Hermano*, Nathan, especially has my gratitude for undertaking some of the archival research and assisting me in getting around, it is in no small part to you all that this book was written at all.

Exterior to that, my thanks go to Chaz Mena, a renaissance man, transplanted English gentleman and thespian-scholar who, through his performance in the PBS show, *Yo Solo*, lodged the subject firmly in my mind. His knowledge of the subject, irrepressible good humour, generous spirit, and material assistance means that I could, quite literally, not have got along without him.

Second but equal thanks must go to René Chartrand, a friend and fellow author at Helion. René, never failed to brighten a day whenever we talked, and as an experienced author, he was able to offer this poor yeoman much pertinent advice and unrestrained material assistance.

It is to the above I also owe many good laughs along the way.

It is to the auspices of fellow Helion author, and scholar, John Reese, with whom I had the honour to share a virtual podium not too long ago, that I owe the appearance of four paintings of the revered historian and artist, Don Troiani within this book, (who was equally kind and helpful to any question I might put to him) for which I am sure we are all thankful, and I am especially grateful that John thought to get in touch with me about the subject of his forthcoming book on African American soldiers in America.

In the vein of making the acquaintance of artistic and scholarly heroes in the production of this book, I am extremely grateful to have a cover created by Christa Hook, whose art, and that of her father, the late great Richard Hook, has always been an inspiration, I would like to acknowledge the assistance of David Rickman behind the scenes in the research of the finished scene, I also offer my sincere appreciation to the office of Augusto Ferrer Dalmau for being so helpful in arranging for me to use the work of Spain's foremost historical fine artist and to the Museo Ejercito in Toledo for their assistance, and patience with my Spanish. I am similarly grateful to the San Antonio chapter of the Granaderos y Damas de Gálvez for their permission to reproduce some photographs of their unit, and to Dr Robbie MacNiven, I too, offer my thanks for his photographs, friendship and kindly assistance. The Louisiana State Museum also has my gratitude for their assistance with an image of New Orleans.

Thanks, as well go to, Dr Alexander Burns, of the *Kabinettskreige* blog, another podium comrade, who was kind and considerate enough to offer thoughts on sources and helped bridge the gap between the British and the American fields of study. To J. Chapela for help with an order of battle and to Jessica B. Manor, for ideas on sources for the wider Spanish empire, too much of which alas could not be included.

The support of many generous podcasters and creators have been especially valuable to me in spreading the word about this book, and to you all, especially *History Hack*, I offer my heartfelt thanks. If anyone has been left out, especially those who chipped in online to help with research books, it is a matter of space, not of neglect that you are not mentioned. I thank you all.

Finally, to the team at Helion's *From Reason to Revolution* series, especially my editor Rob Griffith, and Commissioning Editor Dr Andrew Bamford, I offer my sincere thanks and respect for striving to publish works of history that do not always include, Romans, Vikings and Nazis, and for giving me my first opportunity to speak in public at the series conference at Derby in 2022.

1

Introduction

Spain had no official position on the independence of the United States, but as the largest imperial power in North and South America, opportunities presented themselves that could not be ignored. However, Spain's leaders entered the war cautiously, ensuring they did so to maximise their own advantage. The principal war aim of the Spanish government in the Americas was the control of the Gulf Coast of the current United States, which by extension would mean gaining the control of the southern reaches of the Mississippi and the navigation of the Bahama Channel, lost to Spain by the treaty of Paris in 1763. Emphasis was placed the reconquest of what was then termed West and East Florida by the Minister of the Indies, José de Gálvez and communicated in the instructions issued to colonial governors, as well as outlining objectives in Europe, the Caribbean and Central America. Many of the objectives targeted former Spanish possessions that had been lost in the Seven Years' War, (and before that in the case of Jamaica,) and creating a basis from which to reassert Spanish monopoly in the Gulf-Caribbean region. Spain, or at least the government in Europe, approached a patriotic war with a cold and business-like appraisal, and they did so, much more slowly and independently than either the Americans or the French liked.

But considering grand schemes to be a fantasy, the likes of Royal Commissioner Francisco de Saavedra succinctly summed up the considerations of the key statesmen of the Spanish empire when he outlined the basic realities of engaging in a conflict from a political and economic point of view. If the king went to war, he was essentially contracting to tax his subjects. The decline in profits for domestic products as opposed to the inevitable rise in foreign products during such a time ensured economic destabilization whether the war was successful or not, and quite apart from the efforts of the enemy. When taxes were inevitably enforced to offset the cost, the oppression caused dissatisfaction. Therefore, in addition to the loss of life, the act of being at war would, for the duration of it, and even if it was successful, damage the country. It was essentially a very risky investment that would only return profits if the conflict terminated in Spain's favour, whereupon 'conditions change: domestic products rise, foreign ones fall –

Carlos III was one of the great enlightened despots of the eighteenth century, he pushed through aggressive reforms throughout his empire, and key to this was the resumption of Royal Monopolies in the Gulf Coast Region, for which West Florida and Campeche needed brought back under Spanish control. (British Library Flikr)

that is the moment to raise taxes in order to liquidate loans that have been negotiated.'[1]

In April of 1779 Carlos III had sent notes to London and Paris offering to act as mediator to treaty talks that would be held in Madrid, but the condition that the contested colonies be treated as independent in fact, was unsupportable to the administration of Lord North.[2] Therefore the Condé de Floridablanca, the chief minister of state and architect of his country's entrance into the conflict, had instructed the Spanish ambassador in London the Marques de Almodóvar, to inform Lord Weymouth (Secretary of State for the Southern department,) that the 'pile of stones, which is only a matter of expense and care to them [The British] disturbing to us and an impediment to permanent friendship,'[3] was the price of Spanish neutrality. The government of Carlos III, then already in strategic talks with the French, knew well enough that the British would not give up a pebble of their precious pile of stones without a fight, and would make Gibraltar the key treaty condition for either Bourbon power to end the war. On 12 April, the Treaty of Aranjuez was signed in secret between Spain and France, renewing the old Bourbon family compact, and laying out the Spanish war aims to retake Gibraltar, The Floridas, the expulsion of logwood cutters and settlers from the bays of Honduras and Campeche and the recapture of Minorca.

Through the spring and the early summer, it was not certain in London or America if the Spanish court would actually have the backbone to commence hostilities, and Benjamin Vaughn, the advocate of reconciliation, and correspondent with Benjamin Franklin, was unsure if the court had 'any firmness.'[4] The question looked to be on the way to resolution on 2 June 1779, when the aged Whig MP, Thomas Townsend, had risen in Parliament and began asking a string of questions, he said that he 'wished to learn what was the present object of the war in America? How it was to be carried on?'[5] As so far as he could see the army was not sufficient, (broken up as it was across

1 Aileen Moore Topping (ed.), *Journal of Don Francsico de Saavedra de Sangornis 1781-1783* (Gainsville: University of Florida Press, 1989), p.xxvii.

2 Griffith, *War for American Independence*, p.545.

3 Griffith, *War for American Independence*, p.544.

4 Benjamin Vaughan to Benjamin Franklin, 9 April 1779, *Founders Online, National Archives*, <https://founders.archives.gov/documents/Franklin/01-29-02-0246>, accessed 21 July 2023. Original source: Barbara B. Oberg (ed.), *The Papers of Benjamin Franklin, vol. 29, March 1 through June 30, 1779* (New Haven and London: Yale University Press, 1992), pp.290–297.

5 John Stockdale, *The Parliamentary Register: Or History of the Proceedings and Debates of the House of Commons* (London, John Stockdale, 1802), vol.XII, pp.219–220.

the Atlantic and Caribbean), to allow General Sir Henry Clinton to act in any other manner than on the defensive. Amongst many others, he wanted to know if any more offers had been given by the Americans, and if so, he felt it was prudent to treat with them, and asked further if unconditional submission was still the object of administration, the reasoning for this was given in a following question, which was to ascertain,

The British capture of Havana in 1762 had been a great blow to Spanish military prestige. When the siege of Pensacola began Galvez made sure to reference it prominently in his initial correspondence with Major General Campbell. (Anne S.K. Brown Military Collection)

> If what was asserted by his honourable friend [Mr Burke], on Monday last was true, viz. that the negotiation with Spain was broken off, he would say our case was desperate, for he hoped we would act manfully, and by our spirit repel the threatening danger; but could not avoid thinking it to be very alarming. America and France already in open war with us; Spain arming, and a cloud hanging over Ireland, afford us a rather gloomy prospect.[6]

He was answered by Lord North that unconditional surrender had never been a goal of the administration rather the issue was whether the colonies were to be preserved in their connection to Great Britain or renounced. 'He never had, in endeavouring to obtain this end [the preservation of the colonies], once thought of overturning the liberties of America; his sole view was to assert the just and natural rights of this country.'[7] Of the Spanish he

---

6   Stockdale, *Parliamentary Register*, vol.XII, pp.219–220.
7   Stockdale, *Parliamentary Register*, vol.XII, p.221.

British Prime Minister Lord North. (British Library Flikr.)

confirmed that their mediation was at an end; however, at that juncture the court of Madrid remained friendly and asserting protestations of neutrality, while admitting to no agreement between them and Spain.

By 14 June, whenever the subject of Spain arose in the House of Commons it was in regard to an inevitable breakdown of relations and their entry into the war. Burke assured the House that Spain was hostile but reserved his evidence. The possible entry of the second Bourbon power into the fight urged the opposition to call for heightened efforts to reconcile with America, and if Congress would not treat with this administration, then another should be formed.

On 16 June, Lord North announced that de Almodóvar been recalled to Madrid, and had delivered a manifesto to Lord Weymouth, which would be laid before the House the next day.

North then had to weather the storm of outrage from the opposition benches, with Burke pointing out the scorn with which their warnings regarding Spain had been met,

> Good God! With what joy have they triumphed as it were in our ignorance and folly! Spain we were told, time after time, could have no interest in joining our enemies. Spain had colonies of her own, and would not set so bad an example, as to succour or aid those rebellious ones of America: besides that, Spain was naturally inclined to peace with Great Britain … Oh, sir, how have we been deceived! How have we slept night after night, and dreamt of the faith of Spain! How long have ministry retired to their beds, full of wholesome advice and admonition on the previous point, and walked morning after morning, trumpeting their assurances of the pacific disposition of Spain![8]

Burke's impassioned rant ran to such a length that the speaker called him to order and bade him desist unless he had a motion to make. At this, he said 'Sir … the impeachment of the minister' and here he pointed at Lord North 'would be a very proper one.'[9] The House rose in a tumult of ministers calling out 'Move! Move!' And it was some time before order was restored.

---

8   Stockdale, *Parliamentary Register*, vol.XII, p.421
9   Stockdale, *Parliamentary Register*, vol.XII, p.422.

The anger arising from the negotiations with the Spanish would return some weeks later, when the papers regarding it were called for.

The next day the Spanish manifesto, which stopped just short of a declaration of war was read to the House. Firstly, it pointed out that the mediation of Carlos III had first been accepted, but then treated with bad faith, while numerous offences to Spain had been carried out including violations of the Treaty of Paris. As Great Britain had no interest in Spanish mediation, Carlos would act likewise, though his offer, originally made between September and October of 1778 would remain.

> Notwithstanding the pacific depositions of his Majesty, and even the particular inclination he had always had an expressed for cultivating the friendship of his Britannic Majesty, he finds himself under the disagreeable necessity of making use of all the means which the Almighty has intrusted him with, to obtain that justice which he has solicited in many ways, without being able to acquire it.[10]

Six days later the aged Earl Nugent, having listened to the great disadvantages the country now laboured under opined that 'Spain and France were both vulnerable; the former mortally vulnerable in many parts. Spain might be conquered by her own doctrines. She might be deeply wounded in South America. Let us go and preach up independence there; not only preach it up but assist South America in the obtainment of it.'[11] The Marques de Almodóvar left London on 18 June, and his household followed him on 6 July.[12] The opposition blamed the government for mishandling, or for ever entertaining Spanish mediation, their disappointment stemmed from lack of progress to treat with the Americans and the embarrassment of apparently being lied to by the administration regarding what they found to be an insincere offer of mediation. David Hartley, MP for Hull, a Whig, Abolitionist and friend of both Wilberforce and Franklin, whose signature would in time adorn the upcoming Treaty of Paris spoke at length on 22 June on the infamy of the war and Spanish mediation.

> If there be any sense of national honour left in this country, such a proposition should have been considered as a declaration of war on the part of Spain; I know the answer that an Earl of Chatham would have given upon such an occasion. The answer which that great man, who carried the name of this country to the highest pinnacle of human glory gave to a Spanish minister upon a proposition similar to this, in the year 1761 was this: 'It will be time enough to make such propositions when you are in the possession of the Tower of London'.[13]

10 Stockdale, *Parliamentary Register*, vol.XII, pp.446–448
11 Stockdale, *Parliamentary Register*, vol.XII, p.490.
12 Thomas Digges to Benjamin Franklin, 6 July 1779, *Founders Online, National Archives*, <https://founders.archives.gov/documents/Franklin/01-30-02-0036>, accessed 21 July 2023. Original source: Oberg (ed.), *The Papers of Benjamin Franklin*, vol.30, pp.56–59.
13 Stockdale, *Parliamentary Register*, vol.XII, p.560.

Such was the circumstances in Parliament when Spain entered the war, which had formally been declared on 21 June.

As has been said, and as the manifesto made clear, for the Spanish this war was about redressing a balance. It also, as was made clear by some ideas voiced in Parliament, was necessary to maintain a balance in the Americas in so doing. Spain had entered the revolutionary age thinking it had emerged into the age of enlightenment, and without really realising it was unconsciously laying the groundwork that would allow the empire in the Americas to crumble. Although pleased in principle to offer aid to the rebellious colonies, Spain wanted no revolutions in theirs. Rather, since the middle of the century, a sweeping array of Bourbon reforms which were also concerned with the profitability and security of the empire as well as its tranquillity, tried to head off such unrest. These reforms ironically tended to break as much as they fixed, and sometimes lead to exactly what they were trying to avoid. The Spanish empire in America was Hispanic rather than Castilian, built as it was, on and with conquered indigenous populations culturally retrained to be catholic farmers through the mission system and the *encomiendas*, the end of which brought a new character to the frontier. The peoples of the Spanish Americas and those who existed in its orbit reacted in different ways to the wind of change, and in some cases drove political and economic change themselves.

One of the defining events of the Spanish frontier, and indeed the empire, in the eighteenth century was the creation of the *Comanchería*. The establishment of which over the first half of the century was the most significant event to occur in the southwest since the Pueblo revolt of 1680, a conflict that in itself put an end to the *encomienda* system in New Mexico and made the Pueblos rich from trading stolen Spanish horses. By 1710 the Pueblo horse traders had caused a cultural revolution amongst the Ute-Comanches who were setting to make themselves masters of the grazing land, buffalo ranges, and slave markets of the southern plains.[14]

Foreign occupation of the eastern seaboard, and the sale of iron, and muskets through Canada and along the Ohio, Mississippi and Missouri created an equally unseen and dangerous ripple outwards into the unknown reaches of the Great Plains, where even by the 1750s there was no real European presence. However, the Europeans still made themselves felt. Nations who were displaced by the British or armed by the French moved west, and using their more powerful weapons, drove other nations out in search of new places to live. Then in turn, usually by their exposure to eastern weapons, they too were able to dominate those who they encountered. People who had never seen a European before came to know the power of a gun to use on their traditional enemies. The clash of the gun people and the horse nomads caused a halt in the westward movement of southern native groups searching for new opportunities, but also encouraged the formation of confederations, such as the Nortenos of the Red River Region, and the power of European muskets and horses, when mixed, created in the Ute-Comanches, a new

---

14   T. R. Fehrenbach, *Comanches: History of a People* (London: Vintage Books, 2007), p.119.

military, political and economic force, unseating the Apache from what had been called the *Apachería* and encouraging widespread raiding as the ripples of displacements spread into New Spain. The establishment of the *Comanchería*, not only made Bourbon reforms moot between Louisiana and New Mexico but was one of several American political realities that made the treaty of Fontainebleau in 1762, which ceded the Louisiana territory to Carlos III, absurd. Great problems lay ahead for provincial governors who received effective orders to push the frontier north, but these were based on the illusion that Spain controlled everything on the maps prepared for the Council of the Indies. In fact, between 1762 and 1780 the Comanches rose to surpass the Spanish as the main mercantile and military presence in the southwest, especially in the west, under powerful leaders like Cuerno Verde and Ecueracapa. Their progress was both concerning, unstoppable, and revealing of a sophisticated political and societal structure which allowed centralised leadership to drive military and economic policies that the Spanish had not been aware of. The response to which further unbalanced Spanish progress northward as espoused by Jose de Gálvez who blindly forged ahead without realising, he was trying to fix the wrong problem. The formation of the *Provincias Internas* and the war to supress the nations within them, was the remedy he chose but the initiative crumbled, except in part, in California.

When war broke out with Britain, the *Camino Real* between New Orleans and San Antonio became vital to the transport of cattle for New Orleans. Knowing he would need supplies of beef for the war effort, Bernardo de Gálvez despatched Francisco García with a letter for the Governor, Domingo Cabello, requesting cattle. García arrived in San Antonio de Béxar on 20 June 1779 and this triggered a flurry of activity from the Governor to requisition a large herd. He was aided by Fray Pedro Ramírez de Arellano of Mission San José, the Father President of the Texas missions, by August, 2,000 head were ready to drive. Hundreds of horses were also arranged for the guard. The core of the Louisiana beef came from the ranches between San Antonio and La Bahia, comprising 30 major spreads and at least 13 smaller grants, and during the war period over 15,000 head of cattle were sent to New Orleans.[15]

The continuing conflicts with the Apaches and Comanches made moving large numbers of animals highly dangerous, and the passage of these herds fed the simmering pot of frontier tensions. In June 1780 Don Christobal Ylario de Cordoba, was driving 1,000 cattle to Nacogdoches for the Louisiana war effort. He and his 20 men had reached Arroyo de Nogales where they were set upon by an estimated 100 Comanches, who scattered the herd and killed a drover. Perhaps hoping to be better placed to raid the cattle herds and the ranch country around Béxar, a large band of Comanches encamped on a ridge between the Colorado and the Guadalupe rivers. This was a large encampment, and the Spaniards who rode out to attack it under a *subteniente* named Alférez Valdéz decided to await reinforcements, but by

---

15   W. Granville, N.W. Hough, *Spain's Texas Patriots: It's 1779-1783 War with England During the American Revolution. Part 5 of Spanish Borderlands Studies* (Midway: SHHAR Press, 2000), pp.15–17.

the time they had crossed the Guadaloupe the Comanches were gone, only to return suddenly in scattered groups through September, raiding ranches, miles away, including Fuerte de Cibolo.

Quite apart from emerging empires, older colonial legacies also made progress difficult, and the veneer of Spanish control less pristine than some might have liked. In Louisiana the first Spanish governor, Antonio de Ulloa, found the French Creoles he was to govern difficult to deal with. Being a man of such accomplishment and intellectual renown that he found it easy to give offense, even if it was unintentional, this and a populace that was suspicious and sometimes hostile to the incoming Spanish did not help matters when it came to equitably resolving the conflicting issues that arose from one regime replacing another, and by 1768, after many misunderstandings, Ulloa and the Creoles were in a delicate state.

In the lengthy list of grievances drawn up by the agitated Creoles, Ulloa was accused of threatening (amongst other things) the following: Acadians with slavery, a six mile no-flogging zone around the city as his wife was disturbed by the cries of those being beaten, and worst of all, flooding the markets of the colony with tortillas. The tallied list was as much a sounding board for personal grievances as accusations of real mismanagement, but one thing was certain, the New Orleans gentry did not like Ulloa and especially disliked Spain's restriction of free trade.[16]

The first part of the Creole Rebellion of New Orleans lasted from 27 October to 16 November 1768. After a planning phase, the guns at the gate of New Orleans were spiked and a petition, signed by 500 people calling for the banishment of Ulloa and a restoration of their rights as French subjects, was laid before the Superior Council, who took it under consideration. Meanwhile a mob of 400 Germans and Acadians took over the city on the 28th, forcing Ulloa and other Spanish officials to seek shelter on ships anchored on the river. The next day the rioting got worse, and there were fears that Ulloa would bombard the town, prompting the Council to call for the insurgents to quieten down on pain of having their petition dismissed, but then quickly pressed for Spanish withdrawal and a restoration of French control.

Ulloa sailed for Havana in the middle of November, but the victorious Creoles did not enjoy their victory for long. Such treasonous behaviour could not be tolerated, and the next year Spanish rule was restored by *Teniente General* Alejandro O'Reilly. He was a hard man, and he made his position plain, securing New Orleans with an overt display of Spanish military might. The ringleaders and instigators were arrested and tried for treason, five of whom were sentenced to the gallows but due to the lack of a hangman were shot; the rest were dispatched to the dungeons of Havana.

The most dramatic popular rising was Tupac Amarru II's, which was much larger than both the Louisiana debacle and possibly even that of the British colonies as well. Indeed, it represents a true popular rebellion, as it began in objection to the injustices meted out on the Quechua by the *Corregidores*, who

---

16   John Walton Caughey, John Walton, *Bernardo de Gálvez in Louisiana 1776–1783* (Gretna: Firebird Publishing Company, 1998), p.14.

A view of New Orleans circa 1765. The British had every intention of taking the town in 1779, and but for the speed of the Spanish attack that year, and the successful defence of St Louis in 1780, they might have succeeded. (Courtesy Louisiana State Museum)

were tasked with enforcing the existing law and the Bourbon reforms. In the autumn of the 1780, the heavy hand of the *Corogidores* responsible for taxation across the Andean communities was proven to be a yoke too heavy to bear, when Tupac Amarru hanged a *Corregidor* and raised a Quechua rebellion which strove to create a new society and government in Peru. Tupac, or José Gabriel Condorcanqui Noguera as he was known before the rebellion, was similar to the other leading patriots of Spanish, and indeed British America, in that he was an educated nobleman of significant influence, occupying the position of *Kuraka* which means, superior, or, principle, and was approximate to chief or headman but represented a much more formal rank in the Spanish empire and traced back to the rule of the Incas. In the Thirteen Colonies the patrician rebels in Massachusetts and Philadelphia demanded their rights as British subjects under the constitution set up between 1666 and 1688, and upheld in 1714, and when they were denied them, stirred up public outrage with enlightenment rhetoric that painted George III as a malevolent tyrant, who would not forbear to stop at mere taxation but would surely make all the freedom loving inhabitants of the colonies as powerless as slaves. As valid as their claim of unjust taxation might have been, much of the padding was little more than rabble-rousing.

To Spanish eyes it was a *Criollo* problem that had gotten out of hand.[17] Few heeded the fact that they too had a *Criollo* problem born of a disaffected patrician and bourgeois class, and an oppressed lower class represented at its lowest tier by slaves and *Indios*.

In Peru the Quechua population did literally stagger under the burden of taxation and oppression as a conquered people. Tupac Amaru no sooner hanged the *Corregidor*, Arriaga on 4 November of 1780 than he embarked on his campaign, moving swiftly to gather support and supplies, he made a swift tour of the surrounding towns, locking up Spanish officials and royalists and making speeches in the plazas outlining his plan in the cause of Quechua liberty. An end to the *Mita*,[18] taxes and the *Corregidors* were central themes, in the future he wanted to throw out all the Spanish laws and create strong new ones; the head tax alone would be retained and paid directly to him. He sent letters to other *Kuraka's* ordering them to arrest the *Corregidors* and said that the King had grown tired of his orders for the relief of his *Indio* servants being ignored and had issued Tupac Amaru an extraordinary decree that validated his actions. The Quecha rising was popular at its root, but also distinctly Catholic and royalist, with the rebel field-sign being a simple woven cross and a stitch of red embroidery to show their status as good Christians,

---

17   *Criollo* being the Spanish version of creole, which referred to people of European ancestry but who had been born in the colonies.

18   Enforced Indian labour quotas for the mines.

EVERY HAZARD AND FATIGUE

and all would know that the soldiers of Carlos III wore red cockades in their hats. The response in the immediate area was surprising to the Spanish, who had no idea of what was brewing until it boiled over, many fled, while others simply put their heads down, as up to the middle of November, Tupac Amaru had given orders that no Spaniard was to be harmed. It is possible that he hoped to at some stage show that his motives were born out of true faith to the king, whose agents and ministers were dealing unjustly in his name, and that at some point down the line the beneficence that can only come from an enlightened despot might indeed right the wrongs that Tupac Amaru and his people had experienced when he was José Gabriel. Yet he went further in private and spoke of making himself the head of a new government, and when on 16 November he issued a decree emancipating all African and Afro-Peruvian slaves.[19]

In a supreme irony, at the time the Spanish were undertaking their final attempt on Pensacola, which in its way would aid the independence of the United States, the great Rebellion of Tupac Amaru II, which at its height saw 40–60,000 rebels in some manner of revolt, was crushed. After failing to take Cuzco, between December 1780 and January 1781, the rebels were cornered in late March and defeated in early April, where Tupac and his family were captured. Large-scale executions of patriot commanders and leaders occurred soon afterwards, and the leader of the rising was not spared. Tupac Amaru and his family were executed in a gaudy and ghastly public spectacle, 10 days after the final act of the siege of Pensacola, which, it was hoped, would send the message that liberty was the gift of the King, and it was granted under his terms or none.

The repression of popular risings in Louisiana and Peru and the resistance in the *Provincias Internas* and on the southern plains, were a good reason to remain at arm's length when it came to aiding a provincial government throw off a colonial master.

The minister of the Indies, Jose de Gálvez (the uncle of Don Bernardo) laid out very clearly to, Diego José Navarro Garcia de Valladores, the aged *capitán general* of Cuba in June of 1779, that

> There is no positive order or political basis for the United States to be seen or considered under any concept but neutrality, since not acting as subjects of Great Britain, they do not deserve our hostility; and not openly being friends of the Spanish nation, they should not benefit from our war efforts. Thus … limiting aid to them to what is demanded by the right of hospitality.[20]

In his book on the influence of sea power, Captain Mahan summarised the Spanish effort in the Gulf of Mexico and West Florida as detrimental to the wider Bourbon alliance, 'Their only bearing upon the general war was the diversion of this imposing force from the joint operations with the French, Spain here, as at Gibraltar, pursuing her own aims instead of

---

19   Charles F. Walker, *The Tupac Amaru Rebellion* (Cambridge: Belknap Press, 2014), p.49.
20   Gonzalo M. Quintero Saravia, *Bernardo de Gálvez: Spanish Hero of the American Revolution* (Chapel Hill: University of North Carolina Press, 2018), p.145.

concentrating upon the common enemy, – a policy as shortsighted as it was selfish.'[21]

This accusation is overly harsh, for while Spain certainly, and quite naturally, pursued her own interests as a priority after the disaster of the Seven Years' War, they contributed to the French alliance, and unofficially to the war effort of Congress in other ways. Quite beyond her naval capacity, which it should be added France was loath to do without in the Caribbean, the Spanish colonies offered a uniquely useful opportunity for trade with the United States. The United States, or the confederation thereof, did not have a stable currency, nor easy access to friendly ports, the hard currency was indeed the Spanish dollar, which was traded at $30 to the pound, and by this stage in the war Congress's specie was all but failing completely, putting strain on the alliance with France, and by extension Spain, as the French often sought aid from the Spanish. The famously worthless Continental dollar, quite literally considered worth less than the paper it was printed on, was not reassuring anyone, let alone their specie fluid allies who were essentially pouring money down a hole with little hope of recompense. With debates going back and forth over the worth of a dollar in 1779, Congress was eager to obtain ready sources of cash. Restrictions on trade, which were usually onerous in Spanish empire were relaxed, and Diego Navarro instructed the secretary of Spain's agent at Congress, Francisco Rendon (his superior, Juan de Miralles having died), to arrange for the purchase of 3,000 barrels of flour as an opening gesture, which under the new dispensation would be paid for in Spanish silver at $30 a barrel. The opening of markets in New Orleans, Vera Cruz and Havana, brought about a conflict with French ambitions, who with equal self-interest asked that the relaxation of the royal monopoly be kept hidden from all but a few trusted merchants as they worried the lucrative opportunities of the Spanish trade would disrupt their alliance with the Americans. The contract was given to Congress's commercial agent, Robert Morris who had sensibly kept his ear to the ground in Cuba and obtained the flour from the French depot in Maryland. By 1780 over 3 million *Pesos* had been paid to Congressional agents, which also aided the Spanish in obtaining supplies. [22]

Aid to the Rebels had begun much earlier than that but under similar lines. As a neutral power, Spain could, without reservation, allow the sale of goods to anyone who had a licence to trade with them. Congress not only needed hard currency, but the materials to fight a war. In 1776, the Louisiana merchant, and agent of congress, Oliver Pollock secured two shipments of gunpowder for $1,850 from the Royal stores. The next year a consignment of goods, delivered tax free by a merchant named Miguel Eduardo of Havana to the Governor by royal order, were deposited in a warehouse at New Orleans. The invoice listed '6 cases of quinine, 8 cases of other medicines, 108 bolts of woollen cloth and serge, 100 hundredweights of powder in 100 barrels, and 300 muskets with bayonets in 30 boxes.'[23] The goods were listed for sale

---

21 A.T. Mahan, *The Influence of Sea Power upon History 1660-1783* (Boston: Little Brown & Company, 1884), p.517.
22 Topping (ed.), *Journal of Saavedra*, p.106.
23 Caughey, *Gálvez in Louisiana*, p.88.

Benjamin Franklin was one of the main contractors for arms, ammunition and equipment from 1777, organising vast cargos of war materials to be bought and delivered to New Orleans for the American War Effort. (British Library Flikr)

as unsuitable for the kings' regiments in Havana for the cloth, and merely mundane other goods for the powder and muskets, the subterfuge was completed by decoy barrels of unoffending items, pre-opened for casual inspection. The next year, Benjamin Franklin had contracted for covert shipments of 215 bronze cannons, 4,000 field tents, 30,000, bayonets, muskets, and uniforms, with 51,314 musket balls and 300,000 lbs of powder through the firm of Gardoqui and Sons.[24]

By the end of 1777, Bernardo de Gálvez's first year as governor of Louisiana, $70,000 worth of goods had been bought and sent up the river to the upper Ohio. The operations of George Rogers Clark were financed and supplied in large part by Oliver Pollock who in turn was supported in his activities by Gálvez, who had secret orders to encourage the rebels however he saw fit, and again there was a certain symbiosis, as a great deal of the materials that kept the Spanish navy at sea could be obtained in the back country of the separatist colonies, as was told to Gálvez in a letter from Patrick Henry. In August 1779, Pollock established credit with Gálvez and took out a $74,000 loan from the government of New Orleans, a grateful Pollock was to suggest a portrait be commissioned of the governor to commemorate his service to congress.

What can be seen here was essentially a way to use the Mississippi to bypass the British blockade. Using the peninsula of Florida as a shield for merchants to reach the rich trade centres of the Spanish empire. This not often realised fact brings home the importance of the western theatre of the wider war. If the war was to continue, it was vitally important to Congress that they or a friendly or neutral power should control the Mississippi and the Gulf.

In a wider sense the economic shadow-alliance with Congress, the siege of Pensacola, and the operations before it, took place just outside the orbit of the new Franco-American alliance, but was characteristic of the new face of the war, where the goal of American Independence had to get in line alongside and in some cases behind those of the Bourbon allies, and by its end was a rising concern to the evolution of the British Southern Strategy.

That being said, a war was still being fought by the United or Confederated States on the continent. On the subject of his returning to America, Earl

---

24   Robert H. Thonhoff, 'The Vital Contribution of Spain in the Winning of the American Revolution: An Essay on a Forgotten Chapter in the History of the American Revolution', *Granadaros y Damas de Galvez*, <http://granaderos.org/vital.html>, accessed 2 August 2023.

Cornwallis, then grieving the loss of his wife in England, wrote that 'I am now returning to America not with views of conquest and ambition, nothing brilliant can be expected in that quarter; but I find this country [Britain] quite unsupportable to me. I must shift the scene, I have many friends in the American Army; I love that army, and flatter myself that I am not quite indifferent to them.'[25]

Given the general sense of stalemate that had hung in the air since even before the evacuation of Philadelphia and the Battle of Monmouth, Cornwallis's gloomy expectations of returning to service sum up the situation quite well. However, the British Commander-in-Chief in North America, General Sir Henry Clinton did have hopes of something brilliant, as in response to orders from Whitehall to prosecute the war based on loyalist and naval power, and to return his energies to the southern colonies, he had proposed refocusing British efforts on the Carolinas and Georgia.[26]

British Commander-in-Chief, General Sir Henry Clinton. Like most senior officers, Clinton had no conception of what to use the garrison of West Florida for beyond a strike at New Orleans. He seems to have abandoned Campbell to the aid of Jamaica, not realising that this too was out of the question by 1781. (British Library Flikr)

That being said, he too was fed up but unlike the devastated Cornwallis he was tired of fighting a war that had so little public support and, so he felt, so little direction or aid from the government. Indeed, in the summer of 1779 he had resigned his command, though he would remain until a replacement could be named, which he hoped would be Cornwallis. While he waited, he planned. The south was considered a loyalist haven, and indeed large numbers of refugees had fled into the Floridas after 1776, and the nations of the Cherokee and Muskogee (Creek) were known to be hostile to the United States. Some evidence of the importance of the loyalist threat to the rebels can be gleaned in the three attempts made to try and take St Augustine, the capital of East Florida, by United States forces between 1776 and 1778, all of which had ended in ignominious failure, and resulted in the appointment of Major General Benjamin Lincoln to the command of the southern district. Clinton, who loved his maps, let his gaze drop below the Carolinas, where the British had been disappointed before, to Savannah and felt that the navy could transport an irresistible force to Georgia before the Rebels' new French allies could interfere.[27]

After receiving positive direction from the government, Clinton dispatched Lieutenant Colonel Archibald Campbell, with 3,079 men to Georgia, which captured Savannah on 29 December 1778, and Augusta (an important hub of Native American trade and diplomacy on the Savannah

25   Franklin & Mary Wickwire, *Cornwallis and the War of Independence* (Northampton: The History Book Club, 1970) pp.115–116.
26   Bicheno, *Hugo Rebels and Redcoats*, pp.159–160.
27   S. Martin, B. Harris, *Savannah 1779: The British Turn South* (Oxford: Osprey Publishing, 2017), p.32.

River) on 31 January 1779. However, through the spring and summer, it became clear to the British that after the poor showing early in the war, the loyalists were not as enthusiastic about taking up arms, as the royal governors and local planters said they were. Isolated and increasingly the target of robust rebel forces under Lincoln, the British came under strain.

Campbell had gone on leave and handed over command to Lieutenant Colonel James Prevost, the son of military commander of East Florida. This change of command saved Charleston as the younger officer was satisfied with simply keeping Lincoln out of Georgia and wound up being bottled up in Savannah facing not only the Continental Southern Army but the French expeditionary force under the Comte d'Estaing on its way back to France, in September. However, the siege of Savannah highlighted the weaknesses of the alliance rather than its strengths. Combined Operations at Rhode Island had already proved disappointing, with Washington observing that d'Estaing 'had not spirit equal to the risk.'[28] To the further disappointment of Congress and the French government, the operation at Savannah ended in dismal and costly defeat when the allies failed to storm the British works in October, and d'Estaing, continuing his journey back to Europe, left the rebels once more isolated.

The success in Georgia spurred on Lord George Germain in encouraging Clinton to make the war a more American affair, and to concentrate on the south. The British government was slowly backing away, hoping perhaps to disentangle themselves to a certain extent now that France, and Spain, would be threatening their colonies in the Caribbean. This attitude, though at face value strange, is entirely in keeping with British global strategy as 1779 drew to a close. For our purposes, this is well demonstrated in the decision to risk the entry of Spain into the conflict in order to preserve, not the posts of Baton Rouge and Mobile which were snapped up by de Gálvez, but Gibraltar.

In 1780, Clinton took Charleston, the largest single defeat suffered by the rebels during the war, followed by one of their worst field defeats at Camden at the hand of Cornwallis, which caused great losses to the Continental Line Infantry of Virginia, Maryland, and Delaware. Although indications were that loyalists were still not coming out in any great number, especially after the Patriot victory at King's Mountain and the horrendous partisan war, Saratoga successes on the scale Congress needed were non-existent between '79 and '80. Likewise, as of the summer of 1780, although the British could now no longer rest in the confidence that the Confederation, as it was sometimes called, could be contained, and dealt with in a little transatlantic bubble, they could view the situation as beginning to turn their way again. Although Washington was not defeated, a stalemate went two ways, and for the rebels a stalemate put immense strain on the colonial economy, with congress increasingly at a loss to see a way forward and how to pay for the war. The perennial problem of enlistments and rewards for time served, not least the recruitment of fresh troops which also raised its familiar head as the enlistments of 1777 came to an end, and without a stable currency, Congress

---

28   Griffith, *War for American Independence*, p.517.

faced a chain reaction, leading to the failure not only of their economy but of the war.[29]

Hopeful British strategy included the isolated garrisons of West Florida. Lord George Germain had sent an order to Major General John Campbell, Commander-in-Chief of West Florida, four days after the declaration of war with Spain on 21 June 1779, calling for him to prepare measures to begin hostile action. Specifically, an attack on New Orleans was envisaged. Germain's instructions might well have been pleasing to Campbell as such an expedition, while risky given the troops he had to hand, would bring to

Vignettes of various Battles fought against the British during the wider American Revolutionary War, including at top left, the siege of Mobile. (Library of Congress)

---

29   Richard Buel Jr, *In Irons: Britain's Naval Supremacy and the American Revolutionary Economy* (New Haven: Yale University Press, 1998), p.144.

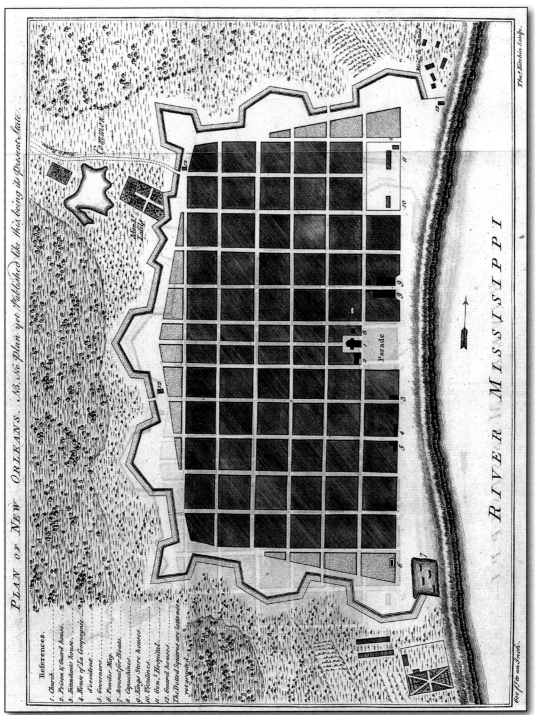

Captain Pittman's map of New Orleans circa 1770. The city represented the frontline of the Spanish empire in the war with Britain and would have come under immediate attack from West Florida had Gálvez not struck first. (Library of Congress)

the territory the naval forces he so desperately needed and a great influx of cash and supplies. However, it was this dispatch that when copied and sent to the Mississippi forts was captured and proved to Bernardo de Gálvez the necessity of an early strike.[30]

Bernardo de Gálvez, was on the eastern frontline of the Spanish land empire, and in his view, this meant he needed to attack before the British. The Spanish had long been prepared to strike, with the colonial government at New Orleans knowing almost as much about British West Florida as Campbell. Brushing off a hurricane that delayed his operation, Gálvez struck in September 1779, before any of the frontier posts could be alerted, though some had been reinforced in preparation for the attack on New Orleans. From Campbell's perspective Gálvez's campaign along the Mississippi to Manchac and Baton Rouge was so swift and successful that they had all but reduced the western part of West Florida before Campbell even heard that Gálvez had opened hostilities.

Campbell actually learned of the defeat just as he was about to embark 500 men on a small flotilla laden with gifts for the Native Americans, having already sent out 300–400 Waldeck troops in anticipation of launching the campaign against New Orleans. 'This news disappointed all my hopes and expectations and converted my attention from that of attacking [New Orleans] to making preparations for Defence of Mobile and Pensacola.' [31]

He was not alone in his frustration, the field chaplain of the 3rd Waldeck Regiment, stationed at Pensacola wrote in October of 1779

> The General was in such a confusing and embarrassing situation that he did not know which way to turn. Should he embark or stay on land? Is this not a damned country, where the greater part of the army corps has been taken prisoner for five weeks, and where a stretch of land of 1200 miles has been taken without the Commander-General knowing it?[32]

---

30   George C. Osborn, 'Major-General John Campbell in British West Florida', *Florida Historical Quarterly*, vol. 27, no.4, p.326.

31   Osborne, 'Campbell in British West Florida', p.327.

32   Max von Eelking, *German Mercenaries in Pensacola During the American Revolution, 1779-1781*. (Pensacola, Pensacola Historical Society, Florida), p.16. Translated by Louis Krupp from *Die Deutschen Hulfstruppen im Nordamerikanischen Befreiungskriege, 1776 bis 1783.*

2

The King's Bread: Gálvez and the Army of Operations

Instead of the usual breakdown of the factory settings of rival eighteenth-century armies, so to speak, an outline of the specific forces at play will be of use going forward, with a slight preponderance towards the less studied Spanish army. Readers wishing modern appraisals of the British Army in North America can do no better than Matthew Hasler Spring's, *With Zeal and Bayonets Only*, and the works on the light infantry tactics of the war by Dr Robbie McNiven.[1]

The British had not seen the likes of Spain's daredevil governor of Louisiana yet in their experiences in North America, and he was the last thing they expected from an officer of Carlos III's army.

Given the diversity of eighteenth-century Iberia, it could be said that Gálvez was born in Andalucía, rather than Spain, when he came into the world in the summer of 1746. His background, coming from one of the country's most multi-cultural regions prepared him well for his service in America.

Mariscal de Campo[2] Bernardo de Gálvez challenges almost every contemporary preconception of what a Spanish general was supposed to be like. True, he was from a well-connected and prestigious family in southern Spain, and depended on that cushion throughout his life, but he tempered that privilege with a single-minded ambition to prove himself worthy of it. Though from Andalucía he had something of the *Extremeño* in him that the *Conquistadores* would have recognised, which is to say he had grit. He also had a sharp and active mind that had been trained well by injury and disappointment, yet he was irrepressible in his confidence that neither, storm, tempest, nor the designs of his enemy (quite literally in all respects) were

---

1   See, Robbie MacNiven, *British Light Infantry in the American Revolution* (Oxford: Osprey Publishing, 2021), Matthew E. Spring, *With Zeal & Bayonets Only: The British Army on Campaign in North America, 1775-1783* (Norman: University of Oklahoma Press, 2008).

2   This rank translates literally as field marshal, however in the Spanish army it occupied a place equivalent to major general in the British Army, and junior to a *teniente general* in the Spanish.

ever able to quash. Far from the idea of a preening don lost in Iberian ideas of honour, Gálvez was a Francophile with something approaching the common touch, making sure his officers and troops knew they could expect to see him share their dangers and hardships, and so imparting to them by example the dedication he expected. Of course, certain ideals of Spanish nobility were absolutely to be seen in his character. He would take no insult, and he also had a strange, almost self-destructive sense of the dramatic when he felt he had an audience, yet he had a way with words and was a commanding presence that was hard to overcome in a council of war. As a general he was careful to prepare before he acted, and then to act with speed and aggression when the time came. It would seem he was personally highly courageous and audacious, which is testified by his willingness to expose himself personally to potential injury or death, and which would be one of his great weaknesses as a senior commander. However, to add another contradiction he was humane in exposing his men to danger. When he took Fort Bute at Manchac, he did so by a brilliant *ruse de guerre* rather than immediately trying to assault, as he knew he could never account for the loss of life when there was another way.

As we shall see, at Pensacola, though he had the means to achieve his goals by sacrificing the lives of his soldiers to the British artillery, he knew he did not have to do so, and it is for this reason that the siege progressed as it did. He tempered this popularism with a regular officer's understanding of where to draw a line, when he worried that frontier soldiers 'reared in freedom and accustomed to independence' had developed too independent a spirit which bordered on insubordination, while his indifference to prejudices that were common in his generation was clear enough, 'What does it matter to His Majesty if one who serves him well is black or white,' he wrote, 'if the colour of his face is negated by the nobility of his heart.'[3]

Gálvez knew what it was to both fight shoulder to shoulder in battle, and also what it was to see generals spend lives recklessly and without profit, as a junior officer he had also quickly shown the talents that made him popular with soldiers. As commandant of Nueva Viscaya and Sonora in 1770 he had ridden a sortie in pursuit of a group of Apaches, and urged his men on when all seemed lost with these words:

> Alone I would go without having anyone to accompany me; and I will either take a scalp to Chihuahua and perform my duty or pay with my life for the king's bread that I have eaten. There is the road from our land, follow it those of you who have faint hearts; but follow me those of you who wish to take part in my glorious hardships, follow me on the assumption that I can give you nothing but thanks for this fineness, but that it will live always in my memory and recollection.[4]

Gálvez was invalided out of the Provincias Internas after being severely wounded in the arm through his *adarga* shield. He was also wounded by arrows and a lance but these must have been blunted by his *cuera* armour.

---

3   David J. Weber, *The Spanish Frontier in North America* (New Haven: Yale University Press, 1992), p.329.

4   Caughey, *Gálvez in Louisiana*, p.63

However, he never forgot that sortie. For five years he acted as an instructor and was briefly seconded to the French army before obtaining a posting with a regiment in O'Reilly's expedition to Algiers.

On 23 May 1775, the fleet of 18 warships, 33 other vessels of war and 344 transports sailed to the bay of Algiers in which they anchored on 30 June. Approximately 24,000 men of the king's army now awaited orders to land.[5] It was the largest armada Spain had sent abroad in decades. A potent signal to the lords of Barbary that the hand of the Catholic King could still reach out and smite them.

Opposing them were the combined forces of the Dey of Algiers and the Bey of Constantine amounting to somewhere around 40,000 men, about half of which were cavalry. Early on 8 July the first division of 8,000 men landed and pushed inland from the beach, screened by light infantry. They experienced far more resistance and far greater numbers than had been expected. The advance was broken up by small clusters of buildings and fields and began to grind to a halt amid heavy casualties. Not long afterwards the appearance of camel herds on the flanks began to panic the dense formations of Spanish infantry, drawn up six deep, so that when the rear ranks became exited or scared, they inevitably began to shoot into their own front ranks. Thinking the Algerian horse had cut off their retreat, the Bourbon infantry began to withdraw. The flanks were badly cut up by the 'Moorish' cavalry, and a costly retreat back to the beach left the ground strewn with the white coats of the Catholic infantry.[6] The Marques de Romana was killed at the head of his brigade, and over 2,700 men killed and wounded with him. No prisoners were taken as a generous bounty had been placed on infidel heads, and some sources count the casualties as high as 5,000 by the time O'Reilly ordered his troops to reembark. One of which was Gálvez, who had received a wound in one of his legs, while serving with the *piquetes* and light infantry. He recovered quickly, and along with many who probably should not have been rewarded, received promotion, before once again returned to teaching at the Military Academy at Avila. At this time, he was described by his friend Francisco de Saavedra, '... he wrote a little song about the expedition and other funny little pieces. He was a man of huge talent and very fond of music.'[7] His bravery and the patronage of his uncle, the minister of the Indies, might be better, saw him brought out to Louisiana to command the Regimiento Fijo de Louisiana, and he became acting governor in September 1776, assuming the full reins of power in New Orleans on 1 January 1777 from Louis Unazaga. Here his Francophilia made him very popular in the former French colony that had ejected its first Spanish governor in 1768, in what one could call a proto-American Revolution. Gálvez married a rich French creole widow and made great strides in preparing the colony for war, which he saw as the reason he was appointed.

---

5   William Dalrymple, *Travels Through Spain and Portugal, in 1774, with a Short Account of the Expedition to Algiers* (London: J. Almon, 1777), p.184.

6   Dalrymple, *Travels Through Spain and Portugal*, p.184.

7   Saravia, *Gálvez*, p.76.

In his operations between 1779 and 1780 he had skirted disaster, gambling that his preparations and skill were enough to overcome difficulties, in the Mobile campaign especially as he lost his supplies, and much of his ships in a foolhardy attempt to force Mobile Bar after his fleet had been damaged by a tropical storm. One imagines the memory of his speech on the Apache frontier came back to him when all seemed lost, as undoubtedly it did when he faced adversity at Pensacola.

Gálvez today is becoming slowly better known, and he is something of a popular hero amongst Hispanic Americans, and rightfully so. At the same time conservative Spaniards see him as a symbol of Iberian excellence and the combination of the two sometimes gives an unpalatable veneer that prevents his story being widely accepted. Spanish triumphalism is a two-edged sword for the reputations of the notable Spanish commanders.

It is all too easy for an anglophone audience to cringe a little when the achievements of what they have been taught to believe was a backwater of the war are vaunted (in some cases to exaggeration) as worthy of acclaim. Indeed, when one is confronted by the short career of Gálvez, it is very easy to take it with a heavy pinch of salt, and to attribute it to luck and fortune, and inferior opponents with less means, or just a Spanish retelling of the *Last of the Mohicans*. Except, if it was all just an anomaly, why did similar expeditions in America during the Seven Years' War and the Revolution, fail? Arguably, Major General Edward Braddock's army of 1755 was better equipped and more professional than the ones that Gálvez led to Baton Rouge and Mobile. Why was Campbell unable to relieve Mobile in a similar overland expedition to that which Gálvez had undertaken in 1779? Though his career was too short and in terms of military operations too limited, to know for sure, what we do know would suggest that whatever luck Bernardo de Gálvez had going for him, he was gifted enough to know how to take advantage of it.

In his admirable book, *The Military Experience in the Age of Reason*, the late Christopher Duffy reported a bleak picture of the Spanish army in the eighteenth century. The reason for this being that it had an awful reputation during the period. From 1718 to 1765 few had a good word to say about Iberian troops, in part due to the failure of the Bourbons to halt the decline of Spanish arms that had generally set in from 1650 under the Hapsburgs. Towards the end of the War of the Spanish Succession, despite Spaniards making up the bulk of the Bourbon forces in the Iberian theatre the British thought them an 'parcel of wretches.'[8]

The year after the siege of Pensacola, the military thinker and educator, Gerhard von Scharnhorst was scathing:

> The Spanish have never changed. Except for their hair, which is now powdered and curled, the soldiers remain in the same condition as seventy years ago. Their generals are totally ignorant of tactics, for they owe their promotion to

---

8   Christopher Duffy, *The Military Experience in the Age of Reason* (New York: Athaneaum, 1988), p.28. See also, René Chartrand, *The Armies and Wars of the Sun King 1643-1715* (Warwick: Helion & Company, 2021), vol.IV.

favouritism, or to long service in garrisons where their only occupation was to arrange the processions to the burnings at the stake, and so on.[9]

This was as much a dismissal as a criticism, but the Gulf Coast campaign refutes it and in turn begs the question whether Scharnhorst was displaying his own Protestant prejudice rather than offering a more considered opinion. This stereotype that the Spanish were a set of powdered and brainless Dons leading a rabble of poorly equipped lazy peasants persisted, and as no one outside of the Spanish themselves really had cause to keep up with the progress of Iberian military activities until the Peninsular War, when British and French officers encountered what was left of the old regular army going to the dogs after the state collapsed between 1808–1809, the negative impression never died. The large gap between 1738 and 1775, in which the army seemed to try and resurrect itself was conveniently overlooked, and the shorter period of application between 1779 to 1796, in which Spanish generals and soldiers showed quite clearly that they still knew how to conduct a war, is largely ignored in favour of the debacle at Gibraltar and the failures against Napoleon. However, it is entirely true that as of the end of the Seven Years' War the Spanish were something of a minor military power and the bungled effort that saw the loss of both Manilla, Florida, and Havana, showed that despite reforms to create a more Franco-Prussian version of the army, much work was still to be done.

It is to this failure to organise a lasting military spirit before 1775 in the eyes of contemporaries, that Duffy is certainly referring to, as he himself found that the most influential writer of military theory outside of France was Don Alvaro Navia Osario y Vigil, Marques de Santa Cruz de Mercenado who was killed at Oran in 1732. The Marques's cumbersome *Reflexiones Militares*, in which the author attempted to cover as many subjects as possible, ran to 11 volumes and found their way into the library of Frederick the Great. Mercenado's opinion of the ordinary soldiers of Spain was only a little better than that of Scharnhorst, and more akin to the faith that the Duke of Wellington had in his rank and file than an outright dismissal of worth.

Organisationally, the forces commanded by Bernardo de Gálvez between 1779–1781 were both evidence of the reforms occurring in the Spanish army, and also the army's somewhat archaic and informal nature.

The royal ordinances of 1768, however, had taken steps to lift the organisational and procedural weight from the generals themselves and tried to create a more modern force that could take the field in the same state of readiness and condition, no matter the talents of the commander. This raft of regulations, focusing on regularisation of the duties of officers, NCOs, and ordinary soldiers of every class, remained the core bedrock of Spanish military doctrine, well into then nineteenth century, and was updated numerous times rather than rewritten.

As a service, the regular army of the Bourbon dynasty in Spain, hereafter known as the metropolitan army, was in a constant state of change, however

---

9   Duffy, *Military Experience*, p.28.

The entry of the Bourbon states into the War of Independence gave it a European theatre. The Great Siege of Gibraltar (1779–1783) failed and the capture of the Rock proved to be one of the few strategic goals the armies of Carlos III failed to achieve. (Anne S.K. Brown Military Collection)

the change was hesitant. Between 1748 and 1768 the establishment of an infantry battalion changed six times, ending up for provincial and metropolitan battalions at nine companies of fusiliers and one of grenadiers, with each fusilier company mustering three officers and 77 men, with 73 men in the grenadier company.[10] Each battalion (including the *Fijo* provincial regiments) carried two colours, one bearing the arms of the king and the other the *Cruz de Borgonia* with regimental designations. Each regiment also tended to have a nickname, much as Roman Legions did, like the Regimiento de Guadalajara which had the sobriquet *El Tigre*.

Elements of the metropolitan army had been participating in colonial defence since 1730 and after 1763 it was deemed necessary to increase the number of regulars serving in the Indies. Millions of *reales* was also spent on upgrading fortifications at San Juan de Puerto Rico, Vera Cruz and Havana, plus regular provincial regiments were established, which were to all intents and purposes to mirror the establishment of the metropolitan regiments. The newest were the freshly reorganised Regimiento de Infantería Fijo de la Habana, and the Regimiento de Infantería Fijo de la Louisiana. A distinction needs to be understood here between what would be termed the *Milicia* and the *Fijo* (fixed) regiments, as the latter were in every respect regular infantry, and the Regimiento de la Luisiana participated in all three years of the Gulf campaign.

---

10   Chartrand, *Spanish Army*, p.15.

An interesting aside to the establishment of the metropolitan regiments is found in the *Ordenanzas* of 1768. 'The commanders of the Warships or commissioners who carry out the embarkation in Transports, [to America] must give a table to all the Officers, their wives, and children.'[11] Bills for food were paid for out of the pockets of the officers, daily, who were all required to go on half pay while at sea, the other half being assigned for expenses. Officers' wives were not the only women to be mentioned either, as a subsequent instruction required the women and children of the troops to be paid and rationed from the navy supplies like their husbands, with a sergeant receiving 40 *maravedis* a day from the stopped pay of the officers, to a private's eight, the implication being that a family would earn twice the wage of a single man. Camp followers and other types were not considered regimental women, such soldiers who smuggled unauthorised women onto a ship or into a camp, and especially if they tried to 'live scandalously,' with such females that were termed 'publicly frivolous women' either openly or in disguise were to suffer arrest and punishment.[12] The moral wellbeing of the battalions, and the individual who would have to investigate such a charge, was the chaplain, who was to care for the souls of every soldier, wife, child and servant, or otherwise dependant, in the camp. The *sergento mejor* was required to present lists by company, irrespective of sex or station, of the names of True Catholics within the battalion, as presumably opposed to *conversos*. Guards were expected to give salutes not only to officers, but also people associated with them, such as their wives, whether the husband was present or not.[13]

In his initial campaigns up the Mississippi and against Mobile, Bernardo de Gálvez utilised companies of militia, colonial regulars, and metropolitan regulars, besides volunteers and naval support. Bernardo de Gálvez himself had never commanded so many regulars as he did during the siege of Pensacola. This is not to say that militia did not serve in the Pensacola Campaign. Famously Gálvez was able to call upon the organised or disciplined and emancipated militia of Havana and New Orleans, consisting of *blanco* (white), *pardo* (mixed) and *moreno* (black) companies of state equipped troops. Since the reforms of the Conde de O'Reilly new companies of *pardos* and *morenos* had been added to the garrison of Louisiana, so as to come into line with the other major cities of the Indies, and Gálvez used them as vanguard troops. It seems that, as per the regulation of 1776, all provincial militia battalions adopted flank companies, with each battalion maintaining service companies of grenadiers and *cazadores*, made up of the most able-bodied volunteers for duty beyond their region. By the time of the siege of Pensacola the emancipated militia of New Orleans had won a reputation as skilled light infantry.

Light infantry played a vital role in Spanish operations, but the corps was in its infancy at the time. Though the sources are vague, Gálvez constantly

---

11   Anon., *Reales Ordenanzas para las Fuerzas Armadas de Español* (Madrid: Seretaría del Despacho Universal de Guerra, 1768,) Tomo I, pp.222–223.

12   Anon., *Ordenanzas*, Tomo I, pp.215, 222–223.

13   Anon., *Ordenanzas*, Tomo I, p.275.

referred to *cazadores* and *infanteria ligera* in his reports. The metropolitan army maintained specialised light infantry regiments, which at the siege of Pensacola were represented by the Voluntarios de Catalunya, which had been formal regiments in the line of battle as the first and second Regimientos de Catalunya since 1763. It was the second Catalunya that served at Pensacola.

Additionally, Gálvez seems to have made extensive use of *piquetes*, troops drawn from the *fusiliero* companies to mount guards and act as detachments for special assignments, who are referred to, sometimes, as *infanteria ligera*.

Gálvez 's army represented a vast swathe of nations in the best tradition of eighteenth-century Bourbon armies. For a start there were men from the colonies serving in the regular and militia establishments, such as *Sargento* Manuel Rodriguez, who was born in Mexico City in 1759, and was serving in the marine battalion when he gallantly defended Dauphin Island outside Mobile Bay, with a *piquete* of 18 men against HMS *Mentor* on 5 January 1781.[14] Juan de Villebeauvre had been born in Brittany sometime between 1735 and 1737. He had gone to the Americas with the Compagnies Franches de la Marine, winding up at New Orleans, and when Louisiana was ceded to Spain, he elected to trade one white coat for another, being made a *sub teniente* in the Regimiento de la Luisiana in 1767, he served in the 1779 campaign and took the surrender of Natchez, where he remained commandant.[15]

Famously, the *Gálvezton* brig, and the galley flotilla of New Orleans, was commanded by a militia *teniente coronel*, named Don Pedro George Rousseau, who had been born in France and volunteered for the Continental Navy in Virginia. After capturing some British ships on the Mississippi, he became one of Gálvez's most trusted officers.[16]

Amongst the more obscure members of the Louisiana militia was Miguel Dragon, who was born in Athens in 1739 as Michalis Dracos, and found his way to New Orleans as a merchant when it was still French. He married Marie de Montplasir in 1755 and remained after 1763. Dracos was in the militia when the American Revolution broke out, in 1776 he and Marie had a daughter, who does not seem to have survived infancy, and the next year another girl was born, Marie Celeste, who would have been two years old when her father marched off with Bernardo de Gálvez to fight the British, in the city's company of artillery. Dracos was a *sargento* then but eventually reached the rank of *teniente*, serving in each of the operations of the Gulf theatre.[17]

Spanish noblemen from Extremadura and Andalucía were of course present like *coronels* Ezpeleta, Miró, and *Brigadier* Gironimo Girón de Moctezuma, Marquis de las Amarillas, a descendant not only of one of the oldest families in Malaga but also of the last *Mexica Tlatoani*, who had been second in command at Mobile.

---

14   Jack D. Holmes, 'French and Spanish Military Units in the Pensacola Campaign,' in William S. Coker and Robert R. Rea (eds), *Anglo-Spanish Confrontation on the Gulf Coast during the American Revolution* (Pensacola: Gulf Coast History and Humanities Conference, 1982), p.153.

15   On Villebeuvre see, Jack D.L. Holmes, 'Juan de la Villebeuvre: Spain's Commandant of Natchez During the American Revolution', *Journal of Mississippi History*, vol.37 (1979), pp.97–126.

16   W. E. Clement, *Plantation Life on the Mississippi* (Gretna: Firebird Press, 2000), p.157.

17   Louise Pecquet, *Some Prominent Virginia Families* (Lynchburg: J.P Bell, 1907), pp.162–163.

Francisco de Miranda, the future father of Venezuelan liberty, was born in 1750 to a successful merchant of little lineage from Spain and a *criollo* mother of good family and wealth. The caricature of the puffed up, preening *criollo* with pockets that were deeper than his intellect, who in the words of the historian, Miguel José Sanz, abused 'the prerogatives of their birth because they were ignorant of what these were for,' was one that was well established and Miranda himself would grow up to fulfil at least part of that stereotype.[18] Indeed, when Miranda was born his father Don Francisco was embroiled in a legal battle with the old *criollo* aristocracy regarding his right to identify himself publicly as a captain in the militia of the city. A position in the militia carried with it a title, importance, and social standing, and especially so in the viceregal capitals. In Peru, where all classes could engage in commerce without stain (internally at least) of class distinction, wealth and nobility was no bar to being a trader, and those who had made names in the colony since the founding of Lima traded upon them and in the creation of wealth also created a colonial aristocracy. Outwardly however the *peninsulares* smirked at how they went about garnering badges of their wealth and position. Namely, in lieu of the ability to be granted noble titles, they avidly sought posts in the militia into which the richest and best connected would undoubtedly rise to the top. The most prized title *criollos* could often aspire to was, *coronel*, and they poured much of their wealth into their regiments, creating gaudy, and to many minds absurd, battalions of *Indios* and mixed-race soldiers, commanded by shopkeepers and grocers. Nothing could be more representative of the drive of the *criollo* classes to rise in status than by the ostentatious branding of themselves with military ranks, and in so doing so identified themselves to outsiders as unforgivably American.[19]

From 1771 to 1780 Miranda pursued claims of nobility and a military career in Spain and North Africa slowly becoming disillusioned with the system in the Iberian Peninsula as he had in Caracas, but as yet he was a *capitán* with friends and connections. In 1780 Miranda joined the forces being sent out to the Caribbean as the Army of Operations under *Teniente General* Victor de Navia, in *Jefe de Escuadra* Jose de Solano's fleet, and was further given the position of aide de camp to *Mariscal de Campo* Manuel de Cagigal. The expedition, numbering some 10,000 men, sailed in April, and would arrive in time to add its weight to the siege of Pensacola.

Men like the Conde de O'Reilly, and Miranda's commandant in Morocco, Don Juan de Sherlock, the defender of Mellila, represent an important facet of the Bourbon Spanish army of the eighteenth century; the Irish. The Irish regiments of Spain were not as famous as the Brigade Irlandaise of France, but was equally respected in the Spanish army, and it was impossible to escape the influence of émigré families that came over at the turn of the century to serve in the Catholic armies for the eventual

---

18   Robert Harvey, *Liberators: Latin America's Savage Wars for Freedom, 1810-1830* (London: Robinson, 2002), p.19.

19   Jean Descola, Michael Heron (trans.), *Daily Life in Colonial Peru 1710-1820* (New York: The McMillan Company), pp.207–208.

restoration of the House of Stuart, and Irish liberty. Of course, after almost a century abroad, the Hibernian character of the Irish regiments was becoming distinctly Hispanic. Gálvez had the Regimiento de Hibernia with him at Pensacola, commanded by *Coronel* Arturo O'Neill de Tyrone y O'Kelly who had been born in 1738 in Dublin and had served with the Hibernia for 28 years. His ties with his commander went back to Algiers. The forming of personal connections throughout the army had been the main positive outcome of that operation. The Hibernia was an experienced regiment, but many of its company level officers were young and owed their positions to family connections. A glimpse of some of its officers give a flavour of it character. There was *Capitán* Juan Brickdale, who had been born in England in 1756, and had entered the Hibernia as a cadet in 1772. *Capitán* Juan Hogan was born in 1756. His father had once commanded the regiment and he had joined as a cadet in 1767. *Teniente* Cornelio O'Kenny, who had been born in 1740, entered as a *cadete* in 1763. Newly promoted *Sub Teniente* Josef Trapani was an Italian. Having been born in 1738 he had joined the regiment in 1755. Though old for a subaltern, Trapani had entered the Hibernia as a private, and so was that rare species of officer that had risen from the ranks. Finally, *Sub Teniente* Tomas O'Donoghue, born in Spain in 1762, had become a *cadete* in the Hibernia in 1777, being promoted in 1779.[20]

At the age of 34, Bernardo de Gálvez was about to lead yet another army, 'of all conditions, nations and colours,'[21] as he had against Florida on the Mississippi. He knew his officers, and even the troops who had never served with him were eager to do so. They were gathered between New Orleans and Havana in unprecedented numbers for the young general. It was to be the largest Spanish operation of the American Revolution, but Pensacola was to be a challenge unlike any he had faced before. He was no longer commanding as the governor of Louisiana, but was what today we might term, supreme commander of an army group. Inexcusable delays in getting the operation started meant that, all told, the British had been preparing their fortifications for two years, including a period of about a year between March 1780 and 1781, in which they could not quite believe they had not been attacked. Gálvez shared their confusion, and by the time he got to Pensacola, he had to contend with a system of earthworks, and a garrison over twice the size of any he had tackled before. On 26 April 1780 a letter was delivered to Fort Panmure, Natchez, from Alexander Fraser of the British Indian department. The *commandante*, De Lavillebeuvre, forwarded it to Gálvez, the contents of which more than hinted what he could expect at Pensacola.

I have the pleasure to acquaint you that Mr. Swanson McMain with 5 ships more with goods likewise 5 frigates and 2 74-gun ships are arrived at Pensacola likewise G[eneral]. Clinton expected daily from Savanna with troops from whence he set

---

20   W. S. Murphy, 'The Irish Brigade of Spain at the Capture of Pensacola, 1781', *Florida Historical Quarterly*, vol.38, no.3, pp.223–224.

21   Saravia, *Gálvez*, p.149.

A view of Pensacola, in West Florida circa 1770–1776, engraving by George Gould. This gives an idea of how Gage Hill commanded the town and how ships would have to fire over the rooftops to hit it. The new earthworks built between 1778–1781, which represented the prime objective to the Spanish, occupied the hill behind the large house in the centre right of the picture. (Library of Congress)

of a long time agoe [*sic*]. We had at Pensacola before the arrival of these shipping 1,500 troops with 1,500 Indians so that if the Governor Gálvez does go there I hope he will meet with a warm reception.[22]

This time the British were ready.

---

22   Lawrence Kinnaird (ed.), *Annual Report of the American Historical Association for the Year 1945* (Washington: US Printing Office, 1949), p.377.

3

Jailbirds and German Troops: John Campbell and the Garrison of Pensacola

Major General John Campbell of Strachur was a contrast to Gálvez in that he fitted the contemporary image of a British general quite well. He had been born in 1727 and so would turn 54 in 1781. He was a hereditary clan chief in Scotland, and also just happened to bear one of the most common names in the British officer corps. His long record of service went back to the Jacobite Rebellion, where he had been wounded at Culloden, serving in the Earl of Loudon's Regiment. From there he had joined the 43rd Highlanders (later renumbered the 42nd), and had been wounded again in the attack on Ticonderoga in 1758. After rising to major in the 17th Foot he became the lieutenant colonel of the 57th, which he commanded between 1775 and 1778. He had seen active but not very arduous service during the New York campaign, with the pinnacle of his time fighting the rebels being when he took the fort at Paulus Hook in New Jersey. Upon promotion to brigadier general, he was ordered to sail from New York to bring reinforcements to Pensacola, the capital of West Florida, and shortly after his arrival was further advanced to the rank of major general and became commander-in-chief there in March of 1779. Unlike Gálvez, Campbell is not a celebrated man: few know his name, and those that do often find it hard to distinguish him from the gallery of other Campbells who served in the eighteenth century. As an officer he was conventional, and at times was accused of being timid as well. However, there was a stolidity and good sense to John Campbell that asks us to remember that although he was not shaped in the heroic mould, it did not mean he did not always know his business, especially with the means at his disposal. It took him from the summer of 1779 to the spring of 1780 to be able to regain his equilibrium against Gálvez, by which time West Florida on the Mississippi and Mobile had been lost. Then, having had things simplified, he set about building up the fortifications of Pensacola and gathering as many troops as possible against the inevitable Spanish attack, hoping against hope that he would receive some naval aid.

Under ideal situations Pensacola was quite a strong place to defend, especially from the sea. It sits on one of the larger bays on the northern curve of the Gulf of Mexico, sitting at a midpoint between the Florida peninsula and New Orleans, fed from the north by the Escambia and Black rivers, the mouths of which are separated by an isthmus like projection of land that almost cut it in half. The eastern side of which the British maps sometimes call Chester Bay, presumably after the governor, Lieutenant Colonel Peter Chester. A settlement called Campbelltown lay to the north of Pensacola on the Escambia side. A muscular arm of the coast reaches out from the east and narrows as it approaches the mouth of the bay, now called Gulf Breeze, enclosing it but leaving a passage to the sea and terminating at Deer Point (Cabo Venado). This isthmus is shielded to the south by the sinuous stretch of hard packed sand called Santa Rosa Island, which runs like a sparkling coral ribbon for some 52 miles east to west and creates, not only its own channel, but the access point to the bay which is and was just over a mile wide between its most western point and the mainland at what in 1781 was called Barrancas Coloradas, or Red Cliffs. The town and harbour itself, noted for the length of its quays, the sandy streets, and the intolerable boredom of being stationed there, occupied a spot at the edge of the western shore of the bay between the mouths of two bayous and below a low but distinctive plot of high ground which the British had called Gage Hill.

Many of the names of Pensacola Bay dated back to 1693, when Don Carlos de Siguenza y Gongora surveyed harbour. It was this Mexican mathematician that observed the strengths and weaknesses of the anchorage which remained as relevant to attack and defence almost a century later. The fortifications on the Barrancas and the Siguenza point on Santa Rosa was his idea, however all attempts to place a fort on the sandy island were foiled by the weather and lack of funds to erect stable fortifications, and as we shall see the necessity to cover the channel with artillery from both sides was to prove a critical weakness.[1] There was very little originality in the placement of defence works by the British, who rarely strayed from the blueprints of their predecessors. The early Spanish fortifications and some French additions had all more or less succumbed to fires and enemies by 1750, and a hurricane wrecked a promising defensive work on Santa Rosa Island, altering the nature of the sand dunes so as to make it impractical for habitation. However, the fort at Barrancas Coloradas was once again in place, courtesy of the British by 1781.[2]

This was the main seaward defence, mounting 11 guns, with a ditch, a palisade, and a blockhouse that stood just up the bay from the fort at Tartar Point. A ruined fortification, a signal house, and a block house were the only defences on Santa Rosa, these being in poor repair, and there had not been the means to build a complimentary battery at Siguenza point to create a crossfire between there and the cliffs. Pensacola was described by Bernard Romans as it was between 1769 and 1775, when it had 'about a hundred and eighty houses in it, built in general in good taste, but of timber: the town is laid out in an oblong square, near the foot of a hill, called Gage hill; and by means of two rivulets of excellent water which almost surround it, is

---

1   Faye, *Fortifications of Pensacola*, p.151.
2   Faye, *Fortifications of Pensacola*, p.163.

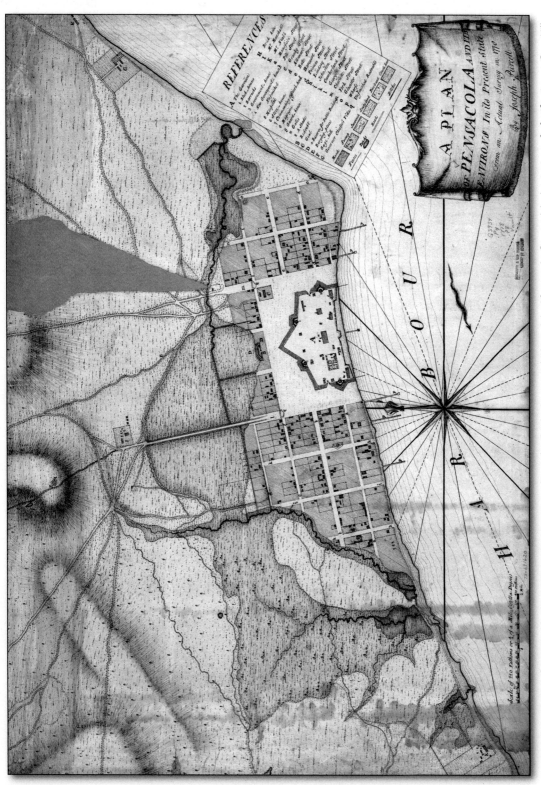

Joseph Purcell's map of West Florida. This 1778 survey gives extraordinary detail right down to which roads had fences, the flora and the beginnings of a fortification on Gage Hill. (Library of Congress)

the best watered of any I know on the continent.'[3] By the time the Spanish arrived, the town was defended from Gage Hill, not the plaza itself. About 1,200 yards from the centre of the town was a large, elongated fort. It was composed of a regular star-fort from which stretched a hornwork that ran south and incorporated two blockhouses that protected the road to Mobile and occupied the middle slope of the hill, which was long and shallow, but rose subtly for another 900 yards. At the peak, Campbell constructed what became known as the Advanced, or Forward, Redoubt, also called the Queen's Redoubt, which was a half-moon work, surrounded by a ditch and abattis, and to which was added two wings as the siege progressed. In between the two, 300 yards from the advanced work and 600 from Fort George, was a circular work, called the middle, centre, or Prince of Wales's Redoubt. This was added after the advanced redoubt to connect the two main works and was sometimes also called the circular redoubt, indeed one Spanish map calls it El Fuerte de Sombrero, as it conjured the shape of a low crowned hat.[4] All told it was an impressive chain of earthworks. Critically, however they offered no protection from the water, and the most important fort to not be built was that which should have been at Siguenza Point.[5]

When Major General John Campbell had arrived in Pensacola in January of 1779, he had found that the many dismal reports he had been given of the state of the province were more than accurate. He wrote to Lord George Germain in March of 1779, that he lacked money and credit, had no vessels for navigation, no artificers to repair or build new works and even if he had there was no provisions or materials to do it with, all of which placed a great burden on the troops of the garrison, whose far too few artificers lacked sufficient engineers stores to be properly employed. The work to upgrade the defences probably cost about $50,000 and was a testament to his industry that the fortifications were in such a good state in 1781.[6]

The woes of Campbell seemingly had no end, however, for he even found his troops were unsatisfactory, summing them up to Clinton as 'jailbirds and German troops' in February of 1779.[7] After 17 men of the Maryland Loyalists had deserted to New Orleans with 100 pounds of ammunition he branded them Irish vagabonds, and deserters from the rebels who were highly untrustworthy because of the 'instability of their disposition.'[8] Quite where he got this impression of the loyalist regiments is unclear, but he made a similar allegation against the 60th Foot. That being the case the loyalists had good reason to be dissatisfied. The men of the 3rd Regiment of Waldeck were damned as unfit for wilderness operations, and unsurprisingly, Campbell only had confidence in what was left of the 16th Foot.

---

3   Bernard Romans, *A Concise Natural History of East and West Florida* (New York: R. Aitken 1776), p.303.
4   Medina Rojas, Francisco De Borja, *José de Ezpeleta, gobernador de la Mobila, 1780-1781* (Francisco: Escuela de Estudios Hispano-Americanos, 1980), p.117.
5   Faye, *Fortifications of Pensacola*, pp.277–282.
6   George C. Osborn, 'Major General John Campbell in West Florida', *The Florida Historical Quarterly*, vol.27, no.4 (April 1949), p.318.
7   Osborne, 'Campbell in West Florida', p.321.
8   Osborne, 'Campbell in West Florida', p.321.

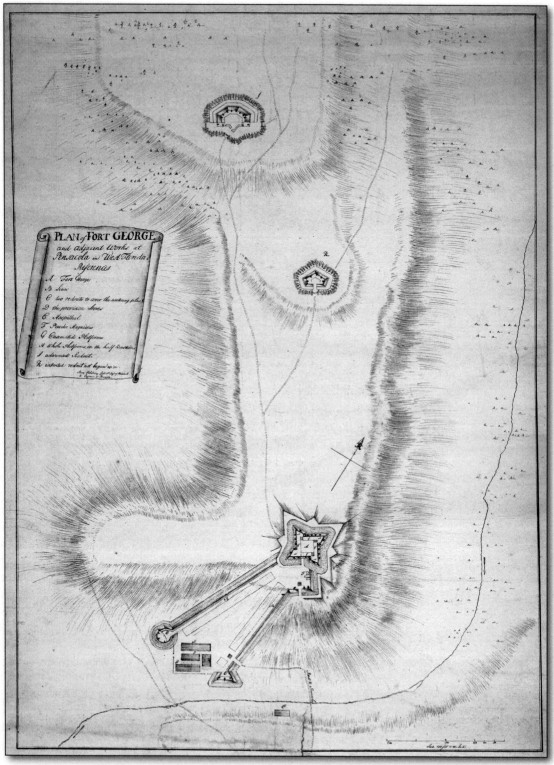

A superbly detailed Plan of Fort George and adjacent works at Pensacola drafted by the acting Chief Engineer Henry Heldridge of the 3rd Waldeck Regiment, circa 1780. It clearly shows the original extent of Fort George on the lower plateau of Gage Hill, and the long extension to connect it to the blockhouses on the Mobile Road. Note the abattis and the lack of flank batteries on what became known as the Queen's Redoubt but which is here termed the advanced redoubt. (Library of Congress)

A North View of Pensacola, on the Island of Santa Rosa, Drawn by DOM. SERRES.
1. The Fort. 2. The Church. 3. The Governors House. 4. The Commandants House. 5. A Well. 6. A Bunge.

This engraving from 1768 mistakenly assumes that Pensacola stood on Santa Rosa Island and can be viewed from the north while on the water. However, it confirms some descriptions of the mostly timber built town, interspersed with older Spanish buildings. (Library of Congress)

His correspondence throughout the siege would show he was not a popular officer, who had no great pride in his troops, though he did take pains to keep them clothed even at the risk of annoying General Clinton. Captain Elias Durnford of the Royal Engineers seems to have had more of the personal touch, and an idea of charismatic leadership than Major General Campbell.

Finding naval support was also a constant battle. Campbell requested two sloops be stationed in the harbour to transport the heavy guns and garrison troops for the fort, and he deemed it of paramount importance to base a squadron at one of the ports on the gulf which could control the Mississippi. Campbell did have two sloops in Pensacola, but he deemed them in a wretched state. He was very concerned that these were the only warships to be had and complained that he had 'not a single gun mounted to prevent the enemy from entering.'[9]

Of the many places a soldier could be stationed in the Americas, few had a kind word to say about West Florida. Unlike even East Florida, this was a frontier posting of the unhealthiest reputation, and had little by way of comforts. Lieutenant Hugh Mackey Gordon of the 16th Foot, who was Deputy Quartermaster General and Deputy Inspector of Provincials, as well as one of Campbell's aides de camp, thought Pensacola to be 'the worst part of the world'. He found 'nothing to be had but lean beef and pork except the poultry which is extravagantly dear and it is so damned hot fish stinks before it can be boiled,' he added that 'the only thing this pleasant place abounds

---

9   Osborne, 'Campbell in West Florida', pp.321–322.

in is a Beautiful white sand which circulates freely.'[10] Further he bemoaned coming 'from a pleasant, plentiful company into a most wretched one.'[11]

The cost of simple items such as bread and flour at Pensacola was a source of great disquiet to the garrison, especially as their pay barely met their everyday expenses and bat and forage allowance was deep in arrears. Campbell explained the situation to Clinton in the late spring of the next year.

> … permit me to observe that Your Excellency has omitted answering the prayer of Lieutenant Colonels Stiell [Former Commander in Chief] and Dickson [Commander at Baton Rouge], and Captain Johnston's [Commander Royal Artillery] Memorial which was for a similar allowance of Bat Baggage and Forage money to that of the other Troops under your Excellency's Command, and I have now to add that the Regiment of Waldeck think themselves particularly aggrieved in being detached to so disagreeable a part of the world where there is a scarcity … of provisions much beyond that of New York... and yet where the usual consideration of Bat … & Forage money for the year 1779 has hitherto been denied them; I formerly kept them in temper by waiting for your Excellency's Answer to the memorial above-mentioned; I have now soothed them by communicating to them this application in favour of them and the troops serving in West Florida: as I trust to receiving a favourable answer.[12]

In the end this favourable answer took until February of 1781 for Campbell to receive. The majority of the Germans especially hated Pensacola. Only a few months earlier, in January of 1779, the chaplain of the 3rd Waldeck Regiment, Philipp Waldeck, had caught his first sight of Pensacola from his transport ship, 'Normally, when we enter a harbour, everyone is anxious to see the city. But here one could already see from aboard ship that this was a miserable place.'[13] The impression was not improved after they had landed.

> We walked about in order to take a closer look at the city, which makes a miserable, sad impression. Pensacola is laid out rather spaciously and, if one counts all of the structures, the number of buildings is approximately two hundred. These have all been built since the last war when this pitiable territory was given to the English Crown. The houses here are all constructed of pine wood, quite light and airy, as the climate here requires. There are still three of the old Spanish buildings here: an old, decaying structure in which the governor lived; another dilapidated structure in which the Indian colonel [superintendent], Stuart, lives; and a powder magazine. I don't know where the stones came from for this last building, for there are no stones available here. The streets, if that is what they are supposed to be are full of sand, in which one walks about up over ones shoes, as

---

10   Hugh Mackay Gordon to Edward Winslow, 20 March 1779, *The Winslow Papers*, <https://web.lib.unb.ca/winslow/index.html>, accessed 29 June 2023.

11   Christopher New, *Maryland Loyalists in the American Revolution* (Centreville: Tidewater Publishers, 1996), p.83.

12   The National Archives (TNA): PRO 30/55/23/34, Campbell to Clinton, 13 May 1780.

13   William E. Dornemann, 'A Diary Kept by Chaplain Waldeck During the Last American War Part III', *Journal of the Johannes Schwalm Historical Association*, vol.3, no.2 (1986), p.49.

one would in Germany in the snow. This sand is so hot in the summer that one's shoe-soles and feet burn in it.[14]

He did admit that the weather at the time he landed was not much different in temperature to summer in Germany, and the newly built barracks was large and comfortable, but the chaplain's struggle with sandy shoes would continue.

As can be imagined any regiment that was sent to West Florida that did not already have supremely impressive field maintenance standards was bound to end up wrecked by the time it returned. A tour of two to three years being common. Even then, clothing had a nasty habit of rotting on a soldier's back, shoes went dull, mouldered, and cracked as the oil normally used to condition them attracted roaches, and regulation blankets that were supposed to last seven years, were worn out in four in West Florida. In the course of the three years from 1765 to 1767 the 31st Foot, stationed at Pensacola, lost six officers, five officer's ladies, and three officer's children, 190 men, 23 enlisted men's wives and 41 enlisted men's children to sickness, and child mortality. It was said that the regiment buried half its effective strength before being relieved.[15]

The Swiss professional soldier, Brigadier General Frederick Haldimand, who did a great deal to improve things in the early part of the British occupation made his intention to fix things plain when he took command in 1767, as he had not been appointed, so he said, merely to 'preside at the funerals of brave troops.'[16]

It was hard and unforgiving work, however, in the summer troops could only work in the morning and evening, and in winter the storms often destroyed what had been accomplished. As such, labour parties from the regiments were augmented by enslaved labour (rented for the purpose). Additionally, soldier's families were given extra rations. Which was no small gesture, as in 1768 the 31st Foot had 80 women 68 children with them, the 21st had 71 women and 59 children, and of these 151 women, 30 were pregnant.[17]

Away from all that was familiar and subjected to the harsh climate and military discipline, standards were hard to keep up. The usual amenities of grog shops and places of entertainment were to be found in town, skittles were popular, as were drink and dice. 'There was nothing among them [the soldiers] but cursing fighting and drinking,' and Lieutenant General Gage was prompted to muse that there seemed to be a contagion in the climate.[18]

The alcohol and the heat certainly had their part to play. A drummer of the 34th faced a court martial for beating his wife. In the course of the trial, it appeared that the lady had been frequently and exceedingly intimate

---

14   Dornemann, 'A Diary Kept by Chaplain Waldeck', p.51.
15   Robert R. Rea, 'Life, Death and Little Glory,' in William S. Coker (ed.) *The Military Presence on the Gulf Coast* (Pensacola: Gulf Coast History and Humanities Conference, 1978), pp.25–27.
16   Rea, *Life, Death and Little Glory*, p.25.
17   Rea, *Life, Death and Little Glory*, p.25.
18   Rea, *Life, Death and Little Glory*, pp.28–29.

with a surgeon's mate, whereby the drummer was said to have been 'injured in the most tender part.' The unfaithful couple being caught in the act, the drummer had apparently chastised the woman on the spot, for which he was placed under arrest, however the presiding officers at court martial seemed to have approved of the summary justice and Major Robert Farmar, then a serving officer in the 60th, who had become a prominent landowner by 1781, was furious when the court failed to uphold his disciplinary measures.

The climate and jealous husbands were not the only peril either. It paid for officers and men to go about armed if they were on an excursion. Captain Elias Durnford was in the habit of strolling on Santa Rosa Island with his ladies, and on one particular jaunt encountered a large cat of unusual size, likely a Puma. Durnford tried to fire his pistol at it, only to find the charge had been drawn, and so stared the beast down until it retreated.

According to the Dutch botanist and cartographer, Romans, the shelter of Santa Rosa Bay was infested with mosquitos, which forced all people of sense in the area to use mosquito nets, and a type of tent called a Baire, which was made of a 'light coarse cloth, like canvass gauze.'[19]

In April 1780, Germain had bemoaned the disappointing speed at which British forces had been deprived of the king's land, and instructed Campbell to focus on the defence of what remained until reinforcements could be sent to allow him to act offensively.[20] In the meantime, he urged a strong show of support and good will to the Muskogee nations and their neighbours. As Campbell had cited the defection of the Choctaws as a main reason for the fall of the lower Mississippi, which resonated in a way with London as, one of the more curious passages in the Spanish manifesto of injustices ran: 'The dominions of the crown in America have been threatened, and they [the British] have gone to the dreadful extremity of raising the Indian nations, called the Chatcas, Cheroquies and Chicachas, against the innocent inhabitants of Louisiana, who would have been the victims of the rage of these barbarians, if the Chatcas themselves had not repented, and revealed all the ... English had planned.'[21]

Whitehall advised that Superintendent of Indian Affairs, Alexander Cameron, go on a grand tour of the villages of the Choctaw, Chickasaw, Creek, and even Cherokee nations, and attempt to form either a hostile or neutral bloc that could either harass the Spanish or at least not ally with them.[22]

Meanwhile through the summer of 1779, the Spanish once more called upon their vast colonial resources to pile war materials into Louisiana, not only that but money and powder was sent up the Mississippi to Fernando de Leyba at St Louis (through the auspices of Oliver Pollock), to fund and supply the operations of George Rodgers Clarke between the Ohio and Missouri. The *Audiencia* of New Spain assured the *capitán general* of Havana that food, provisions and 800,000 *pesos* was to be afforded him.

---

19   Romans, *Natural History*, p.227.
20   Osborne, 'Campbell in West Florida', p.328.
21   Stockdale, *Parliamentary Register*, vol.XII, p.444.
22   Osborne, 'Campbell in West Florida', p.326.

In February 1780, Campbell wrote to Clinton that the fate of the province was in the balance and outlined the steps he had taken to secure it, unaware that as he was writing Bernardo Gálvez was approaching Mobile. The year was to prove decisive in the struggle for the Gulf Coast. Despite the gravity of Campbell's thoughts on security, the British commander waited too long to launch an expedition to relieve the garrison, electing to await official news that the post was under attack instead of acting on information imparted by deserters. When the expedition did set off, the weather had turned bad, and the regulars did not see dry clothes again until they returned to Pensacola. Despite dramatic reports from the Spanish of their proximity, the man body had only gotten as far as the Tensaw river by the time Mobile surrendered.

Except for two men who drowned at the Perdido river, Campbell lost no men on the expedition, but was blamed for his inactivity and it cannot have made him look good to his allies who joined the expedition either. He can be seen to be a cautious but capable general with a surprisingly resilient force despite his complaints about it. Due to his small numbers, lack of faith in his own troops and feeling cast off, overwhelmed, and abandoned, Campbell preferred to fortify what he could rather than attack. As such he willingly surrendered the initiative for the majority of 1780, never knowing how close Gálvez had come to defeat after being essentially shipwrecked trying to cross Mobile Bar.

Nerve would appear to be the great divide between the two generals, and the Spaniard appeared to have the lion's share. This is not to do with numbers and backing being more readily available to the Spanish, as this only became available as successes demanded reward. In 1779, Gálvez lost most of his supplies and transport in a hurricane, while a third of his force was hit with disease on the famous *Marcha de Gálvez*, yet he still successfully removed the Mississippi from West Florida, showing that were the positions reversed, it is unlikely that Mobile would have been taken. That being said, when his problems were reduced to what was clearly in front of him, Campbell would prove stolid in defence of his forts.

Though the siege of Pensacola is extremely well served by diarists and official reports, we have no front-rank views for the British side or detailed narrative descriptions of personal activities. As such a brief explanation of how the British army conducted itself in combat will be necessary to give character to the numerous skirmishes and actions that occurred after Gálvez brought his forces onto the mainland.

The British Army in North America, which was spoken of with such fondness by Lord Cornwallis, was an accomplished fighting entity. Not in the sense of the linear warfare that people popularly perceive in the eighteenth century but in a rougher, looser type of combat which no army that operated on the continent could be ignorant of. In 1785, Major General William Harcourt, writing after the war lamented that the British infantry were lacking in discipline, as opposed to that of Prussia, due to their time in America and upon the whole whether 'loose files and the American scramble would not have been preferred,' by the officers of the army.[23]

---

23   A.P. Kup, 'Sir Charles McCarthy (1768-1824), Soldier and Administrator', *Bulletin of the John Rylands Library*, vol.60, no.1 (1977), p.60.

Far from being a sign of indiscipline, the fact that the British Army could be accused of this at all tells us much about the impact of the eight years of service in North America, and the previous 20 years besides. The reputation of Yankee militiamen as expert bush-fighters was a potent one, but by the time of the Philadelphia campaign it had been more than shown that with the right training, the regulars were just as dangerous in the woods. By 1778, troops that had seen active service in New York and Pennsylvania had an updated tactical vocabulary, which made allowances for a mode of warfare that suited the conditions in North America. The light infantry doctrine of the British Army had its foundation in the Manual Exercise of 1764, from these came Lieutenant General George Townshend's instructions of 1772, which in turn influenced the expanding of the light infantry by Major General William Howe at his camp of instruction at Salisbury in 1774. This in part had been based on Howe's own experience in the French and Indian War and was practically progressed by field operations against the rebels between 1776 and 1777. No troops that had served during this time could be ignorant of loose files and the American scramble, and many officers reported great satisfaction at whipping the rebels at their own game, comparing it in some cases to a good day's hunting. Indeed, no incoming troops from Britain were left in their close order lines for long. In September of 1777 the then ensign, John Enys of the 29th Foot, described his regiment becoming practiced in Harcourt's so-called scramble.

> During our stay here, our party went into the woods a little way to practice treeing as they call it, that is to say the manner of hiding ourselves behind Tree Stumps etc, etc, etc and at our return the Major was pleased to say the men had exceeded his expectations tho I could see very plainly our awkwardness diverted the Indians and Royalists [Loyalists] who are by far better hands at this Work being bred to the woods from their infancy, and accustomed to this manner of hiding themselves to shoot deer, and other wild beasts.[24]

This entry could well have spoken to the regiments, of West Florida. With the understanding of the prevalence for open order operations we can presume that with the commencement of hostilities, the regiments had practiced treeing as well, but likewise would have been seen as less than proficient by their allies. The regular troops at Pensacola, therefore, had the theoretical capability to skirmish as a battalion, but Campbell described them as not properly adapted to what was termed, *petite guerre*, and they were badly worn down by their long posting to what was universally acknowledged to be terribly unhealthy climate.

The six or seven companies of the 16th Foot, or what was left of them by 1781, had been garrisoning various parts of the Floridas since 1768 and if later documentation is anything to go by, they numbered barely over

---

24 John Enys, Elizabeth Cometti (ed.) *The American Journals of Lt. John Enys* (Syracuse: Syracuse University Press, 1976), pp.24–26.

three officers and 107 men at the end of the siege.[25] As Campbell wrote to General Clinton in May of that year; 'It will give me the greatest satisfaction imaginable if your excellency can spare me one British Regiment in the room of the 16th Regiment who are worn out in the service, and such of the men as may be judged fit for service, with your approbation, to be droughted [sic] into the 60th regiment, as they want a number of men to complete.'[26]

Though the 60th (Royal American) Regiment of Foot had a reputation for being excellent light infantrymen during the French and Indian War under Henri Bouqet (who coincidentally died in Pensacola), the 3rd and 4th battalions of the 60th had been raised in 1775 and were sent from England to the West Indies. Eight companies were then sent to West Florida. Both the Waldeck regiment and the 60th took heavy losses during Gálvez's rapid conquest of the Mississippi and Mobile. Although already badly understrength even after less than six years, (by 1780 the four Companies of the 4/60th mustered barely 98 men between them), by the time Mobile fell the 60th had lost seven companies as prisoners to the Spanish.[27] One (likely amalgamated) company of the 3rd battalion was all that was left in the garrison at Pensacola when the Spaniards came, and amounted to about four officers and 129 men.[28]

As for the 3rd Waldeck, it is known that the Germans adopted treeing and scrambling tactics in North America and did so with extreme efficiency at the Battle of Long Island. However, it is to be gathered from Campbell's sentiments that the 3rd Waldeck were not fit for wilderness service. In 1780, after only a single summer at Pensacola, *Oberst* Johann Ludwig Wilhelm von Hanxleben reported that the regiment's strength stood at only 371 men, due to disease, fatigue, and the loss of four companies to the Spanish at Natchez. Like most of his soldiers, Hanxleben would have gladly exchanged a summer in Florida for a year in service to the Devil.[29]

The rampant dissatisfaction was most marked with the northern Loyalists and Germans. General Clinton, clearly did not anticipate the effect on morale when, writing in 1778, he explained that he intended to employ foreign troops and provincials for far flung garrisons like St Augustine and Pensacola as their 'loss to this army will not be so much felt.'[30]

The Provincial troops from two regiments, one from Pennsylvania and the other from Maryland, were sent from New York to Jamaica with Campbell. It was a decision that was bound to make an unhappy garrison even more unhappy. The muster-master general of the provincials, Edward Winslow, wrote:

---

25   Albert W. Haarman, 'The Siege of Pensacola: An Order of Battle', *Florida Historical Quarterly*, vol.3, no.44 (1965), p.195.

26   Historical Manuscripts Commission, *Report on American manuscripts in the Royal Institution of Great Britain*. (London: HM Stationary Office, 1904), vol.1, p.431.

27   Lewis Butler, *Annals of the King's Royal Rifle Corps* (London: Smith, Elder & Co., 1913), vol.I, pp.220–221.

28   Haarman, 'Siege of Pensacola', p.197.

29   Friederike Baer, *Hessians: German Soldiers in the American Revolutionary War* (Oxford: Oxford University Press, 2022), p.304.

30   New, *Maryland Loyalists*, p.82.

The sending [of] Provincial Troops on such services has become [a] matter of consideration among 'em; they have generally censured the measure as unjust & not consistent with the original compact. This assertion arises from an idea that all or most of the provincial corps were Local & intended to defend particular provinces from which they could not be removed but by their own consent. Contracted as this sentiment may at first appear there is some reason for it … Most of the recruits enlisted expressly for the term of two years, or during the continuance of the rebellion; there is not wanting among them men of sufficient cunning to suggest those terms imply an option in the soldier whether he will continue in service after the expiration of the first period; quibbling and dishonourable as this suggestion may seem to a European gentleman; it is a tolerable pretence of an American labourer.[31]

The Maryland and Pennsylvania regiments were similarly plagued by issues of being ill clothed, stricken by smallpox, and the threat of being unified into one corps, which caused an argument between the rival senior officers. Lieutenant Colonel James Chalmers of the Maryland Regiment had left to plead his case to Clinton in New York. This move, prompted Clinton to deny permission to amalgamate. It is no surprise therefore to find a great deal of desertion from the Provincials and the Waldeck Regiments.

---

31   New, *Maryland Loyalists*, p.83.

4

The Most Fortunate People in the Universe: The Allied Nations

During the siege, Campbell had 500 warriors with him at Pensacola, of which between 40 were Muskogees and eight were Chickasaws. According to a report from the Indian Department, 744 Choctaws had been present as of 10 February, but a reduction occurred between then and the beginning of the siege in March. Cameron reported that the Chickasaws were then, 'all out a-hunting,' as were the Muskogees, but modest numbers arrived to replace outgoing Choctaws by the spring. In terms of army hierarchy Campbell would have more or less assigned them as a division under command of Superintendent Cameron, who thought Campbell had mishandled their allies from the start. 'We have two-thirds of the Choctaws in our interest' he wrote in February 1781, 'and if I was not too much afraid of incurring more expense to government, I would have had the whole of them in our interest last fall.'[1]

Campbell disliked Cameron, seeing him as a man with ideas above his station. Having your largest source of manpower under the theoretical command of a man you neither liked nor respected either as a professional or a gentleman, and who returned the sentiment, was never going to be easy. Meanwhile Cameron certainly felt he knew better than Campbell.

Cameron attributed the failure to keep the allies close to Campbell's penny-pinching. Which in itself was a response to the wilful, though strategic, spending of Cameron's illustrious predecessor, John Stuart. The superintendent was aware that the commander in chief wanted spending in his department cut, but at the same time refused to pay bills he had authorised. Likewise, Campbell was at that point refusing to pay bills incurred by initiatives begun under Stuart. Despite pleas from the wealthier inhabitants that they would personally start a fund to equip the Choctaws and keep them at Pensacola, Cameron felt unable to go around his superior

---

1   Cameron to Germain, 10 February 1781, in Davies (ed.), *Documents of the American Revolution*, vol.XX, p.59.

officer in that way, especially as in February he had run out of funds and gifts. The Choctaws, he wrote were,

> … ready and willing at all times to turn out against the enemy, and I must really say of them that they behave with more civility and sobriety than any Indians I ever knew, but the want of proper white leaders among them is now very evident to every person. I am not, however, without fear of losing some of them.[2]

Prior to the final expedition against Pensacola, Bernardo de Gálvez sent a letter to Campbell asking him, in the name of humanity, to send his indigenous allies away. Gálvez's appeal to not use Native American allies in the coming fight was based both on strategic and personal considerations. He was most firm and disciplined with his own less numerous allies, but having seen how effective indigenous warfare could be against static positions, especially when the warriors were well equipped and supplied, he truly despised the irregular warfare practiced on the frontier.[3]

He had written on the necessity of winning the surrounding nations to the side of Spain in 1777,

> With the existing forces in this province, it is not possible to resist the slightest enemy attack without the Indians on our side … All of the northern part of the province is covered by a multitude of Indian nations settled in British territory, living with the same unrestraint and freedom as all of the Indians in New Spain, without any loyalty or friendship but to those who give them more; with this in mind, and in the event that war breaks with the British, it is necessary (even at all costs) to attract the savages to our side. This, I think, will not be extremely difficult, for two reasons. First because even today they have a certain attachment to the French, with whom they have lived many years; and second, after being properly pampered with our gifts, they will agree to everything we ask of them.[4]

Alexander Cameron reported, with some frustration, that 'Gálvez will even humble himself so low as to kiss their warriors from ear to ear and to pay them every respect that is due to great chiefs. He sent for them to visit him in Orleans.'[5] However the governor's uncle had seen fit to discourage the expensive practice of indigenous diplomacy as practiced by the French and the British, opting instead for his costly frontier wars, and as such there was no funding for a regular supply of gifts and entertainments that this particular mode of diplomatic relations required. The result was a great disinterest of the majority of the Muskogee nations towards Spain, though throughout the war the loyalty of the Choctaws would sway from one side to the other.

2   Cameron to Germain, 10 February 1781, in Davies (ed.), *Documents of the American Revolution*, vol.XX, p.59.
3   Caughey, *Gálvez in Louisiana*, p.189.
4   Saravia, *Gálvez*, pp.100–101.
5   Saravia, *Gálvez*, p.186.

In the first two years of the war, Stuart had told the southern nations that the war was not something they needed to concern themselves with but by 1777 it was clear that the British were no longer reticent about calling 'upon the savages,' as Lord Dartmouth put it.[6] Stuart, knew the potential of indigenous warfare. Many frontier diplomats had seen the devastation a well-armed nation could wreak on an isolated area. Relentless raiding could create a zone that inevitably became uninhabitable.

Despite the horror many held at the idea of employing war-bands, Stuart urged that 'no time be lost in employing the Indians of the different nations to give all the assistance in their power to such His Majesty's faithful subjects as may already have taken or shall hereafter take arms to resist the lawless oppression of the rebels and their attempts to overturn the constitution and oppose His Majesty's authority.'[7] Alexander McGillivray, a mixed-race member of the Muskogees was of the opinion that this would be relatively simple, as, 'Indians will attach themselves to and serve them best who supply their necessities'[8]

Few of the European Americans truly wanted the involvement of the other American nations but the pool of manpower they could bring to the war in the back-country was too tempting a resource not to draw on. In April 1780, when it seemed that Gálvez would strike at any moment, Campbell had a similar attitude to his Spanish opponent, but he was ruefully grateful to have around 1,235 Muskogees, 236 Choctaws and 31 Chickasaws encamped nearby. However, like practically all his troops, he more or less despised or pitied them as 'a mercenary race ... the slaves of the highest bidder without gratitude or affection; However, ... I am afraid that Europeans themselves have brought them these principles.'[9]

Campbell's revulsion at the apparent mercenary attitude of his allies speaks of his general ignorance on the subject. He had no experience with this sort of diplomacy and no faith in the generous and open policy of Superintendent Stuart who warned Governor Tonyn in St Augustine that, 'We court Indian help; we do not command it.' A proverb Campbell ignored if he was ever aware of it.[10]

The apparent mercenary nature of the Muskogees, Chickasaws and Choctaws was evidence of the fact that by the eighteenth century practically all eastern American nations were dependent on some sort of European trade for their subsistence. Although they were still able to support themselves with agriculture and hunting, European materials and tools had replaced those of their own manufacture. Stuart had been very free with distributing goods to the neighbouring nations, spending around $100,000 on gifts and supplies, which meant that when Campbell tried to cut back, the tri-nation group between Florida and the Mississippi suffered.

---

6   O'Donnell, *Southern Indians*, p.30.

7   Saravia, *Gálvez*, p.183.

8   Saravia, *Gálvez*, p.183.

9   Saravia, *Gálvez*, p.184.

10   Stuart to Tonyn, 21 July 1777, in Davies (ed.), *Documents of the American Revolution*, vol. XIII, p.72.

That being said, Campbell's attitude shocked Superintendent Cameron, who must have quickly realised that, the general had every intention of using allied warriors as a force-multiplier but no clue how to go about it, and little appreciation that as allies who chose to assist from free choice, they would expect reward commensurate to the risk.[11] 'He thinks [Indians] are to be used like slaves or a people void of natural sense.' Cameron wrote vexedly, which was a great shame to him as, 'Never was Indians better affected to government than the Choctaws now in our interest … I have it not in my power to use them as I am sensible, they deserve.' After Stuart's reckless spending, Campbell was within his rights to keep a tight hold on the purse-strings, however this would allow the Spanish to be unknowingly much more persuasive in keeping the southern nations in a neutral position. Ironically, Gálvez would later suggest an Indian policy based on Stuart's model with the intention to keep the peace by making all neighbouring and vassal nations totally reliant on the colonial power.

The Muskogee speaking nations of present South Carolina, Georgia, Alabama, and the nascent Seminole nation of Florida, still represented the largest group of potential allies, enemies, and trade partners for either side, however. The majority were known to be friendly with the British but there were some, especially in Florida that were not. An important faction of what the British called the Lower Creeks was the Alachua.[12] They were the founding branch of the Seminole nation after their leader Cowcatcher settled at Cuscowilla during the War of Jenkins Ear. They were thought to be sympathetic to the British but were interested enough in Spanish trade and protection that they sent a delegation to Cuba. Visits to Havana were quite common between 1761 and 1776, on one occasion a chief named Thlehulgee returned from a trip there in the autumn of 1766, well dressed in Spanish clothes, with various chiefs and warriors taking passage with Spanish ships and fishing vessels to Cuba into 1772. The mouth of the Apalachicola and Tampa Bay were common spots to see the ships drop off their passengers, with large groups coming to welcome them home in some cases.[13]

While few of the allies of either European side were named and properly identified, and while both European generals had their own opinions about the usefulness of native allies, the general fitness of the warriors as self-contained military units within wider war-bands was never in doubt. In 1781, royal commissioner, Francisco de Saavedra, called the American Indian nations allied to the Spanish 'Faithful friends and implacable enemies.'[14] A sentiment that would have been acknowledged by most of the British Indian

---

11   Cameron to Germain, 31 October 1780, in Davies (ed.), *Documents of the American Revolution*, vol.XVIII, pp.219–222.

12   Localism was a major factor in the south, and in the Muskogee confederacy would refer to themselves as coming from a specific town, or region, as such though the British categorised the Coweta for example as part of the Lower Creeks, and the Tallapoosa as from the Upper Creeks, they all formed part of a wider Muskogee confederation.

13   Mark F. Boyd, 'Spanish Interest in British Florida, and in the Progress of the American Revolution', *Florida Historical Quarterly*, vol.32, no.2 (1953), p.93.

14   Topping (ed.), *Journal of Saavedra*, p.183.

department and the commandants of the *Presidios* along the frontier of New Spain. The words of an unnamed chief, of an unnamed tribe who came with only 10 men, to Bernardo Gálvez may have inspired these words. 'Thirty times have we seen thus globe of fire be born and die before arriving at thy presence. We come to aid the Spaniards, believing them to be more just than other white men. Although we are a small nation, our assistance is not to be despised, because we know how to shed our blood for our friends, and we are accustomed to drink the blood of our enemies.'[15]

Saavedra wrote that during the siege of Pensacola, where his role was very much one of an observer, he:

> … applied himself to getting acquainted with the nations who had gathered to assist us … There were Indians of various nations, the principal ones being the Choctaws, the Creeks or Tallapoosas and the Alabamas … The Choctaw nation formerly was numerous and formidable, but their number declined notably. At present the Tallapossas are the strongest and most bellicose nation known in these districts, and Americans, Englishmen, and Spaniards vie for their friendship with equal ardour. The Alabamas are brave and warlike, but their number is small; nonetheless an alliance with them is valuable for those who possess Pensacola and Mobile … the heads of the Choctaws are flattened in an operation practiced on infants from the moment of birth. The Alabamas lengthen their ears have them pierced in several places, and wear earrings of strange shapes … Amidst their barbarity they consider themselves to be the most fortunate people in the universe.[16]

Though it is strange that he should ignore the Chickasaws, the Alabamas he refers to were a distinct, if minor entity, of the Muskogee confederation, of which the Tallapoosas formed the largest part.

Saavedra's comments regarding the attitude of the allied nations towards war are probably the most useful and, in his musings, he sometimes displayed a marked sympathy, which was not necessarily common, and admiration for their way of war.

> These nations know of no other occupation than hunting and warfare. The first satisfied their needs, the second assured their independence. The only advancement that until the 1780s they had obtained from their contact with Europeans was the improvement of their means of destruction – substituting guns for the bow and arrow – but because the nations were not capable of manufacturing those weapons, far from profiting from them, they had lost much in the exchange, and became dependent for the acquisition of the tools most necessary for their subsistence and defence on trade with their greatest enemies.[17]

The need to obtain high status goods and tokens of friendship, as demonstrated by chiefs like the Seminole, Tunapé, who actively sought alliances with Spain, also hinted at a new dynamic within the southern nations. The eighteenth

---

15   Topping (ed.), *Journal of Saavedra*, p.178.
16   Topping (ed.), *Journal of Saavedra*, p.176.
17   Topping (ed.), *Journal of Saavedra*, p177.

century saw a great shift in the way powerful figures gained their position, where once a leader or chief, would have accrued notoriety through acts which set them apart as religiously and spiritually gifted, a wave of young up-and-comers had realised the same authority could be obtained by those who provided the most European trade goods and firearms.[18] In the Choctaw nation, the claim to leadership based not on the spiritual realm but on material wealth could get a man killed, as happened to Red Shoes in 1747 and as was threatened to Franchimastabé in 1796.

Saavedra went on from his enlightened thoughts to admire the fighting qualities of the warriors he had seen, something many Europeans found no trouble in admitting, but with a familiar codicil.

No portrait exists of any war leaders of the Muskogees, Choctaws or Chickasaws who came to Pensacola between 1780–1781. However, descriptions state that colourful head-scarves wrapped like turbans were worn by them, as well as European military adornments, such as in this portrait by Trumbull of Hopothle Mico from the 1790's. (New York Public Library Digital Collections)

Generally, the Indians of these nations ... are vigorous, well formed, tall and extremely agile ... They have quick comprehension and abundant cunning, and, within the limited sphere to which their close attention is reduced, no people can boast of surpassing them in intelligence. Their character is energetic and decisive, passions operate in them with all their natural vigour, and they are as capable of a remarkable generosity as of a horrendous act of vengeance.[19]

With ample time to observe in 1781, Francisco de Saavedra added that, 'they are the most accomplished hunters in the world. Their bodies, hardened by hardship, resist all the vicissitudes of the nomadic life without being affected ... They have a marvellous patience for enduring inclement weather and for remaining immobile for days and nights in one spot, lying in wait for some game bird or animal.'[20] Saavedra claimed that war bands and hunting parties could traverse 20–25 leagues per day, and that not only could they see farther than normal men, and discern tracks in the forest, some, given the right conditions, could follow prey by scent, and further, that some could determine the nationality of human quarry by means of scent.

---

18   O'Brien, *Choctaws*, pp.1–9.
19   Topping (ed.), *Journal of Saavedra*, p.177.
20   Topping (ed.), *Journal of Saavedra*, p.182.

Their aim with a musket is extremely accurate. Throughout the siege we saw them give amazing proofs of their marksmanship. They acquire this accuracy by dint of practice, for in addition to their continuous performance in the hunt, even when they are idle, they usually have a stick in hand, and they aim with the stick at any object that passes before them. In war they apply the same skills they use in the hunt, because for them War is nothing more than a hunt for men. They will do always in small parties. They never meet the enemy face to face, nor do they fight with him strength to strength. They try to catch the enemy unprepared, and their entire military science is limited to the craftiness of the Hunter.[21]

The reason for this was not due to cowardice, Saavedra acknowledged, rather,

They are extremely prolific in stratagems, and if they were capable of union and order they would be the best light troops in the world in countries filled with dense forests like those of America. Amongst them the most acclaimed warrior is he who knows how to prepare his ambush and do great damage to the enemy without exposing himself to danger. The most glorious action is regarded as a calamity when some of them who engage lose their lives. A chief who would contend for mastery in hand-to-hand combat would be treated like a rash man unworthy to command them.[22]

That being said, hand to hand combat after a volley from cover was absolutely something that a warrior expected to encounter. A mixture of the will to subdue the enemy with club and hatchet, plus the scarcity and value of powder and ball, meant warriors sometimes only fired one volley before charging to secure scalps and loot, or fleeing to find a safe place to reload.

The warriors were no less religiously motivated than their protestant and catholic allies. If anything, even more so. Medicine, or physic as was sometimes used, is an overused term, but it was what the contemporary Europeans referred to the rituals and observances of Native Americans, and even the aura that the warriors believed was exuded from them when going into battle.

When Choctaw warriors went to war, they left what might be termed the ordinary sacred world, a place governed by ancient entities, such as the sun, which was *nanapisa*, 'the one who sees', or the witness; the eye of that which watched over the world. Their rituals, even the symbolism of how they built their houses, all included circles, eyes, crosses, and hands, which altogether expressed a sacred reverence to the sun. The Choctaws were reluctant to hold important meetings and councils when the sun did not shine, and though it is a myth that American Indians did not fight at night, to act out of sight of the light brought little honour to a warrior. After completing their rituals, organised by the *Tichou Mingo*, who was something of a lieutenant to the 'war-chief', who in Muskogee circles might have been represented by the *Tustanagee Thlucco*.[23] They were set apart from the ordinary world and drawn

---

21   Topping (ed.), *Journal of Saavedra*, p.182.
22   Topping (ed.), *Journal of Saavedra*, p.181.
23   This is both a name and a title, meaning Big Warrior. A famous headman who resided in Tuckabatchee was considered a paramount chief amongst the Muskogees in the early nineteenth century.

A sketch of a ritual observed circa 1758 in French Louisiana, where an important figure is elevated in connection with the sun. Solar rituals were common amongst the Mississippian nations, the origins of which went back to the mound builders of Cahokia. (Library of Congress)

very close to the supernatural. Each warrior entered a fight in a high state of focus, and various methods were used to maintain this sense of being until the time of killing came, such as regular war dances, war-songs, painting the skin in the colours of war and death, the close attention to omens and signs, the imbibing of the Black Drink,[24] and restriction to various kinds of food which only one chosen warrior was allowed to prepare.

Saavedra noted that the warriors he encountered greased their bodies with a noxious substance that kept the bugs and venomous reptiles away, which is possibly some subset of the bear grease noted by von Waldeck, but unfortunately does not tell us what it was made of and, 'For their rations they carry a portion of cornmeal, cassava or beans enough to sustain them for one week.'[25]

Each man might carry a musket, a war-club, a knife and a hatchet, the intent being to surprise an enemy, destroy him without loss and leave with the spoils, marking the scene with clubs and painted sticks to show who had done the act. The very paint they wore conveyed supernatural abilities, 'My face is painted so they cannot see me,' ran a line from one song. Once completed, the warriors could cleanse and reenter the normal world.[26]

Chaplain von Waldeck agreed that the warriors were impressive men and mused on their ability to become European style soldiers.

There were many especially handsome young men, few of whom were under six foot tall, who through their style of life are accustomed to long marches. What a wonderful regiment could be made of them. But would they accept discipline?

---

24   A tea made from Yaupon Holly which in the right quantities had emetic qualities associated with cleansing and was often given in less potent quantities at ceremonies and on marches. It was not uncommon for European officers to be invited to drink it as well.

25   Topping (ed.), *Journal of Saavedra*, p.183.

26   O'Brien, *Choctaws*, pp.38–39.

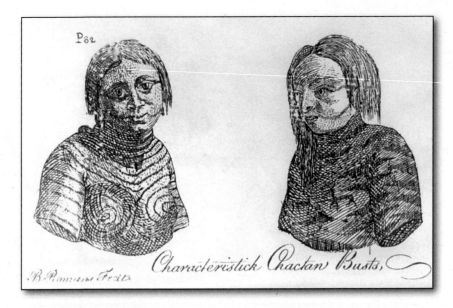

A crude study of two Choctaws people from Romans' concise natural history showing intricate body decoration. (Library of Congress)

Discipline is something about which the know nothing. Even the chief does not control them, but each one does as he believes necessary from an inborn sense of honour of being a good warrior. To hear the singing of their feats prior to an engagement instils a greater desire for further accomplishment than any reward of honour in other armies.[27]

Saavedra was quick to assure his reader that their disinclination to prolonged combat and the lack of discipline observed by von Waldeck was not out of lack of valour, as each warrior showed a great serenity the closer he came in proximity to eternity even in the face of tortures, but he decided that the American Indians were too small in number to respect the callous loss of lives more common to Europeans. He recounted how a famous Tallapoosa warrior told him:

… in the world there were three races of men, white, black, and red; that the first and the second were innumerable, and therefore the loss of some of them was not a cause for grief; but that there were very few of the third, and therefore it was necessary to preserve them with great care. For this reason, during the siege, they were quick to harass the English every time they were ordered to do so, but never could they be persuaded to attack those Indians who were allies of the English, and when one day our parties brought in one of them who had been killed, our Indians even gave a great funeral and buried him with demonstrations of intense grief.[28]

27 Bruce E. Burgoyne, 'A Diary Kept by Chaplain Waldeck During the Last American War Part IV', *Journal of the Johannes Schwalm Historical Association*, vol.3, no.2 (1986), p.27.

28 It is notable that in his general account of the siege, Saavedra never mentions active participation of the pro-Spanish warriors, but the aspects of a civil war were certainly there, and not often pointed out. Topping (ed.), *Journal of Saavedra*, p.181.

For the Choctaws it was the same, for between 1747 and 1750 they had suffered a destructive civil war between the three main branches of the nation, and since that dark time, had ensured that whatever treaties each party pursued it would not lead down that path again.[29] However this did not extend to other nations, for whom sometimes there was a great enmity. 'I remember with sorrow my old village that the English caused to be destroyed by the nations that listen to their word, after having killed our warriors and made our wives and children slaves,' lamented Mingo Emitta, a chief of the *Okla Tennap*, Choctaws in 1729.[30] A bitter war between the Choctaws and Muskogees had lasted from 1765 to 1777, and an arbiter of the peace had been John Stuart.

Stuart of course would have been the first to point out that with nations like the Choctaw and the others, it all depended on the war-leader. Men of great renown in war, such as Franchimastabé,[31] or men of great spiritual abilities like Taboca, could expect a high degree of discipline from their warriors. A precursor to the Spanish conquest of Baton Rouge and Natchez had been the raid of James Willing in 1778, where a modest force of rebels had sailed down the Mississippi on a plundering mission that had laid bare the weakness of the British frontier, but without any lasting result for the Americans.[32] The British response was slow, something that Gálvez had noted, and by the time they reached Natchez, the rebels had flown. A large Choctaw force had been amongst the easiest to recruit to secure the frontier, under Franchimastabé, who the Muskogee called Abecochee (killer). The 155 strong war-band manned the fort for a month, with Franchimastabé organising three rotating watches to secure the town. 'Their conduct during their stay there was such as gave universal satisfaction … it was not within the power of anybody to behave with greater regularity and discretion.'[33] Upon the Choctaws taking their leave, Franchimastabé gave this address to the inhabitants,

> We are now obliged to go to leave you. We are not afraid of our enemy but of the fever that will give no notice of its approach. In case you are threatened with attack from the rebels remember we are behind you. Write to our beloved man [Stuart] who will acquaint us and we will always be ready to follow him out to your assistance and protection. But, on the other hand. Should you offer to take the rebels by the hand or enter into any treaty with them, remember also that we are behind you and that we will look on you as Virginians and treat you as our enemies [34]

---

29 O'Brien, *Choctaws*, p.10.
30 The British divided the Choctaws into three, the West and East Parties, (*Okla Falaya* and *Okla Tannap* respectively), who by this time were mostly pro-British, and the Six-Towns (*Okla Hannali*); O'Brien, *Choctaws*, p.27.
31 His name, as a title, or epithet, meant literally 'he took a Frenchman and killed him,' or 'French killer'. O'Brien, *Choctaws*, p.28.
32 See Robert V. Haynes, 'James Willing and the Planters of Natchez: The American Revolution comes to the Southwest', *Journal of Mississippi History*, vol.37 (February 1975), pp.1–40.
33 O'Brien, *Choctaws*, pp.40–41.
34 O'Brien, *Choctaws*, pp.40–41.

Here the war leader showed not only a fair grasp of the political situation, and how to make the settlers behave, but also a keen sense of the wellbeing and indeed perhaps hygiene of his warriors. War leaders of this level and headmen had the power to revoke titles and warrior status, as such their word was law. When he returned home to West Yazoo Village, he and his warriors were greeted as heroes by the women and a grand ball game was held, along with the traditional four days of fasting, dances, and rituals to cleanse them and allow them to celebrate with the non-combatants. This was certainly the welcome the warriors at Pensacola hoped to receive after defeating the Spanish. The British categorised, native leaders in three ranks, Great Medal Chiefs, Small Medal Chiefs, and Captains, and Franchimastabé was a Great Medal Chief and highly regarded by Stuart.

Despite his words being laced with the odd snide remark about civilisation, Saavedra seemed to have got beyond this during the siege and was not afraid to note that, 'The cruelties and injustices that the whites have inflicted on them, are deeply engraved in their hearts and are perpetuated in their families as the most important parts of their history.'[35] Indeed, he offered this as the reasoning behind the common idea that American Indians were cunning and faithless, remarkably asking his reader to try and understand why they would naturally be inclined to dirty tricks when surrounded by so much foreign avarice. 'The usual thing is that all these nations regard whites with irreconcilable hatred, especially Anglo Americans, whose vexatious proximity, usurping their lands every day, is reducing them to poverty.'[36]

Saavedra's contemplations on the future, derived from his time spent in the company of the small party of Muskogees that had joined the Spanish, and his understanding of the history of the last century, led him to conclude a dark and perilous result, 'Therefore it can be predicted that in less than a century one of two things will happen: either the savage tribes, dragged by the torrential tide of trade and civilisation, will be assimilated into the mass of the Anglo-Americans and the other nations that surround them, or an aggregation of inevitable causes will complete their extermination.'[37]

---

35 Topping (ed.), *Journal of Saavedra*, p.183.
36 Topping (ed.), *Journal of Saavedra*, p.185.
37 Topping (ed.), *Journal of Saavedra*, p.185.

Circles played a great part in the iconography of the Choctaws and other southern nations. These were thought to represent the sun. Dances and councils took place in circles, and war-parties would sleep in such a formation as well. Engraving circa 1758. (Library of Congress)

5

A Delightful Peninsula: The Landscape and Terrain

Cartographers divided the landscape into types. Romans had 'pine land, Hammock land, savannahs, swamps, marshes and bay or cypress galls'[1] Purcell's itinerary of the roads between St Augustine and Pensacola showed swamps, oak-lands (probably equivalent what Romans called Hammocks), pine-lands, and old fields (approximate to Romans's savannahs), as well as ponds and galls.[2] Both Purcell's map and Romans, show that the pine lands were by far the most common,

> …pine land, commonly called pine barren … makes up the largest body by far, the Peninsula scarce being anything else, but about a hundred miles toward the north west of St Augustine, and two hundred from the sea in West Florida carry us entirely out of it. This land consists of a grey, or white sand, and in many places a red or yellow gravel, [and] it produces a great variety of shrubs or plants.[3]

The term pine land came from the predominant species, the Yellow Pine, and Pitch Pine which Romans surmised were sub species of the same tree, both of which made excellent timber, and beneath the tall poles, grew bizarre carpets of Dwarf Palm and wire grass. The vast expanses of this terrain meant that it was typical to find large herds of cattle being kept there, and in the savannahs that grew in the clearings between the pines.

Romans also wrote that, 'In West Florida the pine land is also frequently found rocky, with an iron stone, especially near where the pines are found growing in a gravelly tract, which is frequently the case here.'[4] An unusual anecdote as most people were of the firm opinion that rock and stone were mostly alien to West Florida, especially along the coast. Purcell briefly

---

1   Romans, *Natural History*, p.15.
2   TNA: CO 700/Florida54: A Map of the Road from Pensacola in West Florida to St Augustine in East Florida, 1778.
3   Romans, *Natural History*, p.16.
4   Romans, *Natural History*, p.17.

This view of a Confederate Camp belonging to the 9th Mississippi Infantry in April 1861 during a later siege of Pensacola shows the sandy pine-land terrain that dominated the landscape around the town. Attributed to J.D. Edwards. (Library of Congress)

described the Pine Lands, which were the most common terrain on his map 'They are high and low: the soil is generally very poor and sandy. The low in wet weather in chiefly underwater. The high is in places pebbly and stony and valuable but for its Timber.'[5]

Hammock-land occurred most commonly where the pine met a creek or inlet, 'The hammock land so called for, it's appearing in tufts among the lofty pines form small spots of this kind, if seen at a distance, have a very romantic appearance, the large parcels of it often divide creeks, or rivers, from the pine land.'[6] It was very fertile ground, and home to diverse species of oak, walnut, hickory, mulberry, palm and magnolia amongst other flora, including a plant called *Illicium Floridanum anissum stellatum* (starry aniseed) which was 'first found growing near Pensacola by a free Negro (Pompey) formerly belonging to Chief Justice Clifton, which Negro in his way is a curious herbalist.'[7] In Purcell's map, these are the Oak Lands, 'Their growth is chiefly Oaks, Hickories and Mulberries, the soil in general is middling good but light, and in places as about the Coosa Old Fields, Appalatchi and St Pedro the soil is richer and have Walnut trees and small Canes; appears to be fit for the culture of Indigo, Corn and Pulse of all kinds…'[8]

So called savannahs were to be found amongst the sandy pine lands and hammocks, which were low-lying grassy wetlands, 'notwithstanding the black appearance of the soil, they are as white sand as the higher land round them … they are a kind of sinks or drains to those higher lands, and their low situation only prevents growth of pines in the. In wet weather the roads leading through them are almost impassable.'[9] In West Florida specifically there was a characteristic type of Savannah,

> … they consist of a high ground, often with small gentle risings in them, some are of a vast extent … the largest to my knowledge is on the road from the Chactaw [sic] to the Chicasaw [sic] nation, and is in length near 40 miles over from north

---

5   TNA: CO/700Florida54: Purcell map.
6   Romans, *Natural History*, p.17.
7   Romans, *Natural History*, p.17.
8   TNA: CO/700Florida54: Purcell map.
9   Romans, *Natural History*, p.22.

to south, and from one end to the other, a horizon, similar to that at sea, appears, there is generally a rivulet at one or other … in one or two of them I have seen some very small remains of ancient huts, by which I judge they were formerly inhabited by Indians … in some I have seen fossil shells in great numbers.[10]

Unsurprisingly the savannahs made fertile grazing ground for the semi-wild cattle, and if a planter was savvy and chose his ground right, the water from the cypress swamps offered excellent opportunity for the cultivation of rice, and in terms of drinking water Romans confidently asserted that all of the springs in West Florida were good. Purcell called these Grasslands, Old Fields and described them as variable,

> … those of Appalatchi, Coosa, St Pedro … chiefly grown up with oaks, hickories, mulberries, pines and small canes … The soil is in places rich and in others light, but in general good, it appears to be fit for the culture of Wheat, Indigo, Tobacco, Indian Corn and pulse of all kinds. The other old fields are in general grow up with oaks and pines. The soil light and sandy. The Appalatchi and St Pedro Old Fields bear the marks of once having been large and flourishing Spanish settlements, strongly posted by the ruins of Forts, Churches and other Buildings, the canon and church bells that are found lying about; The Broad Roads; and the remains of Causeways and Bridges that are to be seen to this day.[11]

Swampland was never far away in West Florida, and both cartographic and botanical sources identify them as full of water-oaks and cypress amongst others, and that they were mostly flooded unless they rivers were low. Along the gulf coast of the present United States, east of Lake Borgne and the mouth of the Apalachicola, there are many bays, inlets, and sounds, which through the course of history have been used as havens and centres of trade, and refuge from the storms and waters of the Gulf of Mexico. The majority of the terrain around them was characterised by landscapes like these, and it was amongst the pine, oak, meadow and swamps of Pensacola Bay that the longest siege in North America to that date played out.

---

10   Romans, *Natural History*, p.23.
11   TNA: CO/700Florida54: Purcell map.

6

As Yet 'Unattacked'

The morning after Campbell sent his report to Clinton regarding the failure to relieve Mobile an ominous sound was heard from the sea; the low frequency thumps of distant artillery carried by the breeze indicating ships signalling to one another. The firing was heard again in the evening, assuring every mind that a large number of vessels was at sea. Though many hoped it was a convoy from Jamaica, it could also be the Spanish reinforcements from Cuba, and Chaplain von Waldeck could not help but muse in his diary how quickly events can overtake a situation, as barely 14 days before no one had considered that all of West Florida might be lost.

On 27 March the *Earl Bathurst*, what Campbell called an Ordnance ship, mounting twenty-four 9-pounders and six 4-pounders, under Captain Francis Le Montais, was sent out to identify the fleet. At 2:00 p.m. it became clear that the sails were Spanish. Chaplain von Waldeck heard the news an hour later. He expected that the enemy would anchor at Santa Rosa and occupy the harbour the next day. He wrote morbidly that Pensacola had never had much of a lucky star shining over it. Though, as it happened, he was wrong to be so pessimistic.

Counting 21 ships in the squadron, two of which were estimated to be ships of the line, Campbell was by no means any more confident that he was not about to lose the entire province in the space of a month. On the 28th he began what seems to have been intended as a running letter to Clinton, expecting that 'the fate of Pensacola will probably be determined before this can reach your Excellency.'[1] His entry for the next day notes that the enemy fleet had grown to 29 ships and correctly suspected they were only awaiting Gálvez to march overland from Mobile to begin landing.

Campbell did not offer any insight into his plans to his commander-in-chief but when the Spanish did not land immediately, he began moving his troops into the fortifications above the town. As Chaplain von Waldeck wrote 'everything is stirring here. We have packed and at ten o'clock are to move into our camp at Fort George. Just after ten o'clock the Regiment marched off

---

1   TNA: PRO 30/55/22, Campbell to Clinton, 28 March 1780.

with flags flying. The cannon of the battery in the garrison were tipped over and everyone moved to Gage Hill.'[2]

Camps were laid out and tents erected, with Hanxleben given command of the encampment, and as tends to be the case, the tents were then moved within 24 hours. Meanwhile on the 29th von Waldeck wrote, 'Work on the defences is being pushed strenuously so that the soldiers are almost never idle, and as a consequence, the general has ordered an extra half pound of bread be issued to each man. Our campaign cannot last long, it must be decided in a short time.'[3]

The Spanish had been seen under sail in the evening and the rumour was that they had landed troops, but the next day the horizon was empty, and to the surprise of everyone still toiling in the earthworks, it appeared that the enemy had gone. They reappeared briefly again before finally dropping from sight. Miraculously Pensacola had been spared.

Gálvez 's actions in the Mississippi and the capture of Mobile were met with great satisfaction in Aranjuez when on 15 June *Teniente* Manuel González of the Regimiento de España laid the report before the king, Gonzaléz was made a *capitán*. A third of the value of the spoils of Mobile was distributed to the men and the assembled conquerors were verbally thanked by Gálvez in Fort Charlotte. John Adams remarked shrewdly that this blow signalled the end of British West Florida. British newspapers reported some rather sensational versions of the event and even accidentally prophesied the fall of Pensacola, assuming it had fallen after Mobile, which is perhaps what prompted Germain to assume the town had fallen when he wrote to Campbell in April.[4]

In France reports of the successes along the Gulf were met with approval, and in Spain, Gálvez 's star was certainly rising, though some ministers had hoped for a stronger blow. Gálvez agreed, when he wrote on 20 March that, 'We cannot consider without pain, that if the expedition from Havana had joined us in time the British would have suffered as much as in Saratoga.'[5] The Minister of the Indies lambasted the naval commanders at Havana, making the point that the king's ships were for attacking and pursuing the enemy, not hiding in their harbours.

Counter to this, Spanish naval officer *Teniente General* Juan Bautista Bonet was overheard by *Coronel* Esteban Miró, Gálvez's emissary to Havana, exclaiming that the fuss over the gulf ports was in essence silly, as Cuba was more valuable than 50 Mobiles and Pensacolas, and outright said the king's orders should be disobeyed or at least carried out with discretion. His fleet of 15 warships, 20 transports, and 2,148 men set sail on 7 March under command of *Capitán de Navío* Miguel de Goicoechea and arrived on 30 March, at which time Gálvez was still hoping to press on immediately for Pensacola. This was, of course, the phantom armada that had so curiously bypassed Pensacola. Gálvez's hopes began to unravel in late April as he could

2   Burgoyne, 'A Diary Kept by Chaplain Waldeck, Part IV', p.26.
3   Burgoyne, 'A Diary Kept by Chaplain Waldeck, Part IV', p.26.
4   Saravia, *Gálvez*, p.173.
5   Saravia, *Gálvez*, p.174.

not persuade the navy to commit themselves to risking the fleet over Pensacola Bar, without Bonet's order. Though some thought they could march overland and take the fort at Barrancas Coloradas, there was not enough confidence that this could be done without a commitment from Havana. When Bonet himself said the fleet could not stay more than three weeks at sea, a council of war held on 4 May saw the army commanders agree that without navy cooperation the attack needed to be called off. When his militia clamoured to go home, Gálvez knew he had no choice, and so Pensacola seemed to have been granted a reprieve.

Campbell and his officers were certainly expecting an imminent attack throughout the summer and could not quite believe as the season came to a close that the Spanish would not make an appearance. 'I have to report,' Campbell wrote in May with quiet surprise, 'that contrary to my expectations Pensacola remains still un-attacked.' He too could not quite believe the Spanish had just left and remained tense until 5 April when on that stormy day, the *Hound* and *Port Royal* were sighted escorting a convoy of British ships.[6]

According to a couple of deserters who came in four days later, it seemed to be the case that the Spanish squadron having expected to see Gálvez encamped at Pensacola, sailed up to Mobile, and upon returning and seeing the new ships from a distance, and mistaking the *Earl Bathurst* and *Port Royal* for ships of the line, that they had elected to abandon the enterprise. Additionally, Campbell almost reluctantly offered what was probably Cameron's opinion that the host of warriors encamped near the town had been some sort of deterrent but was quick to write of his displeasure at having to supply them.

Their delaying the Execution of their Design on this Place May be also in part owing … to a large body of Indians, who have been assembled here for its protection, [but] as these savages cannot be confined to one place for any continuance of time, accordingly their number has been for some time past, from their impatience at restraint, daily diminishing, and they are now reduced, from nearly at one time 1,600 to a few more than 1,100 men women and children, and have positively set their departure at the end of five or six days, indeed nothing but their waiting for presents has for a fortnight or three weeks past prevented them from returning home, and those whose patience was worn out and are gone off have made themselves plunder for their want of presents by carrying with them horses and black cattle belonging to the inhabitants; Even the King's horses have not been spared to a considerable number.[7]

John Stuart's death had been a great blow to the ability to work with neighbouring nations in supplying war-bands, but his successor, Cameron, proved quite capable, if not as adept in forging coalitions. He ventured, that 'the possession of this place [Pensacola] is owing entirely to the great number

---

6   TNA: PRO 30/55/23: Campbell to Clinton, 13 May 1780.
7   TNA: PRO 30/55/23: Campbell to Clinton, 13 May 1780.

Convoys of merchantmen were the main means of subsistence for frontier ports like Pensacola. It was also why food and supplies were so expensive. Similarly, a great deal depended on supply convoys from New Spain out of Vera Cruz for the Spanish colonies in the Caribbean. (British Library Flikr)

of Indians who repaired here to assist, and who waited near a month for the Spaniards; then getting impatient wished to go look for them.'[8]

In truth the Spanish had not appeared because they had been beset by meteorological, strategic, and logistical obstacles since early in the year. However, Gálvez's wish to keep the fighting between regular troops shows us that Cameron was not far wrong in assessing the dread the Spanish commander felt when contemplating the assault through a Florida wilderness infested with war-bands. Campbell had written to Earl Cornwallis on the subject of the Muskogee allies and their relative worth. Cornwallis seemed to agree, and never having been particularly noted for his use of non-European Americans in his campaigns, had little use for the Indian Department either. In a letter of 17 July, Cornwallis outlined to the superintendent in Carolina succinctly what he required of the department and the Cherokee, who had been under extreme pressure from the rebels since 1776.

> I should desire that they may be met in good humour and by civil treatment & a proper distribution of such presents as are send from England for that purpose, but I would on no account employ them in any operations of War … as it is not the intention of the Commander in Chief to make any military use of the Indians, I cannot think myself justified in suffering the Publick to be put to any considerable Expense about them, nor can I consent to any gratuity being given to them further than the usual presents. If their Houses have been destroyed, the Rebuilding an Indian Hut is no very expensive affair and I dare say they will get their usual Crops of Corn this year. I can therefore allow nothing further on the account of provisions than for their Entertainment during their stay at Augusta & in that article when I shall pass the accounts, I shall expect to find there has been no unnecessary Waste. I have ordered all the Indian presents that are here to be sent to Savannah, for the convenience of their being transported to Augusta. The number of Officers employed with the Indians, & their salaries have, I conclude been already regulated, either by Sir William Howe or Sir Henry Clinton. The customary Charges therefore on that account will be allowed for the present, and until I see any reason for altering them. From the report I have received from Pensacola of the Behaviour of the Creeks, they have very little Merit from that Expedition, General Campbell says that they staid [sic] only as long as they could extort presents, that they have consumed great part of his provisions, & left him, just at the time that he expected an attack.[9]

The allied war-bands in question had been coming in with their families since late March, and they seemed to both comfort and concern the garrison, Chaplain von Waldeck, always at odds with himself when it came to his fascination and revulsion with his allies, noted the large numbers that had gathered by April.

---

8   Saravia, *Gálvez*, p.184.
9   TNA: PRO 30/11/78: Cornwallis to Lieutenant Colonel Brown, Superintendent of Indian Affairs, 17 July 1780.

Naturels en Hyver

A Native American with a winter blanket circa 1758 from a history of Louisiana, doubtless many of the allied nations who wintered at Pensacola in 1780/1781 resorted to a mode of dress similar to this in the cold months. (Library of Congress)

We have received reinforcements also, but on whose assistance, little is to be relied, namely three hundred Choctaw Indians, who are divided within their own nation, and three hundred Creeks, of whom a great many are already here, and whole families pass our camp daily. We can trust the Creeks a bit more than the Choctaws, as the Creeks have had a more constant friendship with the English, while the Choctaws tend to favour the Spanish ... The governor announced that in our present dangerous situation the inhabitants were not to sell or trade rum to the Indians as the problems of dealing with drunken Indians is well known.[10]

The strategy of piling allied war-bands into Pensacola was controversial, as only the Indian Department seemed to think it was a good idea, whereas Clinton, Cornwallis, and Campbell all either wanted to discourage it, or saw it as a necessary rather than prudent move.

It was however seen as the best course of action by some of the British commanders in the south. Indeed, it speaks to the width of the net cast to bring as many warriors as possible to Pensacola's aid when, Prevost wrote to Clinton from Savannah on 12 April forwarding information from the Indian Department, regarding the 'endeavour to persuade a number ... to repair immediately to Pensacola to assist in repelling the Spaniards who the Express says had already taken Mobile.'[11] The response was encouraging. Throughout early April the sound of musketry had been quite common, as it heralded the arrival of another war-band, although at first it had greatly disturbed everyone. Von Waldeck recorded:

I was sitting peacefully in my tent when I suddenly heard small weapons fire close to the camp, very much as if an outpost were under attack. We ran from our tents and saw a party of Choctaw Indians, who had been thirty days traveling from their land, here ... I followed them all the way into the city in order to hear their speeches. They camped, spread out in an almost oriental fashion, and smoked from their tomahawks. If one enters among them, he does not have enough hands to greet them all, and they shake hands so vigorously that after shaking hands with thirty of them, it can be felt in the arms.[12]

Campbell would seem to have been persuaded that Gálvez was concerned about his much-maligned allies due to the proposal he received attempting to persuade him to send the war-bands home.

10   Burgoyne, 'A Diary Kept by Chaplain Waldeck, Part IV', pp.26–27.
11   TNA: PRO 30/55/22: Prevost to Clinton, 12 April 1780.
12   Burgoyne, 'A Diary Kept by Chaplain Waldeck, Part IV', p.25.

'The allies', a defamatory caricature from the British opposition party in which Lord North shares a cannibal feast with his allies. The British use of Indigenous military aid drew widespread condemnation from their enemies. (Library of Congress)

The Indians who support the side of the English believe that they do them a service by pillaging and destroying all the inhabitants of the other nation. Those who have embraced the cause of Spain imagine that for the sake of reprisal they can commit the same hostilities against the English inhabitants … In this war, which we wage by obligation and not by hate, I hope that you will be inclined to join me in a reciprocal convention to shelter us from the horrible censure of humanity.[13]

Gávez's letter was written on 9 April, and Campbell read it two days later; by the end of the day word of its contents had reached the Waldeck camp. Campbell replied on the 20th,

… in regard to the proposal you are pleased to make not to employ Indians in our National Quarrels, and the complaints you exhibit against the conduct of Indians … in the British interest I beg leave to observe that I never encouraged countenanced or authorised depredations to be committed by Indians, whether on Spanish, French or English Inhabitants, on the contrary I have always prohibited, restrained and absolutely forbid the smallest act of licentiousness, rapine or cruelty whatsoever, and Such Indians as have obeyed my call, and who have demonstrated their fidelity and attachment to Great Britain, have been kept together under proper orders … for the purpose of resisting an invading enemy.[14]

---

13   TNA: PRO 30/55/22: Gálvez to Campbell, 9 April 1780.
14   TNA: PRO 30/55/22: Campbell to Gálvez, 20 April 1780.

A small miniature engraving of a warrior from one of the southern nations holding a scalp and a snake, armed with bow and arrow from the Revolutionary period. The markings on his skin might be fanciful. (Library of Congress)

Campbell asserted that not one warrior had caused the least infraction while under his orders, and indeed the series of meetings and conferences occurring with arriving war-chiefs and leaders, focused a great deal on attempting to get the allies to desist from taking scalps. Campbell naturally left out the fact that the warriors were at Pensacola to fight, and win reputations, which was really only possible by taking scalps, and as such he could not easily ask for the allied warriors to fight bravely but hold back at the same time. Chaplain von Waldeck blamed the British for mishandling this affair which he said caused some of the war bands to leave. The entire subject, was indeed a sore point which did nothing to ingratiate Campbell with his allies.[15]

A primary reason for the concentration of warriors of the three major southern nations was due to the fact that the young warriors wanted to enter a state of manhood. A Choctaw war leader tried to explain this at Pensacola when the subject of mutilating the dead and wounded came up, he said that he was aware that 'taking scalps was not customary among the white folks, but one should not deny the right to this custom, because they would earn the praise and especially the name of warrior in the tribe, only when they brought the scalps of their enemy's home in triumph.'[16]

Quite naturally the intentional taking of a life was seen as the act of an adult, and so to kill an enemy and have it witnessed, was an important rite of passage for young men and older boys amongst the Muskogee, Choctaw, and Chickasaw nations. Quite apart from the fact that Europeans had encouraged the practice of scalping beyond anything ceremonial, the presentation of hair was without doubt the most effective way a young warrior could prove he had become a man. Upon such an event manhood was confirmed by the conferring of a new titular name, by which all adult men, certainly of the Choctaws, possessed. If Campbell wanted the warbands to stay he could not easily order them to restrain themselves in battle.[17]

Campbell, having firmly stated his innocence in any act of violence committed by his allies, went on, in a somewhat overly formal, and unfocused way to attempt to turn the accusation back on the Spanish before in the end addressing the proposal,

15   Friederike Baer, *Hessians: German Soldiers in the American Revolutionary War* (Oxford: Oxford University Press, 2022), p.306.
16   O'Brien, *Choctaws*, p.43.
17   O'Brien, *Choctaws*, p.28.

In regard to not employing Indians for defence against an Invading foe, I must reject such a proposal as insulting and injurious to reason and common sense, a Compliance to such would justly render me an object of the resentment of my king and country, and brand me with an indelible mark of infamy as the Deserter of the same by not using every means of Defence which God and my Sovereign had out within my power.[18]

Campbell went on to refute as much as possible, the claims Gálvez charged him with, and by the time his reply was dispatched, he had detained the ship in which the message was carried on suspicion of espionage, having entered the harbour by night and awaited discovery in the morning, when she was indeed apprehended. Citing that the Spanish general had not observed the usual laws of military etiquette in sending a flag of truce, he sent his reply to La Aldea de Mobila (a small outpost on the east of the bay), and invited Gálvez, should he have any further proposals, to send a commissioned officer to Murray's Ferry on the Perdido.

Had the numbers of warriors and, critically, the assemblage of important and inspiring leaders remained at Pensacola, the Spanish would have been hard pressed to make any headway in 1781. Indeed, the warriors showed a great inclination to march on Mobile and lay waste to it, an eventuality that did not sit well with Campbell who, despite his complaints regarding the demands of the allies, had to dictate a letter to Alexander Cameron on 27 April, expressing:

his concern at the Impatience of the Indians & requests you will inform the whole of them that they may rely on it, that they will not meet a Spaniard by going to Mobile Point for the whole of them [The Spanish] are certainly embarked, and of course a few Days will determine whether they have laid aside their design on this place [Pensacola] & should they Spaniards arrive in the absence of our Friends, we shall [need] their assistance in opposing their landing ... The General therefore hopes they will relinquish their Intention of going out a' scouting; and he assures them that whenever he hears of the Enemy's having given up their plan of attacking Pensacola; he will call together their leaders to make such Intelligence known to them, to thank them in the name of the Great King for their fidelity and attachment and to bestow on them such Rewards and Acknowledgment of their proffered services as is in his power to give.[19]

It cannot be ignored that West Florida was underfunded and poorly supplied, and keeping the allies at the gates, without anyone to fight was expensive. One can only surmise what the descent of over a thousand allied warriors would have achieved if they had been allowed to go to Mobile with a solid contingent of regulars. Although Alexander Cameron believed the security given by the Muskogee, Choctaws and Chickasaws was worth every penny, and Campbell seemed to agree (at least until the summer), those pennies were mounting up, as the lists of goods and accounts for the Indian Department

---

18   TNA: PRO 30/55/22: Campbell to Gálvez, 20 April 1780.
19   TNA: PRO 30/55/22: Campbell to Cameron, 27 April 1780.

Fuskatche Mico, or the Birdtail King of the Cusitahs by Trumbull in the 1790s. In the summer of 1780, well over 1,600 warriors from the nations of the south and southwest had gathered for a great fight with the Spanish at Pensacola in which they would gain rich rewards and convey manhood unto their young men in battle. By 1781, barely 500–600 remained. These fought bravely but would incur most of the blame from Campbell (New York Public Library Digital Collections)

testify. It should be remembered that many of the warbands and their families which heeded the call of the British had come a long way from home and their usual method of living, though undoubtedly adept at surviving in the wilderness, they did not come with the magical ability to sustain themselves indefinitely, especially not in the setting of a European town, and quite naturally they therefore came with the expectation of being supplied in return for their presence. This extended to food, materials for clothes, and housing. On 15 May 1780, one John White oversaw the burial of a Choctaw chief, in which a coffin and grave were provided, the expense of which the Indian Department invoiced Campbell at $22.[20] The fact a grave was dug for the body, would seem to suggest that European ways were being adopted, for as late as the twentieth century elderly Seminoles (who had of course taken their Muskogee culture into Florida with them) remembered that their ancestors never used to bury the dead in the ground, believing that it would encourage the eradication of their people. Money and material things were not meant to interfere with the swift process of ensuring the departed began their new journey in peace, which meant observing rites within four days, lest the deceased take another soul with them.[21]

A bill for provisions, 'Rewards and Presents to Indian Parties employed in the defence of Mobile and Pensacola' between 1 January and 31 March alone came to £317 16s 5½d, which was over $1,300, and the entire department returned accounts to the lieutenant governor's office, amounting to $3,120.[22]

With provisions so dear at Pensacola, the Waldeck regiment barely had enough money out of their regular pay to supplement their rations. The expenses of the Indian Department for fresh beef during the month of May was nothing less than an eye watering $11,714.[23]

On 13 May, after he wrote his report to Clinton, Campbell was obliged to go out to speak with the allied leaders so as to welcome the principal Muskogee leader, whom von Waldeck called General Reko, which may

20   TNA: PRO 30/55/23/43: Account for the Burial of a Choctaw Chief, 15 May 1780.
21   Steve Wall (ed), *Wisdom's Daughters: Conversations with women Elders of Native America* (New York: Harper Collins, 1994) p.73.
22   TNA: PRO 30/55/22: Account of Extra Expenses, 28 May 1780.
23   TNA,: PRO 30/55/24/16: Bill for Beef signed by Alexander Cameron May 1780.

possibly be a title rather than a name. It was a cordial meeting, but one in which Reko made it clear, though he had come merely to meet the new Indian Superintendent, as his good friend Stuart was dead, his warriors had come to fight and receive gifts of ammunition.

Restless allies were something of a theme as the spring turned to summer. Campbell informed Clinton that, 'I have now to add that the Regiment of Waldeck think themselves particularly aggrieved in being detached to so disagreeable part of the world where there is scarcity and lack of provisions much beyond that of New York,' and the regiment had been toiling industriously completing the earthworks.[24] *Oberst* von Hanxleben, did what he could to keep morale up by instituting a reward of fresh meat every Sunday out of his own pocket, but all the fresh beef in Florida would not hide the fact that what the garrison needed were warships. However, Vice Admiral Sir Peter Parker, naval commander on the Jamaica Station, had limited means at his disposal, and many islands to defend, and Governor Dalling's Nicaraguan operations to support, sparing frigates and a ship of the line for permanent duty at Pensacola just did not seem a sensible thing to do without authority, then later in the year, it became a veritable impossibility.

Cornwallis was so convinced by Campbell's dour presentiments about the fate of the province that in mid-July he was taking steps, as the senior officer in the south, to begin reorganising the command structure of the southern department against the loss of West Florida, assigning Lieutenant Colonel Alured Clarke as commander in chief for all of Georgia and East Florida, 'by the last account from Pensacola I think there is great reason to apprehend its falling soon into the hands of the Spaniards, East Florida will then become an important Frontier & is very likely to be the next object of Spain,' the Earl reasoned that with the field army active in force in the Carolinas, Georgia should remain secure and as such 'I shall therefore submit it to you whether, after Pensacola has fallen, you might not think St Augustine the properest [*sic*] place for your principle Residence.' Cornwallis also advised that should Pensacola fall, Clarke should reshuffle his military assets as:

> The 60th Reg't is by all accounts very bad & very little to be depended on, being chiefly composed of Deserters & Prisoners, perhaps if the Loss of Pensacola should happen, you may think it best to bring that Corps to Georgia & place the Reg't of Wissenbach with some weak Provincial Corps at St. Augustine ... I shall notify to both the Governor, & to the Commanding Officer of the Troops at St Augustine that the King's Forces in both Provinces are put under your Command.[25]

Cornwallis advised that Clarke take a trip to St Augustine to appraise the situation there and the notice of Clarke's command over East Florida and Georgia was dispatched the next day, Cornwallis explaining to Governor Tonyn that he would soon be too far removed from both Georgia and the Floridas to act, and that 'if any misfortune should happen at Pensacola (an event I think not improbable) The affairs of East Florida will require a serious

---

24   TNA: PRO 30/55/23: Campbell to Clinton, 13 May 1780.
25   TNA: PRO 30/11/78: Cornwallis to Clarke, 17 July 1780.

attention, I have therefore thought it for the advantage of His Majesty's Service to appoint Lt Col Clarke to Command the troops in East Florida as well as Georgia.'[26]

Clarke accepted the command and prepared to go to Florida, writing to Cornwallis on 23 July from Savannah, that he hoped he would there be able to go form a plan of defence should a successful attack on Pensacola induce the Spanish to attack St Augustine, where he would place his headquarters. He was already concerned by the report of Lieutenant W. Carylon Hughes of the 60th Foot, lately arrived from St Augustine, that there were only three weeks provisions then in store there. It will be noted that though much correspondence passed between the Carolinas, Georgia and East Florida regarding the defence of St Augustine, none of it voiced any plan or suggestion that Pensacola would not eventually fall, or put forward any plan to prevent it doing so, except for Prevost at Savannah who had written to Clinton at the end of April, and here he merely reminded the commander in chief of the threat to St Augustine should West Florida fall, given the 'unprovided state in which that Garrison [Pensacola] is at present,' and who forwarded Pensacola's request for aid to Governor Dalling.[27]

26   TNA: PRO 30/11/78: Cornwallis to Governor Patrick Tonyn, 18 July 1780.
27   TNA: PRO 30/55/22: Prevost to Clinton, 22 April 1780.

7

Storm, Junta and Tempest

Storm

On 4 May, Gálvez had written to Bonet that due to lack of assistance from Havana, he had had to give up on Pensacola. This was not defeatism, as Gálvez was now determined to go personally to Cuba and get the support he wanted. Mobile was left with a small garrison under *Coronel* José Manuel de Ezpeleta, while the army was sent to back to Cuba and Louisiana until a plan could be decided. The ball was now in Campbell's court, and the British commander hoped that a reinforcement would be sent to him so he could recapture what had been lost, and possibly even take New Orleans. Though, as usual, he would be on his own as events on the high Mississippi had added another layer of isolation to the struggle for West Florida. If Louisiana was the frontier of New Spain, then St Louis was the frontier of Louisiana. The Mississippi and the adjoining rivers represented opportunities for both sides, and it had been hoped in 1779 that if Campbell could take New Orleans, then he could open up the entire river from the south up to St Louis. It was further envisaged that a multi-pronged strike from Detroit, might remove Spanish and rebel influence from the Illinois, Kaskaskia, and Ohio Rivers. Although Gálvez prevented Campbell from attacking, the raid from Detroit actually did take place, organised in 1780 by the British commandant at Detroit, Major Arent de Peyster (an American serving in the 8th Foot). Emmanuel Hesse, a fur trader from St Louis was dispatched with 1,000 warriors from a host of nations, including warriors from as far away as the Lakota, Ojibwe and Ottawa, plus other nations that were supposed to be neutral. Spanish governor Francisco Leyba, with the support of George Rogers Clarke repelled Hesse's raiders at St Louis and Cahokia between 25–26 May. Although the assault sent the territory into chaos, as Clarke struck back against the principle enemy bases connected with the raids, Gálvez 's northern flank was secure.[1]

---

1   John F. Winkler, *Peckuwe 1780: The Revolutionary War on the Ohio Frontier* (Oxford: Osprey Publishing, 2018) p.35.

Gálvez arrived in Havana on 2 August. His personal zeal and personality were hard to combat in person, and by 11 August, he had wrung a promise of 3,800 men from the *Junta de Guerra*, with a promise to request 2,000 men from Mexico and Campeche, and as many as could be spared from Puerto Rico and Santo Domingo. By 29 August, Gálvez was expecting to command over 4,000 men. The plan was to sail to Vera Cruz and take on reinforcements, then sail along the coast to Pensacola, probably picking up the detachments from New Orleans and Mobile along the way. Even Navarro was confident, assuring José de Gálvez that the expedition would receive all that was required to make a 'rapid and happy conquest.'[2]

Ezpeleta wrote to Gálvez from Mobile in September, asking to be alerted as soon as possible so he could get his troops moving, 'So then, let me know it [the sending of the ships] in time and I shall shut the cage up so that the bird cannot escape.'[3]

Through the late summer, while Gálvez argued for his troops, the British were still preparing for the fall of Pensacola. The *Dilligence* packet had arrived in Charleston harbour in early September, bringing reports from Jamaica that a large Spanish fleet was at sea, that the island was to be placed in a state of defence, and that Pensacola still had three ships of war in the harbour, plus two transports and five merchant ships, all being detained for security reasons. 'The Fort on Gage Hill was nearly finished & the Troops in general healthy there but a number had deserted to the Spanish.'[4] As per the suggestion of Cornwallis, the new commander in Georgia and East Florida had taken a tour of the major installations in the company of Major James Moncrief, arriving back at Camden in October, Moncrief wrote to Cornwallis,

> The Fort of St Augustine is in very tolerable repair, but wants a number of Platforms and other little matters which I have ordered. Col Clark is of the opinion that this is the likeliest place in the district of being attacked, and if Pensacola should fall into the hands of the enemy, I think it is very probable. I have ordered Frames and materials to be got ready for four to five redoubts, with an Eighteen Pounder Carronade in each, so that should Col. Clark order the, to be out up with the assurance of the Inhabitants of the place, they may be done in a few days and the Abatis laid in the intervals.[5]

In Havana, on 13 September 1780, Navarro convened a meeting. In attendance were *Jefe de Escuadra* José Solano and *Teniente General* Bonet from the navy, Gálvez, and three others. Navarro was not pleased, as despite having had several meetings with a similar docket that summer, Solano had informed him upon his arrival from Cadiz that the king had ordered the meeting to convene in order that his will be established regarding the seizure

2   Caughey, *Gálvez in Louisiana*, pp.192–193.
3   Francisco de Borja Medina Rojas, 'Jose de Ezpeleta and the Siege of Pensacola', in William S. Coker and Robert Right Rea (eds), *Anglo-Spanish confrontation on the Gulf Coast during the American Revolution* (Pensacola: Gulf Coast History and Humanities Conference, 1982), p.110.
4   TNA: PRO 30/11/64: John Fargie to Clinton, 4 September 1780.
5   TNA: PRO 30/11/64: James Moncrief to Cornwallis, 1 October 1780.

A view of the market place in the city of the Havana during the British occupation. The city was the nucleus of Spanish operations along the gulf coast, money, ships and seasoned troops from Cuba were vital to the success of the campaign between 1780–1781. A 1768 engraving from a drawing by Elias Durnford. (Library of Congress)

of the port of Pensacola. Navarro must have opened the proceedings with resignation, though doubtless hidden behind the mask of a man doing the will of his sovereign. Navarro and his ally Bonet had been doing their level best to leave Gálvez to make do with the small army he already had, but the audacious and well connected Gálvez would get his way. However, Navarro and Bonet would not go quietly.

A series of *Juntas* were convened in the weeks that followed, with the opponents of a large-scale assault on West Florida trying to place the defence of Cuba above Gálvez's offensive priorities, and trying to delay the expedition through negative arguments regarding the feasibility of taking Pensacola, but it was hard to argue down the will of Carlos III, José de Gálvez and the Conde de Floridablanca, or the argument that rumours of British strategy could not dictate Spanish strategy. Gálvez and his allies were straining at the leash to be getting on with the expedition when on 16 October, 12 warships, and 51 transports carrying 3,800 men and supplies from as near as Cuba and as far away as Maryland left Havana.[6]

It could not have been timed worse as it coincided with one of the worst meteorological events in recorded history.

Twenty-eight thousand people lost their lives in the Caribbean between June and November 1780 without a shot being fired by any of the warring sides. The hurricane season of that year is remembered as one of the deadliest

---

6   Chavez, *Spain & the Independence of the United States*, p.181.

The Hurricane season of 1780 brought devastation to the Caribbean. It delayed the Spanish siege of West Florida by about five months, and almost ensured that the British naval squadron under Vice Admiral Parker could not intervene. (British Library Flikr)

on record with eight major systems carving trails of destruction across both isolated and populated areas. Louisiana, already battered by a storm the year before, suffered another hurricane in August, while monstrous systems battered Jamaica, causing great damage to the British fleet anchored there.

Across the western Caribbean, the evening of 8 October was characterised by what would be looked back on as a sinister tranquillity. The air was still, and in the often-used vernacular, seemed to be holding its breath, meanwhile the sky glowed red and fiery.[7]

Night brought with it ominous clouds and curtains of increasingly heavy rain, and wind which built to such a tremendous force that it destroyed much of what lay in its path. Barbados was knocked flat, and turned from a tropical paradise into a hellscape, with uncounted thousands of dead in the rubble of the towns. St Vincent, St Lucia and Grenada were the similarly laid waste over the next two days, and a storm surge flooded and destroyed most of the houses in St Pierre on Martinique.

Jamaica, which had already withstood a severe hurricane 10 days before, now felt the effects of the edge of the storm then carving its way across St Domingue. A hundred leagues from Trinidad the Spanish frigate *Diana* was on its way to Cuba, when on 9 October, the hurricane struck. A week before, her pilots had begun to detect signs of an approaching squall of unusual intensity. They read it in the calm humid atmosphere and the subsequent bright skies being covered by dark clouds. The hurricane battered the ships

---

7   David Ludlum, *Early American Hurricanes, 1492-1870* (Boston: American Meteorological Society, 1963), p.69.

for 48 hours. Aboard the *Diana*, was Francisco de Saavedra, the King's Commissioner, specially appointed to resolve the disputes at Havana.

> The wind ran the entire compass, with violent gusts, and amidst the repeated sudden changes of the winds, which prevented use of the sails, we were at the point of striking the masts, because the frigate lost its equilibrium with the enormous weight of the artillery that it carried over the hatches, and it moved heavily in the swells … the sea became frightful and the darkness of the sky, together with the repeated flashes of lightning, made us believe that the storm was discharging its greatest force off the windward islands.[8]

The frigate intended to sail for the south coast of Cuba from Tierre Firme, following the mail packet route, and as they neared Puerto Rico, the crew and passengers noted the evidence of the storm that had almost wrecked them.

> At various intervals we did indeed encounter masts, planks, chicken coops, a yard with a scrap of sail, a big piece of keel, a part of a side of a ship with a gunport like that of a ship of the line, and other fragments of vessels, doubtless the plunder of the great hurricane that had spread ruin through those seas. [9]

The Great Hurricane did not reach Cuba, but steered into the Atlantic to ravage Bermuda, giving the impression that all was well in the gulf. This was the opportunity that Gálvez and Solano took to sail for Pensacola. According to an anonymous officer of the frigate *Santa Matilde*, it took most of a day for the ships to clear the harbour, and they put out to sea at 8:00 a.m., on 17 October. The weather was fair but only an hour and a half later the wind had risen. A gale was no reason to turn back, and the fleet continued on, keeping together, most likely under topsails and staysails, until nine hours later when the full force of a new hurricane struck and scattered the escort and convoy.

Solano was a 55-year-old career sailor from Extremadura, having joined the navy as a teenager in 1742, participating in the War of the Austrian Succession and the simultaneous War of Jenkins Ear, and travelling across Europe studying naval science. In 1762 he distinguished himself by capturing two British ships off the coast of Portugal, and due to his command and experience with Latin American geography and border disputes, he became *capitán general* of Santo Domingo, and was promoted to *jefe de escuadra*.

The log of Solano's flagship, *San Juan Nepomuceno*, recorded that the storm did not exhibit itself until 10:00 p.m. that night, and detailed how the storm built over the next day. Almost exactly 48 hours after the gales and squalls had begun, her rudder broke. On 21 October the wind shifted violently, and although her steering had been secured, this put undue strain on the superstructure. One by one, *San Juan*'s masts collapsed, and her bowsprit was carried away. All of this occurred from 4:00 a.m., and through the half-light of dawn for three hours the crew struggled to clear the wreckage. With the conditions calming but the sea still running high they were unable to

---

8   Topping (ed.), *Journal of Saavedra*, p.22.
9   Topping (ed.), *Journal of Saavedra*, p.32.

ship another rudder. However, they were able to jury-rig masts by 11:00 a.m., which as the weather calmed down on the 22nd, allowed the crew to regain control of the ship.[10]

The *Santa Matilde* frigate ran before the wind for the entire storm, similarly losing all her masts by the afternoon of the 19th. The crew found themselves alone in the unsettled ocean, by which time the storm system had left them behind. A jury-mast was raised on the mizzen three days later, and sightings were taken from which it was established they were on the latitude of modern-day Sarasota, Florida. Over the next three days temporary masts were constructed from the remains of the damaged ones and stores, while the ship made its way back to Havana. They reached the city on 30 October, trailing behind six other survivors.

> … we all entered the port, the Ships were the *San Juan Nepomuzeno*, completely dismasted and without its figurehead; the *Velasco*, which lost her main and mizzenmasts and the *Santa Gemara* which lost all her masts. The *San Ramón*, which was taking on 58 inches of water an hour and had to throw 11 cannons overboard. The *Guerrero* suffered little. The *Astuto* had its rudder parted and without any sail had arrived here. The Chambeqjin had suffered very little. The frigate *Mercante* [differs from actual hospital ship *Louisianna*] which served as a hospital suffered greatly, so that all her equipment and materials were jettisoned. The loss was 300 pesos.[11]

In the days that followed, other ships made their way into the harbour in similar states of disrepair, Gálvez and Solano, who had transferred his flag, thinking all ships capable of sailing would continue to pre-assigned rendezvous points, appeared a few days apart towards the middle of November having done just that, while others apparently managed to outrun the storm and reached their rendezvous points but had to either go to Mobile or return to Havana when so few others presented themselves.

The hurricane of October 1780 scattered the fleet so totally that ships turned up battered and leaking at Campeche, New Orleans, Mobile and Havana, while others foundered.[12] But both Gálvez and Solano were furious that the majority of the ships' commanders had all turned back to Havana instead of heading for the rendezvous. Saavedra's luck did not improve after surviving the hurricane, as the *Diana* encountered HMS *Pallas* on 6 November, and after a brief fight, was forced to surrender. The Spanish prisoners were taken to Jamaica and Saavedra saw the results of the destruction.

> In Port Royal there is a navy yard of king near which warships cast anchor. I counted as many as fourteen ships of the line at anchor there, eleven of them completely dismasted. I inquired the cause of the damage and learned that thirteen of those ships and some frigates, having gone out to escort a convoy

---

10   Ludlum, *Early American Hurricanes*, p.73.
11   Everett C. Wilkie, 'New Light on Gálvez's First Attempt to Attack Pensacola', *The Florida Historical Quarterly*, vol.62, no.2 (1983), p.199.
12   Wilkie, 'New Light', p.195.

until it sailed out of the Bahama channel, where struck on their return voyage to Jamaica ... by a hurricane so violent that all of them almost perished; all were badly crippled, and eleven had to come back with jury masts.[13]

The majority of this damage was caused in the first hurricane of October, which destroyed Savannah del Mar on 3 October. Peter Parker's squadron, forming half of the strength of the fleet commanded by Admiral Rodney, then at New York with the other half, had lost *Thunderer*, *Stirling Castle*, *Barbados*, *Pheonix*, *Deal Castle*, *Victor* and *Endeavour*, while *Berwick*, *Hector*, *Trident*, *Ruby*, *Bristol*, *Ulysses* and *Pomona* were all dismasted.[14]

Parker's report to the admiralty in November attempted to present a straightforward account of ships lost and damaged, but as the list went on, few hearts could not have been dispirited, and the British maritime capability in the Caribbean and gulf coast could not be described in any terms but that of greatly distressed.

Vice Admiral Sir Peter Parker, who had the most means to actually aid Pensacola but was badly curtailed due to operations in Central America, wider Caribbean defence, and massive storm damage. (Library of Congress)

Neither side was in a good place of course. And if the commander of the Pensacola expedition had been anyone but Bernardo de Gálvez, Navarro could well have been able to successfully redirect Spanish strategy towards Jamaica and the Caribbean. However, Gálvez, confident in both himself and his support in Madrid and Seville, seemed unconcerned at the reverse, and all but immediately began preparing for future *Junta* meetings, intending to at least get the promised 3,800 men. Another weapon that, Gálvez now had, was an old friend, Francisco de Saavedra, who having arranged his formal release with the aid of Governor Dalling's secretary, arrived just in time to make plain the king's will. It will be remembered as well, that Gálvez had conquered both the Mississippi and Mobile in the wake of hurricanes and storms, and it might be argued that the Governor of Louisiana now considered it a sign of good luck. However, the British now had a window, of perhaps three to five months in which to take advantage of the respite the hurricane had provided.

Tempest, La Aldea

Life at Pensacola through the summer was one of work, tempered by anxiety, broken up by discomfort, especially for the Germans, from whom comes the best evidence of day-to-day experiences. Work on Fort George and its exterior

---

13   Topping (ed.), *Journal of Saavedra*, p.37.
14   William Reid, *An Attempt to Develop the Law of Storms by Means of Facts* (London: John Weale, 1850), p.291.

forts continued, with the work largely being undertaken by the troops, and it may be presumed drafted inhabitants and slaves, at the margins of the day, as prescribed by Haldimand. Food continued to be expensive, even that which was derived from extra rations allotted for men who were now either dead or prisoners of the Spanish, and Campbell found it necessary to expend some money to purchase fresh clothing for the Loyalists, which had been lost in a shipwreck and had to be purchased again. One presumes therefore the state of the uniforms in the garrison generally was quite appalling.

> ... nearly the whole of this Garrison have been encamped ever since March last [1780] without Tents or Camp Equipage, have all that time been in constant expectation of attack and under frequent alarms – unremittingly employed whenever off military Duty in Constructing Fortifications and raising Works of a defence, Besides Which we are serving in a disagreeable Climate, and in a sequestered corner of the world where Provisions and the Necessaries of Life are so dear, that even the officers must live upon their Rations.[15]

A low-level raiding war was taking place between Mobile Bay and the Perdido, with raiders setting out to attack and pillage plantations, and patrols being sent out after them but usually to no avail. One such strike from the Spanish side took place on 22 June, and some horses were stolen from the Waldeck camp five days later. Raiding and patrolling continued into July, but on the 3rd news of the capture of Charleston reached the garrison which gave a great deal of satisfaction. Certainly, the officers of the Waldeck regiment wished for nothing more than that some sort of peace would be declared so they could all go home, a wish which made every casualty from sickness or enemy fire all the harder. By the middle of August, it was seen fit to reduce the rum ration enjoyed by the troops, and this on top of the exorbitant cost of food, did nothing for the edgy atmosphere in Pensacola as everyone awaited Gálvez's next move. On 13 August, the *Mentor* sent in a prize loaded with ammunition and some mail, originally destined for New Orleans. The privations recorded within the letters gave Chaplain von Waldeck cause to be philosophical about their own situation. The letters, he wrote,

> ... which held the most bitter complaints about the conductions in Mobile We have no complaints of this nature yet. We suffer shortages of several things here. The Spaniards, however have a surplus of all miseries at Mobile. We are healthy, and they are sick & have no medicine. And most of all the complaints are about the Indians who take scalps so close to their sentries that no one dares to go a half mile into the woods.[16]

This feeling only lasted the day, as he and the surgeon found life in the camp under canvass so unbearable that they returned to the town. As they passed the bark roofed huts that the other officers had copied from their indigenous

---

15   TNA: PRO 30/55/89: Cameron to Campbell, 15 February 1781.
16   Burgoyne, 'A Diary Kept by Chaplain Waldeck, Part IV', p.33.

allies, they bemoaned the fact that until then they had always had good quarters in America.

The humidity climbs to its highest along the gulf coast in August and September, which did not help matters, especially in a garrison that derived whatever luxuries it had from convoys from Jamaica. They were enduring a regimen of water and dry bread in the morning, water in the afternoon, and more in the evening to wash down a pipe of tobacco. The Chaplain compared Pensacola to a prison that the outside world had forgotten and was becoming more and more disgruntled with Campbell, his entry for 3 October makes no effort to hide his feelings. 'There is nothing more to drink here except water. The colonel, who has a special ability to hold out somewhat longer, had a small supply of German cognac of which he made a present of two bottles. No, there is no worse place in the world, Satan and all his angels should be banished to this place.'[17]

Throughout the summer and autumn, Campbell's main focus was in fortifying his post and trying to gather as many troops and supplies together as possible. He wrote with satisfaction to Clinton that some of the previously hostile Choctaws had grown tired of the Spanish, and after venting their displeasure on the neighbourhood of Mobile had come to Pensacola to offer their services, which Campbell was happy to accept, though he was quick to inform them that if they became allies of the British, they would not be asked to do any more indiscriminate raiding.

His terseness was undoubtedly due to an incident which occurred earlier in the summer, when a party of Choctaws killed a party of Spaniards under command of a *sargento*, who were, it was later discovered, a guard for a British flag of truce.

The news of the incident was met with such displeasure by the inhabitants and the garrison, that Campbell felt obliged to report the outrage to Clinton, explaining the facts as he understood them, lest the Spanish have cause to make accusations against him for the improper behaviour of British allied war-bands.

> … having sent a letter by a Sergeant with a flag of truce to Mobile village [La Aldea] for the commandant of that Place [Ezpeleta at Mobile]; the Spaniards thought proper to send as far as the Perdido an Escort of a Sergeant and four Private men with said Sergeant in his return, with whom a party of Chactaw [sic] Indians fell in, immediately after they had parted with our sergeant … the Indians massacred the sergeant and two of the Soldiers, the other two made their escape: I am sorry for the accident of this encounter from the Circumstance only of the Spanish having been employed (as they represent) for a protection and safe-guard although there was no call on them to have furnished an Escort to the sergeant in returning seeing I did not think one necessary to him in going…
> I have further to report to your excellency that accounts received three days ago from the Deputy Superintendent in the Chactaw Nation, represent that People in

---

17   Burgoyne, 'A Diary Kept by Chaplain Waldeck, Part IV', p.33.

the greatest … Tumult and Confusion, from the contest between the British and Spanish Parties.[18]

Alexander Cameron interviewed the warriors who gave him their side of the story. The Spaniards had been encountered by accident when both parties tried to use the same house for shelter on the journey, and no British soldiers were to be seen, when the Choctaw leader recognised the soldiers to be Spanish, he let out a war whoop, upon which his warriors seized the Spaniards with the intent of bringing them into Pensacola. However, the Spanish sergeant refused to surrender and struggled with his would-be captors, throwing some repeatedly to the ground, and at this point the Choctaw leader, a man named Mingo Pouscouche, ordered his men to kill their captives rather than risk a general fight. Cameron quoted Mingo Pouscouche in his report to Campbell, the warrior's testimony suggests a man used to the practicalities of wilderness warfare, and who was coldly frank with Cameron about the entire affair.

> If I wanted to kill these people, I could have done it without the least risk to myself or any of my party, but you may observe that my intention was to take them prisoners, otherwise I would not have suffered by them so much. Since my arrival here the People seem very cool and cross with me and it seems to me that they love the Spaniards; I was told that some of the warriors here said that I knew that the Spaniards came from Mobile to see some of the English safe to Pensacola; but if they said so they told a lie. I have thrown away the Spaniards and if the English should throw me away for killing their enemy, I can go away to some other nation who hates them as well as myself. While I was out I saw men, women and children which I believe were French or Spaniards, and whom I might have killed if I had a mind, but I have been always told by the English never to be guilty of killing people who did not trouble them or me and who lived Peaceably at home, but as the English seem now cross with me, I will for the future kill every Spaniard, woman or child belonging to them that I shall come across [19]

Cameron responded to this chilling vow by assuring the man that he believed his story, and that since he was unaware of the purpose of the Spaniards, it would not be held against him. To which he was able to change Mingo Pouscouche's mind, but he lamented to Campbell that the event had taken place, swearing similarly that he had given no such orders. Indeed, the entire attitude of the British to the defection of these Spanish allies, was dismissive if not disdainful. It is mentioned by von Waldeck as well and it would seem that politics and perception overrode the inclination to accept the help of these warriors based on the killing and in some cases, murder of unsuspecting Spaniards.

The defection of the Choctaw bands at Mobile were essentially the cause of the brutal demises of many unfortunate Spanish soldiers, and Spanish and French inhabitants. The warriors, disgruntled by inadequate compensation,

---

18   TNA: PRO 30/55/89: Campbell to Clinton, 18 September.
19   TNA: PRO 30/55/89: Cameron to Campbell, 29 August 1780.

turned on their former allies and hoped to win favour with their former enemies by presenting scalps, commissions, and gorgets to the British. Cameron listened to their offer of military aid and loyalty, but made no secret about his or the garrison's feelings on the matter, 'I told him that I believed he spoke for nothing, and that they were a deceitful People, which was all I said, being very sick in bed at the time.'[20] On the opposing side, Cameron reported that the Spanish had rewarded Muskogee defectors who had robbed and burned British possessions when leaving Pensacola. Mingo Pouscouche did not slink away however, he was the war leader and imbued with an unshakeable spiritual empowerment, he took every opportunity to emphasise his right to fight the Spanish, who had taken Mobile, where the Choctaws had gathered to receive gifts, and the British should remember and honour their promises of bounties, and that irrespective, he would scalp the Spaniards wherever he found them.

The Choctaws were a new source of information as well as disquiet, as Cameron heard from them that they feared the Spanish would soon take Pensacola as they had Mobile, for, 'As the head warrior of the Spaniards told them that he was determined to have every foot of Ground the English had in this country and drive them out of it.'[21]

This was hardly news to the British commander, but it can only have reassured him that he was wise to continue building up his defences. Regarding the fortifications, Campbell reported in October that,

A work has ... been begun are the Red Cliffs, on an Eminence Whence the Shipping stationed for the defence of the Harbour could be greatly annoyed if not entirely driven off with cannon or mortars. The defences of this work are towards the Land, the Ramparts constructed of Facines and sand; on the Sea side is a Precipice, along the top of which there may in time be formed a Battery.[22]

This place had long since been known as a good spot for a battery. Some further indications of how it might have looked are contained in a map from 1771 surveying the harbour entrance and proposed batteries, which included a work on Siguenza Point that was never completed.

... all the Battery's are to have a shade of three inch Plank laid above the Platforms, with propper [sic] decent to carry off the water and to cover the men while they are working the Guns from being fired on by them men in the Round [fighting] Tops of the Men of War ... The above mentioned shade will be likewise of the greatest use to cover the Guns, Carriages and Platforms from the sun and Rain in Summer and Winter ... All the Batteries are to be built with Loose sand 26 feet thick Faced with Fascines.[23]

---

20   TNA: PRO 30/55/89: Cameron to Campbell, 29 August 1780.
21   TNA: PRO 30/55/89: Cameron to Campbell, 29 August 1780.
22   TNA: PRO 30/55/89: Campbell to Clinton, 31 October 1780.
23   TNA: MPD 1/194: Plan of the Entrance of Pensacola Harbour, T. Sowers, March 1771.

Campbell hoped to emplaced guns there that would cover the channel between there and Santa Rosa. The continued work on the fortifications would be reported again in early January 1781,

> an important redoubt for the defence of this harbour has lately been constructed on the highest ground or surmount of the Red Cliffs, and which entirely overlooks all the adjoining Ground, whereon are mounted eleven Pieces of Cannon, whereof 5 are [Thirty]-Two Pounders towards the sea (two of them also bearing towards the Flanks) the rest, 6 pounders. It is constructed of Fascines and Exceedingly well executed and is furnished with a magazine and Barracks for an … Garrison – any vessel drawing more than 9 feet water must not only pass within a mile of the muzzle of the guns, but is also exposed to be raked fore and aft from her crossing the Bar.[24]

The glacis and covered way of Fort George were also coming along, though lack of tools, the expense of those available, and the scarcity of heavy guns was making progress on the exterior redoubts slow. However, with any luck, Campbell hoped he would have time to construct another redoubt on Santa Rosa Island and do all but seal the entrance to the harbour. That was still a month away however as, unaware of the fate of Solano's fleet, he was still bracing for the Spanish to land as late as 15 November when he had written to Superintendent Brown in Georgia,

> I have every reason to believe the Spaniards will soon invade Pensacola. I trust then you will take every step to secure to me (on my Intimation to your commissioners of such an event) a speedy & effectual Reinforcement of Creek Indians. They have already been a principal cause in deterring the Spanish from attacking this place last Spring; and they have it still in their power by frequent attacks and Constant Alarms in short by continually harassing, hanging on the enemy's rear, in case of Siege greatly to impede the operations, if not totally defeat … the Designs of any force they can send against us.[25]

Upon sending such a force, the leaders were to be informed explicitly of what was required of them when they reached Pensacola. Just after the new year, the commander of Pensacola had some cheerful news to impart to headquarters in New York. Campbell wrote to Clinton on 5 January 1781, 'I have to report to your Excellency, this place having once more provisionally escaped a formidable intended invasion and attack.'[26] He went on to detail what he had learned of the hurricane that had scattered Solano's force. The sudden confirmed respite, brought to him via captured ships, left him not only with breathing space but a quandary about what to do with his Muskogee and Choctaw warriors, as,

---

24   TNA: PRO 30/55/89: Campbell to Clinton, 5 January 1781.
25   TNA: PRO 30/55/22: Campbell to Brown, 15 November 1780.
26   TNA: PRO 30/55/89: Campbell to Clinton, 5 January 1781.

Upon the alarm of said invasion, I judged if necessary to order in as many Indians to be assembled to join in our defence as could possibly be collected – These (once called off from their Hunts) will not be satisfied without coming here agreeable to their Invitation, and receiving Presents – Five hundred of the Chactaw Indians having (of consequence) come hither, I have judged if a favourable opportunity for attacking the Enemy at Mobile village on this side of the Bay where they have established an entrenched Post defended with two pieces of cannon and Garrisoned by about one hundred men [27]

Superintendent Cameron put it in slightly stronger terms when he submitted his report to Germain,

General Campbell in about the latter end of December seemed satisfied that the Spaniards had no power to hurt us here and therefore thought it best to order presents to be made up for the Indians in order to send them home satisfied. The Indians were very happy when I told them of this determination but they still expressed their wish of reducing the post at the Village. This I informed General Campbell of, but he would not be persuaded that there was any troops at the Village. The Indians insisted there was, on which General Campbell desired the Indians that they would remain quiet for two or three days and that he would find out the truth of it. But during the night following, a party of the Indians who were out scouting returned and corroborated what the Indians had been saying before. The general sent for the headman of the party and examined him more closely upon the subject, and when he could no longer doubt the truth of the report, General Campbell ordered a detachment from the different corps to be in readiness.[28]

The village was eight miles northeast of Mobile, called La Aldea. A small fishing and farming community on the east side of the bay. Campbell's information, brought in by various scouts and reading parties through the summer and autumn, was quite accurate. The Spanish had built a redoubt of some kind there the previous year after Gálvez left for Cuba, knowing that Fort Charlotte was in a decrepit state and was defended by 190 men, (from the Regimientos de Príncipe, España, and Habana), two 4-pounders, and the Free Louisiana militia, 30 of whom had been awarded medals for their service in the Gulf so far.[29]

After Gálvez and the bulk of the army had left, Ezpeleta in Mobile soon had difficulties with resentful war-bands who felt cheated by a lack of action and compensation, the results of which had been to use a polite eighteenth-century phrase, sanguinary. He also worried about the British counterattacking before he was ready or before Gálvez returned from Havana. Gálvez wrote to Ezpeleta on 20 November 1780 asking him to remain steady, and that he

27   TNA: PRO 30/55/89: Campbell to Clinton, 5 January 1781.
28   K.G. Davies (ed.), *Documents of the American Revolution, 1770-1783* (Shannon: Irish University Press, 1972), vol.XX, p.58.
29   Jack D.L. Holmes, 'Alabama's Bloodiest Day of the American Revolution: Counterattack at the Village, January 7, 1781', *Alabama Review*, vol.29, no.3 (July 1976) pp.209–210.

A view of a cottage on Dauphin Island, Mobile, in 1764. This island was attacked unsuccessfully by HMS *Mentor* at the beginning of 1781. (British Library Flikr)

would not forget or abandon him. 'Do not ever think I am capable of leaving you. With a little more patience and some resolve everything will be solved.'[30]

Ezpeleta was certainly steady, and his eagerness to get along with the capture of Pensacola was by his own admission driving him mad, but he was unaware of the looming danger, and was largely unaided. A reinforcement had failed to enter the channel of Mobile Bay due to a change in the bottom and had instead sailed with its 500 men to Balize.

Campbell was convinced enough of the vulnerability to attempt a strike in order to fulfil his obligations to the Muskogees and Choctaws, and to remove a useful base from the Spanish. 'For this purpose, I detached Colonel de Hanxleden of the 3rd Regiment of Waldeck with one hundred rank and file (exclusive of officers and sergeants) of regular and provincial troops and five Dragoons, and between four and five hundred Indians with a detachment of Artillery and two brass three Pounders.'[31]

Alexander Cameron was more precise regarding the allied contingent '420 Indians crossed the Perdido 12 miles from here on [3 January] under the command of Messrs Bethune and McIntosh, both my deputies, the interpreters and one or two more white men, and marched in front all the way.'[32]

The sloop *Mentor* was sent to support them from the sea. Amongst the provincials was Phillip Barton Key of the Maryland Regiment, an uncle to the poet who wrote the Star-Spangled Banner. Joining them on the march, as one of the 'one or two' white men with the war-band, was former

---

30   Saravia, *Gálvez*, p.188.
31   TNA: PRO 30/55/89: Campbell to Clinton, 5 January 1781.
32   Davies (ed.), *Documents of the American Revolution*, Cameron to Germain, 10 February 1781, p.59.

Maryland Ensign William Augustus Bowles. This individual had been born to a planter's family in Maryland and had run away from home to join the Maryland loyalists in Philadelphia after the British took the city in 1777. Bowles was made an ensign in 1778, as his family was considered respectable in Maryland. After supposedly surviving the heat and Continental lead at Monmouth, in the autumn of the next year he left with his regiment for Jamaica and Pensacola. To believe some of the stories about him, he was apparently charged with being absent without leave and discharged without trial after taking a jaunt into town to tread the sandy streets of the West Floridian capital. This seems a rather less than credible, but some event led him to leave the Provincial service shortly after arriving, leading to the ritual hurling of his coat into the waters. His rebirth was completed when he briefly fell in with a band of Muskogee warriors heading back to their nation after receiving their annual presents from the British at Pensacola but then careered off into the wilderness, striking out to the east side of the bay, to return to the town a few months later in a makeshift boat, using a branch for a mast and a blanket for a sail.[33]

The winter of 1779 was cold, and attended by a frost and Bowles went back to his Muskogee friends on the Chattahoochee, and so we must suppose he lived in or near Ekanachatte, or the Red Ground, a principal Muskogee/Seminole town that stood in modern Jackson County Florida. It was in this period that he seemed to be welcomed into whichever town or village he had found, cemented by his marrying a local Muskogee (though in this case likely Seminole) or refugee Cherokee. Seminole towns were noted places of refuge, and he may have taken up with more than one local woman, as his son became a noted Cherokee leader, but he is confirmed to have married Mary the daughter of Kinache, a mixed-race leader from the Chattahoochee region, who took the name Thomas Perryman.[34] Having traded his red coat for a war shirt and now fought with the Muskogee as a principal warrior. 'Bowles, along with several hundred Indians joined the party, he himself in dress and figure so exactly resembling a savage warrior, that unless he had discovered himself, he would never have been recognised by his old acquaintances, several of whom served in the expedition.'[35] He was a colourful character and one of many Europeans who found adventure and purpose living and fighting amongst their American allies. He was described by Francisco Cerdá, one of the later governors of Louisiana,

The height of Mr. Bowles captures our attention for its stature and for the build of his frame, which is similar to that possessed by the ancient gladiators, qualities combining force and activity ... He boasts several skills – he is an actor without having appeared in more than three plays in his life, a painter, although no one

33 Benjamin Baynton, *Authentic memoirs of William Augustus Bowles, esquire: ambassador from the United Nations of Creeks and Cherokees, to the court of London* (London: R. Faulder, 1791), pp.1–29.
34 James Leich Wright, *William Augustus Bowles, Director General of the Creek Nation* (Athens, University of Georgia Press, 1967), p. 13.
35 Holmes, *Alabama's Bloodiest Day*, pp.214–215.

seems to have seen the results of his skill; alchemist without knowledge of the basics; a navigator without having studied the principles of navigation.[36]

Nor was he the only European in the ranks of the allies. One of the Germans, a deserter named Brandenburg had adopted American Indian ways and was considered, 'as little of a Christian as his Indian comrades.'[37] According to a Waldeck regiment corporal named Steurnagle, this man had been known to the garrison since 1779.

> Among these Indians the Waldeckers found, to their great surprise, a countryman from the town of Konigshagen. This man had in his youth deserted from the Waldecker-Schloss (castle), and after many adventures had fallen into the hands of the Indians, whose costumes and ways of living he had adopted. He became an Indian chief, and acted just like one of them. This adventurer's name was Brandenstein, and generally he was interpreter between the Indians and white men.[38]

Also present was Campbell's attempt at a Legionary unit, the Royal Florida Foresters, who had been the rearguard in the failed relief attempt in the spring. Von Hanxleben's troops left Pensacola on 3 January 1781 and were in position to attack by the 7th. Meanwhile, on the 5th, British ships under Captain Robert Deans (HMS *Mentor*) duped the Spanish batteries on Dauphin Island and attempted to land and steal cattle that were grazing there. A 31-year-old Mexican *sargento segundo* named Manuel Rodriguez, was alert however, and ordered his 18 men to open fire, forcing the British to withdraw.[39]

Dawn on 7 January was foggy, as is common along the Gulf coast in winter, especially after heavy rain the day before. The pale greyness obscured the surroundings of La Aldea to the extent that the guards on the rampart of the redoubt were finding it hard to identify faces and uniforms. Only a dark suggestion of the thick woods presented itself through the murk, rising into more distinct tree like forms, reaching into the obscured sky, their branches laden with the distinctive falls of curling moss. Perhaps the sound of the guards calling to each other in French and Spanish, reached the ears of the von Hanxleben's men through the soft atmosphere, as they moved forward in a single column, bayonets fixed, dragging two 4-pounders as support. The initiation of the attack is not clear, authors such as Holmes, Saravia, and even Ezpeleta, suggest a more cautious advance, whereas the Loyalists report a sudden rush. Von Hanxleben envisioned a multiple pronged attack, as before dawn he had sent Bethune and the warriors to take up positions that would cut off the fort from the water and had arranged to beat a drum as a signal to attack.

Maybe they progressed in fits and starts, marking the calls of the picquets to know where they could pierce the militia cordon and then crossing the

---

36 Holmes, *Alabama's Bloodiest Day*, p.215.
37 Holmes, *Alabama's Bloodiest Day*, p.212.
38 Eelking, *German allies*, p.13.
39 Holmes, *Alabama's Bloodiest Day*, p.213.

200-yard interval between the forest and the works at speed. If so, they were successful and soon reached the camp of the militia.

One of the officers on duty here, was *Teniente* Manuel De Cordoba of the Regimiento de España. He saw the figures moving but thought them to be the militia themselves returning from picquet duty and so raised no alarm. Cordoba was a career soldier from an army family, his father had been a captain in the regiment, and both of his brothers were also officers in the service, one being killed in 1775 as a cadet in the Regimiento de Cantabria during O'Reilly's disastrous invasion of Algiers. *Teniente* Cordoba and his men were taken completely by surprise and bayonetted before they could respond. It would be a hard day when the news reached *Señora* de Cordoba, who had raised her three sons alone, seen them all go into uniform, and had buried one only five years before.[40]

From there, von Hanxleben pushed on to the ditch dispersing his men to the left and right to find an entry point, surprised but undoubtedly feeling confident in not finding any strong resistance. The allied warriors seem to have been left to their own devices. The commotion must have alerted the commanding officer inside the works however, as *Teniente* Ramón de Castro of the Regimiento de Prícipe, realised something was wrong, and reacted quickly, leaping to the defences with great tenacity, as the official report ran. A general volley of musketry blazed along the Spanish earthworks, accompanied by shouts of '*Viva El Rey!*' The Louisiana militia, realising that enemies had gotten behind them men fled for cover.

Lieutenant Benjamin Baynton, recorded that the attackers had come in sight of the redoubt only that morning after five days marching, and had immediately attacked, 'we rushed on with a boldness and intrepidity which deserved, tho' it did not command success.'[41] According to Baynton the Spanish musketry was well delivered,

It was my fate to be shot through my left arm above the Elbow, just as I had got over the pallisadoes. Out of five gallant sturdy fellows I had before the action singled out to follow me at my Side, and in case of necessity, assist me in mounting the works, only two are left to tell the story; and one of them, a Serjeant, who earnestly requested to attend me, dangerously wounded in two places. They fell fighting by my side. I have to lament on this occasion, beside several brave officers, a most faithful & affectionate servant, into whose arms I fell when I received my wound. I cannot help mentioning the poor fellow, because I feel myself hurt at never having it in my power as I could wish, to show him the sense I had of his services, and particularly the warm attachment he manifested in the most eminent danger, and within three foot of the muzzles of the enemy's muskets.[42]

40   Holmes, *Alabama's Bloodiest Day*, pp.218–219.
41   Tod Braisted, 'A History of the Provincial Corps of Pennsylvania Loyalists - Part 5 of 7', *The Online Institute for Advanced Loyalist Studies*, <http://www.royalprovincial.com/military/rhist/paloyal/pal5hist.htm#palbunk>, accessed 6 July 2023.
42   Braisted, 'History of the Provincial Corps'.

Campbell was told that von Hanxleben and his staff were killed or wounded in the first discharge. The bodies of the *oberst*, his adjutant, Lieutenant Stirling, and a Lieutenant Gordon, were found lying together in the ditch. Campbell informed Clinton that 'to the very death of Colonel de Hanxleden this misfortune must be attributed, for after his Death the Waldeck soldiers (5 or 6 excepted) could not be forced to advance notwithstanding every Exertion and endeavour of their officers.'[43] Indeed, a dead Waldeck sergeant was found alone near the palisade, which may suggest the disproportionate number of officers and NCOs standing alone in front of the Spaniards after the first volley. Lieutenant Baynton, who never failed to speak of his experience at La Aldea in the most colourful way, seems to bear out two important details that alongside Campbell create a fairly clear picture of what went wrong. First that only 50 British soldiers were present, and the other 50 were Germans.

> To the honour of the detachment which consisted of only 50 British soldiers, they forced the work and carried it at the same instant against four hundred Spanish troops, who attempted to escape on board an armed vessel which lay off the fort. But from this they were prevented by the savages, who slew many in the water, attempting to seek refuge in their boats. All possibility of flight being thus cut off, they became emboldened by despair and took shelter in their barracks, from the windows of which they annoyed the remaining few of the British, who had escaped in the assault. But more than half of this gallant detachment were killed or wounded. Out of ten officers, three were killed and three badly wounded. Two others of a foreign regiment were exerting themselves to compel, at the points of their swords, fifty of the original detachment, who refused to do their duty.[44]

The redoubt itself was almost certainly the conventional timber and packed earth type. The term pallisadoe used by Baynton, suggests it was of the type constructed later at Pensacola, two parallel lines of logs filled in with earth and packed with fascines. Baynton continued: 'One continual sheet of fire presented itself for ten minutes. You may judge of the gallantry of the Officers, when you read in the papers that out of ten, six were killed and wounded. It was Bunkers hill in miniature.'[45] The wounded officer always insisted that the loyalists had indeed infiltrated the works. 'There remained left in the fort but two officers, with scarce twenty men, who must inevitably have fallen, had they not been forced to fly their vainly imagined victors.'[46]

Campbell's report to New York confirmed it was not quite all in the Spaniard's favour,

> The other troops however appear to have done their Duty, they forced the entrenchment, and were in possession thereof and of the enemy's cannon for near a quarter of an hour, during this time a part of the enemy had pushed to gain their boats at anchor off the Post in this attempt I am credibly informed near forty

---

43   TNA: PRO 30/55/89: Cameron to Campbell, 15 February 1781.
44   Baynton, *Authentic Memoirs*, pp.31–32.
45   Saravia, *Gálvez*, p.189.
46   Baynton, *Authentic Memoirs*, pp.31–32

of them were killed by the Indians and by a few white men that were with them, and the rest drove back towards their entrenchment. On seeing them return our People seem to have abandoned the work without resistance.[47]

The warriors had been engaged throughout the fight, but due to the confused nature of the attack received no directions once the Europeans began the attack.

The Indians were ordered to take post before daybreak on the morning of the 7th between the water of Mobile Bay and the fort on which it stands, and Hanxleden promised Mr. Bethune that he would order the drum to beat for a general storm. But as there was no signal of any kind (which I suppose was occasioned by the death of Colonel Hanxleden) Mr. Bethune did not attempt to storm but with his Indians kept firing at every Spaniard they could see. A body of them at length rushed out of their picquets and ran down the back for the water where they had only one boat at anchor, but the Indians shot them all down and followed them chin-deep in the water to get their scalps which they brought back here to the amount of 40-50.[48]

Word eventually spread that von Hanxleben and two lieutenants had been killed, and the command passed from him and through several other wounded officers, to Captain Phillip Key, as the senior officer still on his feet. Aware that the force had taken heavy casualties and were completely disorganised, Key ordered the retreat.

In the midst of all this danger, Bowles, [who Baynton says had joined the storming party] with the coolness of an unconcerned spectator, very leisurely loaded and discharged his rifle gun at those who were firing from the windows and when the British soldiers called to the ... officers to save their lives by flight, our hero posted himself behind a tree, within a few yards of the work loading and firing alone; and he must undoubtedly have been killed or taken, had not a cannon-ball from the enemy shivered the tree to pieces, and driven him unhurt, to gain the small flying party, already at the distance of a quarter of a mile.[49]

Bowles would be reinstated as an ensign for his part in the action. Of interest here as well is the information reported that very night to Campbell, 'The messenger says the Indians continued the attack after the troops were withdrawn, and still kept up a very smart fire this day at 12 o'clock when he was despatched by Captain Key.'[50] According to Cameron, 'Some of the headmen begged of the troops to return again to the charge and that they did not doubt but they would carry the place,' however their encouragement went unheeded.[51]

---

47   TNA: PRO 30/55/89: Campbell to Clinton, 7 January 1781.
48   TNA: PRO 30/55/89: Cameron to Campbell, 15 February 1781.
49   Baynton, *Authentic Memoirs*, p.33.
50   TNA: PRO 30/55/89: Campbell to Clinton, 7 January 1781.
51   Davies (ed.), *Documents of the American Revolution*, Cameron to Germain, 10 February 1781, p.59.

Meanwhile Ezpeleta and the garrison realised what was afoot, but the British ships had temporarily cut off Mobile from La Aldea, and so there was little he could do. Needless to say, Ezpeleta was ecstatic to hear of the successful defence, and wrote it up with unsparing praise, 'I can report to you that every one of the attacks thrown against us by the enemy has been repulsed, and with these small victories our men are gradually gaining a certain feeling of superiority over the enemy, which could be very useful from now on.'[52]

Ezpeleta clearly had received a rude shock in what was the most recent, and most serious of at least four attacks on La Aldea but was impressed by the quickness with which his men had rallied, and it gave him hope that the enemy would not have done very much at all if there had been forewarning. The Spaniards lost 38 casualties (23 of which were wounded), and Campbell was informed by Key that 37 men and officers were killed wounded and missing from the expedition.

Saavedra wrote excitedly to José de Gálvez when word reached Havana:

> One hundred and fifty men, commanded by Ramón del Castro, Lieutenant of the Principe Regiment, repelled gloriously a corps of three hundred English veterans and three hundred Indians which attacked them during a tempestuous night, having left dead in the very fort, into which they had begun to penetrate, the Waldeck colonel who led the attack and who was the best officer of Pensacola, a sergeant major, an adjutant, a captain of grenadiers, and sixteen men. [53]

Ezpeleta was extremely proud of his soldiers, and praised the courage of the attackers: 'I believe that from what happened they are chastened, since although everything was in their favour, they have lost four officers, who for their courage deserved better luck, and I have no doubt they would have had it if they had not met troops who knew how to confront them, and did not know how to run.'[54]

The Waldeck corporal, Steurnagle, somehow heard a rumour that von Hanxleben had been buried with full military honours, including a rocket salute, but admitted that none knew where he had been buried. The attack had been the largest and best organised since the failed relief of Mobile, and it seems true that with the loss of the Waldeck commander, Campbell had lost a capable lieutenant, but unintentionally he had also signalled that Pensacola was a threat. Ezpeleta sent a runner to New Orleans with a report of what had happened, especially pointing out that British ships still menaced his position. The news was another weapon in Gálvez's arsenal to press for another expedition against Pensacola, as nervous officials in Havana could not ignore the fact that if Pensacola was not now reduced, then all of West Florida might again be lost, and then with it, perhaps, New Orleans.

---

52   Holmes, *Alabama's Bloodiest Day*, p.219.
53   Caughey, *Gálvez in Louisiana*, p.195.
54   Saravia, *Gálvez*, p.190.

Spanish Metropolitan Infantry by Villegas. From left to right Fusilier 2nd Catalunya, grenadier Regimiento de America, fusilier Regimiento de Vitoria, fusilier 1st Catalunya. (Anne S.K. Brown Military Collection)

A wonderful pictorial display of the Spanish Metropolitan Army from 1780, showing also the manual of arms. (Anne S.K. Brown Military Collection)

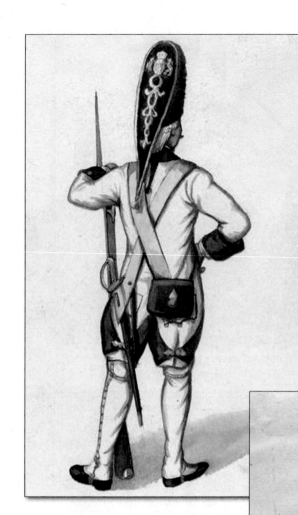

A rear view of a grenadier from a Spanish regiment c. 1778 showing the distinctive cap blazon. The grenadiers were all purpose troops for the Bourbon armies. (New York Public Library Digital Collections)

The Cuerpo Real de Ingenieros, engraving circa 1797. The engineers were at the forefront of the action to reduce Pensacola, and much of the credit for the progress of the siege goes to their remarkably swift construction of trenches and batteries before the British could respond. (New York Public Library Digital Collections)

Spanish 13-inch mortars from 1724 at Fort Ticonderoga. (René Chartrand)

Reenactors representing the grenadiers of the Regimiento de Navarra advance with the bayonet. (Order of Granaderos y Damas de Galvez, San Antonio Chapter)

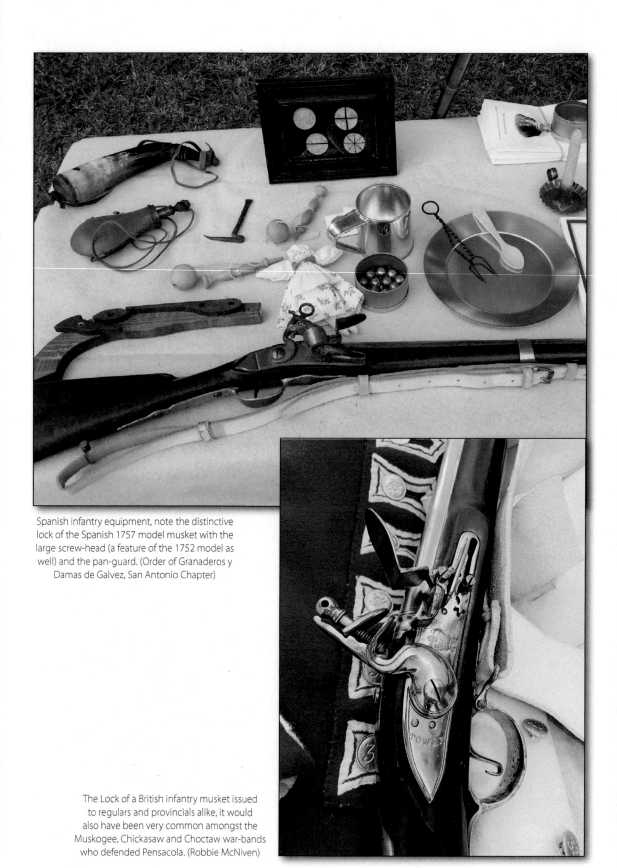

Spanish infantry equipment, note the distinctive lock of the Spanish 1757 model musket with the large screw-head (a feature of the 1752 model as well) and the pan-guard. (Order of Granaderos y Damas de Galvez, San Antonio Chapter)

The Lock of a British infantry musket issued to regulars and provincials alike, it would also have been very common amongst the Muskogee, Chickasaw and Choctaw war-bands who defended Pensacola. (Robbie McNiven)

McBarron's famous painting of the final assault at Pensacola, captures the urgency of the Spanish rush to occupy the ruins of the advanced redoubt after the explosion. As he was illustrating a volume on soldiers in America, he chose to depict grenadiers of the Regimiento Fijo de Louisiana and the Companias Morenos Libres de Havana, rather than the elite companies of the Metropolitan Regiments. (US Army Museum Enterprise Collection)

Por España y Por el Rey, Gálvez en America, by Augusto Ferrer Dalmau. This action-packed scene is likely figurative. Representing many metropolitan and provincial regiments, such as the Navarra, and *Fijo de Louisiana*, with one of the *Fijo de Havana* at the right, marine infantry behind the colours and a militiaman from Puerto Rico. The small inconsistencies do not detract from the power of a piece that Gálvez himself would have approved of. (Augusto Ferrer-Dalmau, Creative Commons: creativecommons.org/licenses/by-sa/4.0/deed.en)

The Spanish Regimiento Real de Artillería, by Beaufort, 1957. (Anne S.K. Brown Military Collection)

Soldiers of a Regimiento Fijo, by Beaufort. Their uniform is very close to the uniform of that of Louisiana and indeed to many metropolitan regiments. (Anne S.K. Brown Military Collection)

Bernardo de Gálvez is wounded by British allied Choctaws while directing the withdrawal of his light infantry during the early stages of the siege. A grenadier officer of the Regimiento de Navarra helps him from his horse, while a senior officer of engineers hold's his bridle, as *Coronel* José de Ezpeleta, riding with *Coronel* Esteban Miró, waves on the 2nd Catalunya, while two soldiers of the Morenos Libres return fire. Behind the stricken commander is a trooper of the Carabiniers of New Orleans. (Original artwork by Christa Hook © Helion & Company 2023)

Private, light company 16th Regiment of Foot by Don Troiani 1777–1781. It was the good luck of the flank companies of this regiment to be detached to the main field army under Cornwallis. The other companies wasted away or were captured in Florida. (Don Troiani)

Fusilier, Regimiento Fijo de Louisiana 1778-1782, by Don Troiani, the bedrock of the New Orleans garrison, this was an experienced and well-equipped regiment, led by capable officers, many of whom were personal friends of Gálvez. (Don Troiani)

Musketeer, 3rd Regiment of Waldeck 1776, by Don Troiani. They went from a relatively comfortable posting to garrison duty in a forgotten part of a foreign empire. Few troops can have loathed West Florida so much as these unfortunate British allies. (Don Troiani)

Fusilier, Morenos Libres de Havana, 1780, by Don Troiani. Whole militia regiments of the blancos, pardos and morenos were rarely assigned combat posts outside of their home city, but the grenadiers and *cazadores*, composed of the fittest men, were used as service companies for field operations. (Don Troiani)

Though the likeness is poor, this miniature of Bernardo de Gálvez c. 1781, seen here wearing the uniform he would have worn during the siege of Pensacola, is possibly intended to portray the fall of Mobile. Note the captured flags at the hooves of his horse. (Museo Ejercito de Espana, Toledo)

As a precursor to his iconic crossing of Pensacola bar, Gálvez sent one of his engineer officers to the flagship to present a British cannonball to the squadron commander, Calvo de Irazabal. As can be imagined, this act, performed in full view of the crew provoked a strong reaction. (Joshua Provan)

A trio of warriors from the Choctaw Nation painted for war, from contemporary depictions and descriptions. Right to Left: A 'medal chief', a warrior on the march and a warrior stripped for battle. The Choctaws wore their hair loose, and decorated with scarves, caps and feathers, in one instance a duck feather cap, complete with bill. The colours of black and red were associated with war and death, and their muskets were also described as being decorated. Until the final stage of the siege the allied nations were the main cause of casualties to the Spanish. (Joshua Provan)

Major General John Campbell was advanced in age and experience in the regular service by 1781. Here seen in a copy of what would appear to be his only portrait, executed sometime after the war. He struggled to defend a poorly funded, under-manned, vulnerable territory. At the heart of his difficulties was the fact he had to depend greatly on large war-parties of Muskogees, Chickasaws and Choctaws for the defence of West Florida, whom he continually denigrated but repeatedly applied to for assistance. (Joshua Provan)

Campbell knew about the reverse long before word reached Havana. A letter dated, 7 January 1781, at 11:00 p.m., was written at the headquarters in Pensacola and addressed to Clinton. Campbell found himself in:

> … the disagreeable necessity of appraising your excellency, That I have this moment received intelligence of the Repulse of the Detachment mentioned in my letter of the 5th ins't, who this morning at break of day attacked the Enemy's Post at Mobile Village - Colonel De Hanxleben thought proper to order a Storm, but was himself killed at the beginning of the Action – Further Particulars are not given … Only (In General) Captain Key of the United Corps of Pennsylvania and Maryland Loyalists reports that, by Colonel Hanxleben's being killed and Captain Baumbach of the Regiment of Waldeck being wounded, the command devolved upon him; whom finding (exclusive of their mishap) two Lieutenants, one sergeant and thirteen Rank and File killed and missing; and two lieutenants, two sergeants and fifteen rank and file wounded, he judged it prudent to order a Retreat, and had got before mid-day to the distance of nine miles on his Return across a Creek, the Bridge over which he had broke down to prevent a Pursuit; when he sent off a message to inform me of the Disaster.[55]

Campbell wrote that Adjutant James Gordon, of the 3/60th Foot, had also been killed, and that Lieutenant Stirling, Adjutant of the Waldeck regiment was missing. Both were deemed by him to be officers of singular merit. News of the defeat and the death of von Hanxleben even reached the army besieging Charleston, with jäger captain, Johann Ewald, recording sadly in his journal, 'How German bones are scattered around in this war.'[56] Perhaps the failure and the loss of good officers and men, plus the damage to prestige in the eyes of the Choctaws, caused Campbell to return to his former gloomy mood, as in February 1781 he brought Clinton to task on the subject of reinforcements.

> Your Excellency's Inability to send us Reinforcements gives me real concern because I can hope for military succour from no other quarter as the conclusion of a letter from General Dalling of the 6th Ultimo will evince – 'To your own judgement and valour of the Troops under your Command, I am … reluctantly obliged to resign you' – I therefore have no Recourse but on the conduct of those Troops and to Naval aid via Admiral Sir Peter Parker having promised us a Forty Four Gun ship to sail from Jamaica on this very day.[57]

Keen to bolster his workforce and numbers, Campbell worked with Governor Chester to secure the services of any able-bodied refugees from Natchez or Mobile who had fled to Pensacola. Those fit to bear arms were formed into a company, paid as Provincial troops, and given the grand title of West Florida Royal Volunteers.

He would have more trouble with his allies, however.

---

55   TNA: PRO 30/55/89: Campbell to Clinton, 7 January 1781.
56   Baer, *Hessians*, p.304.
57   TNA: PRO 30/55/89: Cameron to Campbell, 15 February 1781.

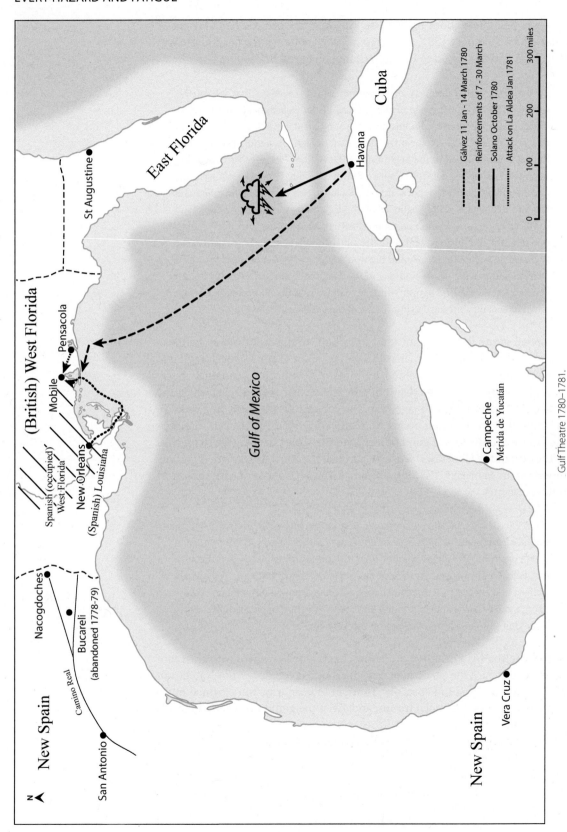

Gulf Theatre 1780–1781.

On the fifth of March about 300 Choctaws, who were sent for and lay at Pensacola for its defence, were served out with some presents and on the day following, they took their departure for their nation. On the sixth received advice from Jamaica that the Spaniards were upon their way to attack Pensacola. Brigade Major Campbell [not to be confused with the commanding general] came to my house and not finding me at home he left Mr. Rose, the Indian storekeeper, to inform me that it was the general's orders that I would send after the Indians and use every means and method to prevail upon them to return once more; that now we should have business enough on our hands.[58]

Campbell's wish to be rid of the war-bands but to always have them near, created an indecision that is painfully obvious when one considers that, twice between November 1780 and February 1781, he told Cameron's deputy with the Muskogee, MacGillivray, to send out messengers to call in the hunters and send the warriors, promising rich rewards, only to cancel as soon as he heard the Spanish were not coming. As such only 40 warriors, who had decided they preferred to winter at Pensacola, were on hand when the Spanish finally did arrive.[59]

The Junta of the Generals

Francisco de Saavedra spent the better part of the autumn, and the beginning of winter in Jamaica as a prisoner, or at least detainee of the British. It had been the patronage of the Gálvez family that had gained him his mission. Not long after the disaster at Algiers, he had been given a post in the Secretariat of the Ministry of the Indies and had proved himself a reliable and trustworthy assistant to José de Gálvez. When news came both of Don Bernardo's victories in Louisiana and his difficulties with Havana, Don José decided to appoint a special Royal commissioner to go out to America where obviously the decisive act of the war would be struck. It was important that this man be the voice of the court in the military juntas, unincumbered by territorial position or military responsibility.

Don José had selected Saavedra and the king approved. Orders were drawn up and powers granted so the *Junta de Generales* in Cuba and the treasury of Havana was to hear his voice as if it was the king's and afford him every cooperation. Saavedra had left on 21 August 1780, and, as we have seen, it was a rough passage. Having hidden or destroyed his compromising papers when his ship was boarded by the British, he insisted he was an official that specialised in economic matters and managed to befriend the secretary to Governor Dalling, who arranged his release. On 2 January 1781, Saavedra

---

58 Davies (ed.), *Documents of the American Revolution*, Cameron to Germain, 27 May 1781, p.149.

59 Michael D. Green, 'The Creek Confederacy in the American Revolution: Cautious Participants', in William S. Coker and Robert Right Rea (eds), *Anglo-Spanish confrontation on the Gulf Coast during the American Revolution* (Pensacola: Gulf Coast History and Humanities Conference, 1982), pp.70–72.

left Jamaica, having made careful observations while there, and landed in Havana on 22 January, where he wasted no time in beginning his task.

Saavedra arrived in the suburb of Christo and went to see his old friend Bernardo de Gálvez that evening. The exchange of news and planning lasted four hours, and one can only imagine Don Bernardo's relief to have Saavedra in Cuba, as his brief would make things go much easier. The day after arriving from Jamaica, Saavedra visited the *capitán general*, who tends to be portrayed by histories of the war as an old, slow reactionary, but might perhaps have had a longer strategic vision than the Ministry of the Indies and the firebrand governor of Louisiana. Navarro was described as 'well intentioned, although somewhat weakened by his great age.'[60] Having been born in 1708. This was the first in a round of calls Saavedra then paid on senior officers and ministers, meeting Don Victor de Navia, Don Juan Bautista Bonet, and *Mariscal de Campo* Don Juan Manuel de Cagigal. Saavedra also met fleet commanders Don José Solano and Don Juan de Tomasco, who, with Don Bernardo constituted the *junta* of general officers, additionally there was Don António de Valle, the secretary of the Havana government, as *junta* secretary.

The intendant of the army, Don Juan Ignazio de Urriza, arranged for Saavedra to stay at the house of the treasurer of the army, Don Ignacio Peñalver. To finish of his busy round of introductions, Saavedra also met with *Chef d'Escadre* François-Aymar de Monteil, the French fleet commander in Havana, 'an ingenious and extraordinarily active man',[61] and the Bishop of Havana at San Juan. Monteil was at Havana with a squadron of the French Antilles Fleet, consisting of ships-of-the-line *Palmier*, *Destin*, *Triton*, and *Intrepide*, two frigates (*Licorne* and *Adromaque*), three brigs, two galeotts and two other vessels. There to combine his forces with the Havana fleet for as long as they might be needed, to safeguard the Bahama channel for the passage of the Spanish convoy from Vera Cruz, and to make use of Havana's excellent shipyards to refit his ships. Monteil, however, said he had gone to Havana in order to participate in Spanish operations, but had been delayed by the damage done in the hurricane season of 1780, after which he had attempted to act the part of the good guest, by only undertaking necessary repairs so as to not impede the Spanish. He hoped to participate in a joint action quickly and return to his station, and was in favour of prioritising the safety of Sainte Domingue directly or via a blockade of Jamaica.[62] Monteil had been arguing for action since the turn of the year and had spoken in the *Junta* in February, that either he must return to St Domingue with a small united French and Spanish squadron, leaving the *Intrepide* in Havana, or be made use of quickly in some expedition against what at this time he considered a far inferior enemy.[63] Gálvez and Saavedra's successful orientation towards the Gulf put great strain on Monteil, who felt he needed to remain until a joint blow was struck. As no opportunity presented itself, he wrote to his

---

60   Topping (ed.), *Journal of Saavedra*, p.99.

61   Topping (ed.), *Journal of Saavedra*, p.122.

62   Rene Quatrefages, 'La Collaboration Franco-Espagnole dans la Prise de Pensacola', in *Revue Historique des Armées*, no.4, 1981, pp.48–50.

63   Quatrefages, 'La Collaboration Franco-Espagnole', p.53.

superior at the ministry of the navy, that he hoped the *Junta* would make a determination soon, but otherwise he was left with nothing to do but chase small corsairs. Saavedra was therefore able to very quickly gather a picture of the forces available to begin operations. 'My primary concern was to inform myself fundamentally about the condition of our land and sea forces, the amounts of money on which they could rely, and the current state of their preparations,' he found that:

> The army numbered fewer than 4,000 men, including the corps that could be added from the garrison of Havana ... The army reached Havana sick and greatly diminished in numbers, in August, that is, in the rainy season and in a subtropical heat. There were no quarters in which to place the men. It was necessary for them to be piled into vaults of the narrow and poorly ventilated fortifications, and as those fell far short of containing them all, it was decided to build a kind of covered barracks or sheds on the parade ground, a humid place and therefore [no] more healthy. With several corps housed there, violent outbreaks of dysentery, putrid fevers, and other illnesses began to occur and in a short time carried off great numbers of men. [64]

The army had to rely on the charity of the church, and apparently all the religious communities offered space for the relief of the army, so that troops could be billeted in the well-ventilated cloisters of the convents.

The hospitals and infirmaries of the Belamites and the pious inhabitants of San Juan de Dios took in as many patients as they could hold. But many private homes were also used, which was much less desirable, in terms of order and cost. Saavedra wrote that it was not unusual for European troops to suffer from the climate in the Americas even in the cool season, and as such the losses of troops in the army of operations was immense in the wet season, dropping in number from an already diminished 7,000 to 3,000 between August 1780 and January 1781. Saavedra opined that it would be impossible to undertake anything without the experienced, acclimated regiments in the Havana garrison. On top of that, the navy,

> ... had experienced many desertions, however, so that 3,000 sailors were missing. The warships were very dirty, four of them were dismasted, all were in need of repair and some careening. In the navy yard there were no masts, no military stores, not even pitch. The army commanded by General Navía had brought only six siege guns, and these were exposed to the elements on wooden rollers on the beach below the Morro, because there was no covered area in which to protect them. It is a remarkable thing that in Havana, where from the year '63 more than 12 million pesos had been spent on fortifications, there should be neither quarters, nor hospital, nor armoury for artillery of medium capacity. The present century had censured Phillip II for not having built one yard of pave road from Madrid to the Escorial, after having spent 12 million *ducados* on the monastery to which he used to go frequently, and for enduring the discomfort being stuck in

---

64   Topping (ed.), *Journal of Saavedra*, pp.101–104.

A view of the Franciscan church and convent in the city of Havana. The religious community of Havana was credited with caring for the hundreds of sick troops from Spain during the interminable delays in beginning the attack on Pensacola. Engraving by Edward Rooker, 1768. (Library of Congress)

the mire almost every year. I do not know how future centuries will judge the lack of quarters and hospitals in the most important stronghold in America, which requires 10,000 soldiers to garrison its forts. [65]

Financial matters were not much better: 'According to information given me by the intendant, the treasury of Havana was in a very bad condition also. At the moment it did not have 1 million *pesos* on hand, and it owed debts of 3 million.'[66] The million in itself had been sent to them after the declaration of war from Mexico, and more was being constantly demanded. The commissioner was however aware of the money and aid promised by New Spain, and he had the authority to organise its distribution. His musings on the subject also reveal how money was passed into the hands of the United States.

In Veracruz there were great stores of packaged flour, vegetables, and meats, but the merchant vessels did not dare bring them because of the danger of corsairs, and warships were few and slow and had many ports of call. The Anglo Americans had supplied this need as much as possible, for in fewer than eight months they had brought to Havana in their light crafts as many as 100,000 barrels of food, but this was a precarious assistance which depended on the degree of vigilance of the

---

65 Topping (ed.), *Journal of Saavedra*, pp.104–105.
66 Topping (ed.), *Journal of Saavedra*, pp.105–106.

English privateers. Moreover, thirty pesos had been paid for each barrel of flour, and in this way 3 million pesos had been exported to the Northern Colonies. [67]

Saavedra's brief was not actually to prioritise Pensacola, it was to identify which target, West Florida or Jamaica, was the more important to the war effort, and to unify the squabbling generals of the *Junta*. After acquainting himself with the situation in Cuba, he decided that the Great Hurricane meant that the idea of coordinating an attack on Jamaica was out of sync with strategic realities in the Americas.

Although he was a friend, Saavedra knew that Don Bernardo had a personal reason to push for Pensacola, 'Don Bernardo de Gálvez sought to take to Pensacola a force great enough to prevent endangering the success of an expedition that would decide his fortune and the fame he expected to win from his superiors and rivals.'[68] Meanwhile, Navía wanted to attack Jamaica, Navarro would reject anything that left Havana without a large garrison, and meanwhile Bonet was worried about the poor state of his ships and did not want to agree to any large-scale expedition lest his resources prove inadequate to the task. These concerns were countered by the fact that a large French contingent would be required to attack Jamaica, and both Saavedra and Solano agreed that the British naval forces in the western Caribbean had been hit worse by the hurricane than their own and would likely be unable to stop an attempt to finish the reconquest of the gulf coast.

Saavedra resolved by 31 January that given the standard campaigning season in the tropics was November to May, and other considerations such as reinforcing Guatemala, the Pensacola expedition made most sense.

On 1 February 1781, Saavedra outlined his revaluation of Spanish war aims in the Indies.

> ... 1) the attack on Pensacola so as to close the Gulf of Mexico to the enemy. (2) aid to the president of Guatemala to enable him to dislodge the enemy from the lands they had occupied on the coasts of that province. (3) dispatch of the fleet to Cádiz so that it would be in the Azores Islands by the time when according to royal orders, the combined fleets of France and Spain would be awaiting it there, and (4) stationing our army and naval forces on the French cape, as Madrid advised, in order to attack Jamaica after meeting with the French wherever the circumstances demand. It is decided that the heads of departments offer reports as to their own branch's feasibility for undertaking respective plans.[69]

Over the next four days of meetings and presentations, it was discovered that the main issues of fitting out the expedition would be bread and ships. Superintendent of the Army Urriza reported that he could provide an army of 4,000 with enough food for three months, despite the lack of funds in the treasury and without convoys from Vera Cruz. However, while there was enough flour, there were not enough ovens to bake it into hard tack fast

---

67   Topping (ed.), *Journal of Saavedra*, p.106.
68   Topping (ed.), *Journal of Saavedra*, p.108.
69   Topping (ed.), *Journal of Saavedra*, p.112.

New Spain provided cattle via Tejas to Louisiana to feed the Spanish army and, thanks to the war fund, millions of pesos through Vera Cruz for both the ongoing military operations and the allied cause. (Library of Congress)

enough that it would be cooled and hardened before entering the ships. This was due to the monopoly held by eight bakeries in Havana, who essentially controlled the price of flour, which was, despite Navarro's efforts to buy Yankee flour at knockdown prices, at that time so exorbitant that ships had stopped coming to the port. This had fostered the creation of a mercantile cabal to import grain illegally. Meanwhile, the navy could not decide whether 12 or 14 warships were required, and Saavedra worried that Don Bernardo was asking for too few men. Gálvez, however, felt that he dared not ask for more in case he entrenched opposition to the operation. The problem was that as of 12 February the number of effective men in the garrison of Havana stood at 2,193, excluding what was left of the forces brought by Cagigal. These men were seasoned to the climate, and as many as possible were wanted. However only 528 were allocated as a reserve for Gálvez and 450 reserved for use as marines. Gálvez, not being a man who particularly cared about opposition, had made his own arrangements, and by this time had all but organised without advertisement the second Pensacola expedition, intending to bring, 1,500 men no matter what the old generals said.

Two days later, on 6 February, there had not been much progress. Saavedra was now finding Bonet, 'basically a good fellow but obstinate in the formalities of authority and irresolute in difficulties.'[70] But the 6th brought news of José Ezpeleta's defence of La Aldea, and this at least allowed the progressive faction to argue that they were running out of time. However, even this was not enough to finalise matters, as a point of contention now

---

70   Topping (ed.), *Journal of Saavedra*, p.121.

existed between Gálvez and Navía over who was to be in command. Gálvez had been named supreme commander of all forces involved in the expedition but whether that came into force while they were in Havana was a thorny subject. A possibility existed that the Governor of Louisiana, as a *mariscal de campo*, would only be able to command his own provincial forces, and Navia as a *teniente general* would command those of Havana. Gálvez shrewdly then began talking about reviewing the drill of the Pensacola army and organising it to his satisfaction. Irked by the younger man's audacity, Navia refused to allow it as he was army commandant. Saavedra now stepped in and called the quarrelling frivolous. He suggested the troops embark at least one day before sailing, without Gálvez taking formal command, then a boat should be sent with a message from Navia conferring command to Gálvez, at which time Gálvez could land on the other side of the harbour and do as his pleased. This was agreed to, a 'comic end of a dispute that could have brought tragic consequences.' [71]

Gálvez was aboard the flagship, *San Ramon*, commanded by *Jefe de Escuadron* Calvo, and met with Saavedra on the 21st to go over the plan once again. The next day the Governor sent a letter to Ezpeleta at Mobile warning him to be prepared as he would either meet him at Mobile or alert him to a move on Pensacola within 10 days. Ezpeleta replied on 5 March, 'The Carnival begins for us right now.'[72] However, delays in weather caused Don Bernardo anxiety as he had already sent ahead for troops of New Orleans to join him at Pensacola and now, he feared they would be overwhelmed if they got there first.

Six days later the weather improved, and with the signs looking optimal, Saavedra came aboard once again to formally accept the plan of action, which was to sail to Mobile and march overland with Ezpeleta to take the Barrancas Coloradas, which would allow the navy to enter the harbour.

On 28 February, at 5:00 a.m., the fleet and convoy set sail, with the *San Ramon* (66), frigates *Santa Cecilia* and *Santa Clara* (34), the chambequín *Andaluz* (20), the packet boat *San Pío* (18) and 32 transports, carrying 1,300 men, and the military train. Although the agreed plan was to sail for Mobile first, Gálvez was too afraid of more delays to do anything but go straight for his long-anticipated target. He gave new orders at sea to sail for Santa Rosa Island, which guarded the entrance to Pensacola Bay.

---

71   Topping (ed.), *Journal of Saavedra*, pp.124–125.
72   Rojas, *Ezpeleta at Pensacola*, p.114.

8

Those With Honour & Courage
(9 March–9 April 1781)

As René Chartrand observed in his book on the Siege of Louisbourg, a siege is a day-to-day affair, and the present author can do no better than to follow his example in presenting that of Pensacola as such.[1] Therefore, the following is a day-by-day account drawn from the combined journals, letters, and logs of the participants.

Friday 9 March

At 6:00 a.m., a great gun was fired from the battery of the Royal Navy Redoubt at Barrancas Coloradas. The signal, sudden and alarming from one of the recently emplaced 32-pounders, in the clear dawn, was held on the moderate north-easterly breeze, carrying the sound of the report to the sentinels in the town and the ships in the harbour and anchorage, before fading away. After coming on deck, Captain Robert Deans of the sloop HMS *Mentor* (18) had his lookouts aloft. From their elevated positions the sailors peered across the bay to the white strand of Santa Rosa, and out to sea. It took about an hour to discover the cause of the alarm. Though it was difficult to tell how far away they were with accuracy, the sails of a fleet had been seen to the south-east. The wind was against them, and they moved slowly, but by 8:00 a.m., Deans knew that they were on course for Pensacola and fired off alarm guns, before dispatching a messenger by boat to the Royal Navy Redoubt, which stood just to the west of the fort at the Barrancas, to confirm the fleet was 'on the coast.' He then changed his position, unmooring and heaving up the best bower to drop down again in five fathoms, closer to what he called the 'block house' at Siguenza Point on Santa Rosa, and between there and the Royal Navy Redoubt. Deans then 'clapped springs on the cable' so his guns could be brought to bear if an emergency occurred while anchored. After this he

1   René Chartrand, *Luisbourg 1758: Wolfe's First Siege* (Oxford: Osprey Publishing, 2000).

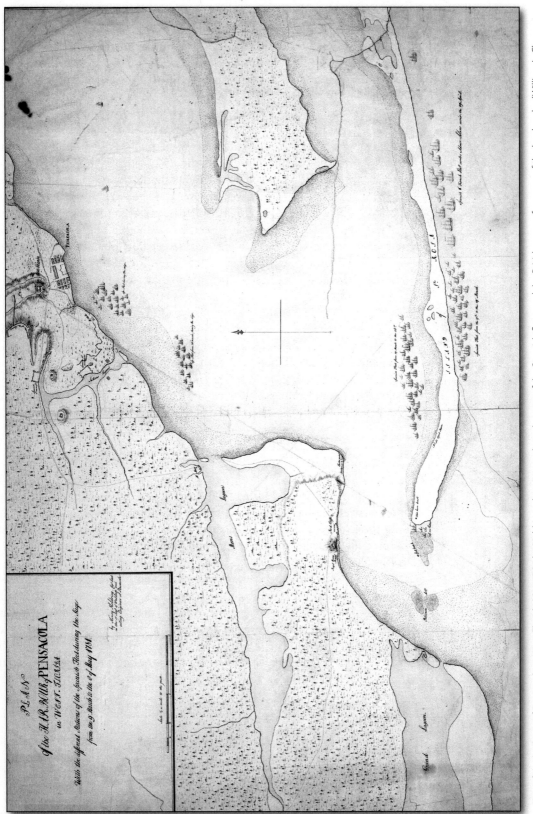

Plan of the harbour of Pensacola in West Florida May 1781 by Heldring, showing each anchorage of the Spanish fleet, and the British names for many of the landmarks. (William L. Clements Library, University of Michigan Library Digital Collections)

continued to observe, being able to report in his log a count of 34 sail sighted from the masthead.[2]

Out across the water to the southeast, aboard the Spanish flagship, *San Ramon*, Bernardo de Gálvez had heard *Mentor's* alarm guns firing, having come into sight of land at about the time the first great gun had fired at the Barrancas.

At 2:00 p.m. in the afternoon Gálvez ordered that all the troops find themselves ready to disembark that night and that each soldier should carry three days' rations; 'it being well understood that the grenadiers and light infantry should be the first to disembark, and that they should pass by the stern of the ship S. Ramon, when two lights should appear thereon.'[3]

By 3:00 p.m., the convoy was dropping anchor about a mile from the shore, and three leagues (roughly 10 miles) from the mouth of the bay. Gálvez was steeling himself for what he expected to be a tough fight to occupy the point of Santa Rosa. It had not occurred to the Spanish, and especially not to those who knew about Pensacola, that there would be no fort or battery emplaced there to cover the other side of the passage. At 9:00 p.m., the Spanish spearhead force of the grenadiers and light infantry under *Coronel* Francisco Longoria was ordered to make ready.

That evening, Commander Chadwick Lindon (Lyndon), commander of the 10-gun brig *Childers*, took his leave of Major General Campbell, (and possibly Governor Chester) and with urgent dispatches for Vice Admiral Parker, weighed anchor at midnight and began to cross the bar, but finding the tide was unfavourable, anchored close to the *Mentor* and waited for the propitious moment. Campbell also sent an express to Savannah.

Saturday, 10 March

At some time between 1:00 and 2.00 a.m., the *Childers* slipped her cable and got over the bar, then stood out to sea, observing the enemy closely until the 23rd, according to Campbell, before coming up on the wind and running for Jamaica, leaving *Mentor* and *Port Royal* as the only ships of war in Pensacola Bay.[4]

An hour after this the Spanish grenadiers and *cazadores* under *Coronel* Longoria were on the move from their beachhead to Siquenza Point. Gálvez had returned to the ships to get the general landing moving as quickly as possible. Surprised and relieved to have met no opposition but eager to take advantage of it. Deans of the *Mentor* had been organising the disposition of what ships were available and trying to get an optimum vantage point from which to view the enemy. By 6:00 a.m., the weather appeared fair with

2   James A. Servies (ed.), *The Log of H.M.S. Mentor, 1780-1781* (Gainesville: University Presses of Florida, 1982), p.164.
3   Gaspar Cusachs, (ed.), Gilbert Pemberton (trans.), 'Bernardo de Galvez's Diary of the Operations. Against Pensacola,' *Louisiana Historical Quarterly*, vol.1, no.1, pp.44-85, (January 1917), p.48.
4   TNA: PRO 30/55/89: Campbell to Clinton, 9 April 1781.

Character of the land along the gulf near Pensacola, Florida. This 1941 image gives a good impression of the terrain *Coronel* Longoria encountered on Santa Rosa Island upon the first Spanish landing in March. (Library of Congress)

a moderate breeze, allowing for some manoeuvre, but with the aid of full daylight, some hours later he 'saw a great many soldiers at the signal house on Rose Island. Came to an anchor. Fired several broadsides at them.'[5]

Longoria's men had been there since 5:00 a.m., according to the Spanish, but apparently not in any great number. They had quickly taken all the structures and works, capturing some sailors from the *Port Royal*, and then occupying the position fully, which far from being a fort was just three dismounted cannons and a partly demolished breastwork of fascines. In the words of *Coronel* Esteban Miró, who was in charge of Gálvez's campaign journal which would be edited and sent to Madrid for publication, 'the English frigates, observing this, commenced a lively fire which caused the troops to move back beyond the range of shot.'[6] The formal account that appeared in the Gazeta de Madrid, added that this bombardment occurred without, 'occasioning the slightest mishap, because the land furnished several small hills that served as shelters, and, besides, some earth was thrown up, for better protection.'[7]

As the day began to turn hazy, the Spanish fleet began coming down the shore towards Siguenza Point, and in the afternoon, Gálvez returned to the island and questioned the prisoners, who informed him that Pensacola was

5   Servies (ed.), *Log of the Mentor*, p.163.
6   Maury Baker, 'Bernardo de Galvez's Combat Diary for the Battle of Pensacola, 1781,' *Florida Historical Quarterly*, vol.56, no.2 (1977), p.179.
7   Cusachs, 'Diary of the Operations', p.49.

strongly defended and supplied, and that aid from Jamaica was expected daily. He then made detailed inspections on the coast to identify where to place a battery to protect the camp and the entrance to the bay, ordering the landing of two 24-pounders, two 8-pounders and four 4-pounders. Also prioritised that first day was ammunition and 150 tents for the troops.

Sunday, 11 March

With the wind now blowing in moderate breezes from the south and the weather still hazy, the Spanish fleet were in a good position to begin sounding the passage into the bay and had anchored accordingly off the bar since moving up from their original anchorage. Meanwhile on Santa Rosa, the first gun battery was finished, and the two 24-pounders mounted. All indications suggested that the Spaniards would force an entrance that very day. Deans of the *Mentor*, who had been observing the Spanish preparations since early morning, prepared to oppose them. He had burned the blockhouse on Santa Rosa and his scout boat had come away with seven prisoners.[8] At 1:00 p.m., having observed the lager part of the enemy warships under sail and standing towards the bar, Deans made sail to dispute the crossing, taking fire from a row galley an hour later but to no effect.

There is no doubt that Deans had some pluck, as the Spanish were indeed intending to navigate the bar. The soundings from the morning having seemed favourable, Calvo elected to act aggressively, and Gálvez hurried aboard the *San Ramon* so as to share the danger. Deans makes no mention of what happened next, but according to the journal of Robert Farmar, 'Some of their vessels attempted to come over the bar but put back. One of their men of war was struck as she was coming over but got off again in about 20 minutes.'[9] The combat diary kept by Miró concurs.

It was much more confusing in the Spanish ships, as the *San Ramon* did indeed touch bottom, eliciting an immediate insistence from Calvo to abort the enterprise, which Gálvez was unable to argue with. The squadron, seeing the flagship return to its anchorage, followed suit. 'All of the night was employed by the Commander of the ship D. Joseph Calbo [Calvo] in lightening it, until it was left in condition to verify its entry, although then, the weather was not favourable to do this.'[10]

Relieved of the necessity of defending the harbour, Deans withdrew. 'At ½ past [two], the Spanish fleet put about and stretched off to the SE. At 3, the Spanish fleet having all stretched to the SE, we bore away to come up above Tartar Point clear of their batteries.'[11]

According to the combat diary kept by Miró, 'The cannons ... located ... on the beach ... began firing on the frigates which [had] made for the mouth

---

8   Servies (ed.), *Log of the Mentor*, p.164.
9   James A. Padgett, 'Bernardo de Galvez's Siege of Pensacola in 1781 (As Related in Robert Farmar's Journal)', *Louisiana Historical Quarterly*, vol.26, no.2 (April 1943), p.315.
10   Cusachs, 'Diary of the Operations', p.49.
11   Servies (ed.), *Log of Mentor*, p.164.

of the Cape [bay] in order to encounter our fleet, but then decided to withdraw until they were located in the interior of the bay.'[12]

The fire was accurate according to the log of the *Mentor*, 'Two of their shot lodged between decks, each of which weighed 26¾ pounds.' At which time he changed his position.[13] Farmar's journal corroborates that, 'The enemy erected batteries on Rose Island which obliged the *Mentor* and *Port Royal* to quit their station.'[14] Campbell agreed that, 'their Batteries being completed and our two ships of war being thereby forced above Tartar Point'.[15]

Calvo was dispirited, 'following more my sense of duty to the king's service and my own honour than the advice of reason, I resolved to force entry with all ships of the escort and the convoy ... but with the entire convoy sailing close to the Barrancas Coloradas, my ship ran hopelessly aground, with the keel crushing in on the bottom. This event left me with the deep disappointment of never being able to enter the port.'[16]

Monday 12 March

The great problem facing the Spanish at this early juncture was not how strong the works of Pensacola were, but how to even get to them. Gálvez met with the officers of the navy aboard the *San Ramon* to discuss this. The abortive attempt to cross the bar had laid seeds of doubt amongst the navy, who met his proposal that shallower draught frigates enter the bay first. But not even Gálvez, who had excellent information regarding the defences as they were in 1779, was certain at this time whether or not the battery at Barrancas Coloradas was able to protect the mouth of the bay, which would render any grounding disastrous. Moreover, the suggestion that the flagship act as a rearguard was taken as an insult Calvo interpreting suggestions he keep his flagship in reserve as an affront to his honour. In the words of Francisco de Miranda who was still in Havana, but who must have later heard the stories, 'Since this happened, the days pass and letters go back and forth, but nothing is done.'[17] Though tempers were flaring, more information had to be gathered, and so in the afternoon of the 12th, having returned to camp and written to Calvo on the necessity of getting into the shelter of the bay so as to be protected from storms, Gálvez sent the commander of the engineers, Don Francisco Xavier de Nava, out to the point of Santa Rosa that more fully faced the battery across the channel with a party of workmen, and orders to begin digging entrenchments. The British at the Barrancas and on the *Mentor* saw this very quickly. Farmar noted that, 'From the fort at the cliffs they fired three shot at the enemy who were erecting a Battery on the point of Rose Island which obliged them to quit.'[18]

12   Baker, 'Combat Diary', p.179.
13   Servies (ed.), *Log of Mentor*, p.164.
14   Padgett, 'Farmar's Journal', p.315.
15   TNA: PRO 30/55/89: Campbell to Clinton, 9 April 1781.
16   Saravia, *Gálvez*, p.197.
17   Saravia, *Gálvez*, p.197.
18   Padgett, 'Farmar's Journal', p.315.

Up at Tartar Point, Deans of the *Mentor* was a little more circumspect, taking a moment to observe the fall of the shot, while his ship was drying her sails and revictualling, 'observed the Spaniards heaving up an intrenchment on Rose Island Point. The fort at the Cliffs fired several shot at them, which they never minded.'[19]

Deans's account is more accurate, but no one paused to wonder why the Spaniards had been so obvious in beginning their works. As it happened, Gálvez had directed his engineer to feign building an earthwork, so as to get a better look at the Barrancas. Both men likely took great note of the elevation and accuracy of the enemy cannons, noting especially that indeed, some of the heavy shot was sighted high enough to hit their position, but there was more to that admission than met the eye. Heartening news came in the mid-afternoon. 'At 3 pm. Second Lieutenant Miguel Herrera arrived in camp from Mobile with word that Don Joseph Espeleta was proceeding on the 16th along the Río Buen Socorro, with 900 men to join His Excellency.'[20]

Tuesday 13 March–Thursday 15 March

Nothing more extraordinary occurred on these days than the beetling of supply boats, carrying supplies of shot to the Barrancas from the British warships, and the slower cruising of the guard-boats. The variable west-south-westerly breezes on the 13th were fresh and the hazy weather continued. Several of the Spanish ships were seen to exercise their topmen, loosing, reefing, and handing the topsails without making any movement. Similarly, to the British, the Spaniards were busy ferrying supplies to the camp on Santa Rosa. Gálvez was tense, the weather, to his mind, was neither here nor there, and the breeze from the southwest often brought strong gales if it settled there, which could force the fleet to move before he had taken the harbour. On the 13th Miró was sent to conduct Ezpeleta and the reinforcements to the bay, so that was something, but that day, the Governor was not pleased to read a letter from Calvo, and several captains, which attempted to convey the difficulties the navy were facing, especially the fact that they had no pilots, and no knowledge of the currents or the depth of the water over the bar. As any passage of the channel would inevitably be slow, Calvo feared his ships would be vulnerable to raking fire from the Barrancas and the enemy warships. After hearing the navy officers refuse to risk their ships without better maps, Gálvez wrote back asking what the possible loss of a frigate would really mean to the king as opposed to the ruin of the expedition. The next day, Calvo's reply attempted to take a patronising tone, 'Your Excellency, do not ignore the art of war, or the rules of military caution, which teach us to avoid extreme danger, haste and delay ... To what purpose will we needlessly send, as sheep to the slaughter, the king's vessels under our command? ... I assure Your Excellency, that I

---

19   Servies (ed.), *Log of Mentor*, p.164.
20   Baker, 'Combat Diary', p.180.

do not want glory at such a cost.'[21] The sentiment cannot have made Gálvez rest easy that night, and he tasked the commander of the brig Gálvez to go into the bay that night and take soundings.

The sea was choppy on the 15th, making the landing of supplies difficult at Santa Rosa, however some vegetables and salted meat did make it ashore, and the 8-pounder battery was completed near that of the 24-pounders. Calvo erred in the war of words by sending another letter informing Gálvez he would need to ask for further orders from Havana. The governor, feeling the challenge to his authority, observed the unsaid allegation of insubordination and fired back that Calvo should not meddle in the business of those whose duty it was to make decisions.

Friday 16 March

The breeze picked up throughout the 16th, but little was recorded save for the reading of the articles of war aboard His Majesty's Ships, and the solemn entry recording the death of seaman Henry Fox of the *Mentor*, who departed this life sometime after 6:00 a.m. In the course of the morning, a merchant vessel, *Love & Unity's Increase*, came alongside the *Mentor* and transferred Mr Davis, a ship's carpenter, and three more seamen as volunteers for the duration of the siege. The *Love & Unity's Increase* was given two 12-pounders, with the necessary ammunition, to take ashore.

In the Spanish camp, Calvo received *Teniente de Fregata* Don Juan de Riano who delivered letters from *Coronel* Ezpeleta, advising Gálvez that he was moving 900 men to the Rio de los Perdidos, and would require launches to ferry the troops across. Calvo heard this verbally from Riano and wrote a letter to Gálvez,

> The moment D. Juan Riano informed me that the army from Mobile found itself on the shore of the 'los Perdidos' River, I ordered that the armed launches be provided with ten days food, and in order that they shall lack for nothing, I have provided to supply a few more from this ship. I will also order the Pio that draws less water, that it go and cover this small expedition as close to land as possible, to free it from any vessel that attempts to oppose it, as also to provide Sr. Ezpeleta a few cannons and provisions if he should need them. I am of the opinion, if your honor desires to make use of it, that the expedition start early, just after nightfall, so as not to draw the attention of the enemies, for they may come out and make some inconvenient opposition, but in this matter you will do what appears best to you. I have elected to direct the launches, my second in command, the Captain of Frigate, D. Andres Valderrama, and the first Lieutenant of ship, D. Antonio Estrada, who carry pilots, a compass and a pilot's mate. God keep your honour many years.[22]

---

21   Saravia, *Gálvez*, p.198.
22   Cusachs, 'Diary of the Operations', p.51.

Gálvez quickly wrote a note approving the measures that Calvo had undertaken, but then tried to open the debate as to who was in command. 'I take advantage of this occasion to ask you, sir, if concerning this issue of entering the port, an operation among those necessary for the conquest of Pensacola, you consider yourself not under my command, since some of the language you used in previous communications has made me think that you, sir, think with too much independence.'[23]

Calvo denied any such independent thoughts but argued he was required by his orders from the navy to behave according to his own judgement. Gálvez had theoretical right to command Calvo, as the latter had orders to follow the governor's instructions but with the usual conditions that he was not to endanger his ships. Calvo had good reason to worry that without proper reconnaissance of both the reach and effectiveness of the British guns and the nature of the bar, he could be risking disaster. Gálvez had a lot of information about Pensacola, and he had probably confirmed to himself by simple observation that the British artillery were at too long a range to hit anything below Santa Rosa accurately. However, his debacle at Mobile would have given the navy little reason to accept his word and just charge in after him.

Saturday 17 March

The rumour in the town the next day was that the Spanish had attempted to land troops at the mouth of the Perdido but had been prevented by the sight of British allied warriors waiting for them. The garbled report must have referred to Ezpeleta's troops but would appear to be much more than a rumour.[24] The warriors in question, however, would likely be the main war-party of Choctaws and Muskogees encamped near the Barrancas Coloradas. Much of the former had been retrieved from the road home at the eleventh hour by Cameron 10 days before, 'I set out after the Indians and overtook them about 18 miles from Pensacola where Mr. Bethune, my deputy for that nation, was dividing some rum amongst them. I spoke to them and told them the Spaniards still threatened to invade us and that I believed that they would make their appearance in a few days.' He had been careful to promise little, and Frenchimabaste, approved,

> … as it was a common talk for twelve moons past; and as to his going back to Pensacola [he] said I never threw away any talks that you gave me but I will not answer for my people returning, for we received but little provisions and the presents the great warrior [Campbell presumably] made us were for nothing; however, you may speak to them as they are here and will answer for themselves.[25]

23   Saravia, *Gálvez* p.198.
24   Padgett, 'Farmar's Journal', p.315.
25   Davies (ed.), *Documents of the American Revolution*, Cameron to Germain, 27 May 1781, p.149.

Cameron managed to persuade 150 warriors to return with him and noted about 500 in total were maintained through the siege.

Deans noted many signals being passed between the enemy ships, but as no hostile movement threatened the British fired a few shots at the Spanish row galleys out making soundings. The *Mentor* set out its guard boats and took on fresh water.

At 4:00 p.m., *Sub Teniente* Herrera arrived on Santa Rosa with more letters from *Coronel* Ezpeleta, advising Gálvez that he was marching to unite with him. The anticipated arrival mixed with the lack of progress seemed to trigger something inside Gálvez. Having had his plans delayed or nearly ruined twice by the weather, he finally lost his patience with the cautious, and to his mind insubordinate, Calvo. Knowing that Riano had situated his sloop and the brig *Gálvezton* with two small gunboats at the mouth of the bay, that afternoon, Gálvez determined to be the first one to force the harbour. This fits entirely with what we know about Bernardo de Gálvez but is also revealing that his audacious character made him difficult to work with. As he had the authority but not the rank to compel the navy and was either unable or unwilling to find a diplomatic solution, Gálvez resolved on a dramatic and calculatedly insulting gesture to sting Calvo into action.

Sunday 18 March

To the British, 18 March was disappointing. Farmar very matter-of-factly noted that 'Gálvez's brig & three row galleys passed the fort at the cliffs & anchored under their Batteries on Rose Island.'[26]

However, there was a great deal of drama in Spanish high command. Tension between the army and navy had been rising since the failed attempt to cross the bar just over a week before. Although it does not surface in the day-to-day accounts, and as such we should be wary to accept wholeheartedly the more melodramatic version as apparently played out in letters, they do need to be examined. The relationship between the commanders had certainly been deteriorating to the point that the letters that passed between them were as much challenges and insults as communications, to the extent that Francisco de Miranda referred to the exchange of letters and insults as sounding like something out of the siege of Troy.

The Homeric antics were only about to become more dramatic. At 2:00 p.m., Gálvez dispatched the engineer officer, Francisco de Gilabert, to the flagship with a message for Calvo, the substance of which was, 'And let him who has honour and courage follow him', and a 32-pound British cannonball.[27]

---

26   Padgett, 'Farmar's Journal', p.316.
27   León Hermanos Parra (ed.), 'Archivo del General Miranda: Diario de lo mas particular ocurrido desde el dia de nuestra salida del puerto de la Havana,' Tomo 1, pp.143–144, *Biblioteca Nacional de Espana, Biblioteca Digital Hispanica,* <http://bdh.bne.es/bnesearch/detalle/bdh0000167999>, accessed 14 July 2023.

Half an hour later, cheered on by the troops, Gálvez, 'boarded the brigantine *Gálvezton* and his arrival was saluted by hoisting the pennant of Chief of Squadron, a procedure which raised expectations in everyone; quickly weighing anchor the ship moved toward the cape with the two gunboats, despite the opposition of the battery [which fired] 70 shots.'[28] The Governor, had correctly gauged that the enemy battery could not protect the passage, and that the channel was deep enough for warships. Of note is the discrepancy between Deans observing the use of the small channel between the sandbank and Santa Rosa, supported by the Heldridge map showing the brig and galleys in the passage, and the Spanish who suggest they sailed very close to the outer side of the bank.

Gálvez was quick to address his troops after the ships anchored, and explained to them what he had done. He even wrote a version of his speech down to send to his uncle.

> I, my sons, went alone to sacrifice myself, so as not to expose a single soldier, not a man of my army, and so the navy could see that there is no danger such as they say, and that I do not want to sacrifice such a respectable Corps, despite all the troubles they have caused me, and the deceptions they have practiced from the beginning … In this predicament … I was forced to take this course of action to set an example, sending Don José Calvo a message through the Engineer Don Francisco Gilabert, who carried the enemy's cannonball, of the same calibre that they were firing, to tell them that those were the ones I was going to confront bare chested while forcing entry into the port, with those with the honour and courage to follow me; and though I hoped to see them following us, I found that they did not, since he, [Calvo] ordered his ships not to move, answering me with all kinds of insults, calling me reckless, and saying that if the enemy's cannonballs did not behead me, the king himself would chop off my head. [29]

Gálvez thanked those who had followed him, especially his crew on the *Gálvezton* commanded by Rousseau and Duparac, and the artillery on a Santa Rosa for their protection. Three cheers for the king were called, and Gálvez ordered a *reale* be given to each soldier on his own account. Gálvez's magnetism and way with words had their usual effect. The frigate captains were suitably overawed by Gálvez's tactics, but Calvo ordered that no ship of the line or frigate was to as much as shorten an anchor cable without his command. At this moment Gálvez was not only at war with the British but his own naval support.

Coronel Longoria went to the flagship at 8:00 p.m. and tried to make amends but Calvo was not in the mood to let Longoria do anything but stand as a guarantor for Gálvez's good faith. The fire from the Barrancas had been very heavy, but they had not done significant damage, nor the British warships, which having failed to obstruct Gálvez's run, shifted their anchorage to the harbour where the *Mentor* had been employed unloading its ammunition and guns for conveyance to the forts above Pensacola. When

---

28   Baker, 'Combat Diary', p.180.
29   Saravia, *Gálvez*, p.200.

the Spanish entered the bay Deans ordered the majority of his crew ashore. Campbell remained detached about the fact he was now cut off from the sea.

> … on the 18th their Batteries being completed and our two ships of war being thereby forced above Tartar Point, they sent in an armed Brig called the Gálvez and three Row Gallies, by a channel close to Rose Island Point and between it and the ten-foot Bank; and the following Day they forced the Harbour and passed the Royal Navy Redoubt with their whole fleet, notwithstanding a well-kept-up Fire from the five 32 pounders all the Time of their Passing.[30]

Monday 19 March

Calvo might well have been furious, but in the morning, he must have realised that there was nothing he could do except let Gálvez have his way. With the Louisiana flotilla in the bay, he could no longer argue that the bar was impassable. Pressured by his own officers to answer the challenge, Calvo allowed the squadron to enter the bay, in order, so he wrote to the Minister of the Navy 'to show him [Gálvez] what the navy could do, on the 19th, the feast of St Joseph, I ordered the convoy to enter, which it did with great fortune, without death, or injury, or serious wounds.'[31]

At 11:30 a.m., two frigates and the chambequín successfully made it through the heavy fire, and over the bar. By 2:00 p.m., the Spanish entered the bay in force, and by 5:00 p.m. they had finally overcome their first obstacle. Gálvez then attempted to take a boat to the Perdido to have a conference with Ezpeleta, but as the wind had risen, it was deemed unadvisable, and he was forced to turn back. Calvo now elected to return to Havana, as he could still claim that the *San Ramon* was too deep of draught to get across the bar and set sail the day after.

Tuesday 20 March

Gálvez now needed to focus on combining his forces and went to inspect likely spots above the Barrancas for Ezpaleta to encamp. The Mobile contingent had a skirmish with some of the British allied warriors near the Perdido, in which Farmar recorded that the Spanish had 10 men killed and one captured, though the Spanish do not mention this beyond that shots were exchanged.[32]

The *Mentor*, with a skeleton crew, progressed up the bay to the mouth of the Yellow River. Meanwhile at headquarters, Campbell received a paroled

---

30 TNA: PRO 30/55/89: Campbell to Clinton, 9 April 1781. The 10-foot bank was a small half-mile-long sand bar that appears on maps separated from Santa Rosa by about 100 yards of channel, 2½ feet deep at the lowest point, see TNA: MPD 1/194: Plan of the Entrance of Pensacola Harbour, 1771.

31 Saravia, *Gálvez*, p.202.

32 Padgett, 'Farmar's Journal', p.316.

prisoner of war officer with a message from Gálvez, 'Most Excellent, … sir: The English in Havana intimated with threats that none of the ships or buildings of the King and private parties be destroyed, burned or torn down under pain of being treated with the utmost rigor. The same warning, I give to your Excellency and others whom it may concern with the same conditions.'[33]

In the afternoon Gálvez took a boat to Tartar Point to inspect the possibilities for batteries and landing troops. Having spotted this, the British responded that evening when the wind had calmed, 'Our troops set fire to the block house on Tartar Point. The enemy fired a great many guns.'[34] These guns were those of Don Juan Riano and the armed launch from the *Gálvezton* which were ordered to open with grapeshot against the beach and trees.

Wednesday 21 March

Gálvez's messenger returned to the Spanish camp accompanied by Lieutenant Colonel Dickson (a prisoner on parole after the fall of Mobile) and later in the day his aide de camp, Lieutenant McKay Gordon, along with one of Governor Chester's aides, which started off an exchange of letters. The letter from Campbell was short and abrupt. Already the tone between the two men was different to those between Gálvez and Dickson the previous year.

> Sir, Threats form an invading Enemy are considered in no other Light than the Finesse and Stratagem of War to forward their own Views. I trust I shall do nothing in my defence of Pensacola (seeing I am attacked) contrary to the Rules and Customs of War, I however consider myself under obligations to your Excellency for your frank invitation – altho' I assure you I shall be determined more by your conduct in answer to proposals that will be forwarded to your excellency tomorrow from Governor Chester in regard to the Prisoners, and from me with respect to the Town etc of Pensacola than by your Threats.[35]

By the afternoon however, Campbell's tone had softened, as he recognised that Gálvez was attempting to set out rules of engagement in order to protect the town, much as he had done at Mobile. In his overly wordy way, the British commander advised that he had abandoned the town to his mercy, hoping that 'the Palm of Victory will fall to the share of the Troops I have the Honor to Command,'[36] as he did not want to bring suffering upon the inhabitants unnecessarily,

33 Baker, 'Combat Diary', p.181; TNA: PRO 30/55/89: Gálvez to Campbell, 20 March 1781. The entire correspondence between Gálvez and Campbell, or Chester, is to be found under this catalogue heading.
34 Servies (ed.), *Log of the Mentor*, p.168.
35 TNA: PRO 30/55/89: Campbell to Gálvez, 21 March 1781.
36 TNA: PRO 30/55/89: Campbell to Gálvez, 21 March 1781.

I do for these reasons propose to your Excellency that the Town and Garrison of Pensacola shall be preserved entire and without wilful Damage by either Party during the Siege of the Royal Navy Redoubt and of Fort George and its adjoining works, where I propose to contend for the Preservation of the Province of West Florida to the British Crown, on the Following Stipulations Covenants and Conditions.[37]

Gálvez was apparently feeling ill by the time this letter arrived, and gave a verbal answer to Dickson, who conveyed it to Campbell, with the promise that he would put it in writing the next day. He did find time to read and reply to two of Governor Chester's letters, however. One informing Gálvez that there was not enough room in the barracks to house Spanish prisoners then in custody, and a proposal that they be set at liberty upon Gálvez's oath that they would not be employed in the fight. The other was to elicit another promise that so long as non-combatants, and especially women would not stray from the town, the Spanish soldiers and sailors would do them no harm. Gálvez seemed to be struck by the generosity of the sentiments offered by the Governor and tried to reply at once.

I have received your Excellency's two letters under date of today, in which you make the propositions that the prisoners of war be set at liberty and that the women and children remain in the City of Pensacola, hoping your Excellency that on my part I will give the most rigorous orders to the troops and sailors in the expedition under my command, that should not cause them the least extortion. The coincidence of finding myself a trifle ill deprives me of the satisfaction of replying to your Excellency upon said particulars …[38]

Dickson was thoroughly briefed in what to say to both the Campbell and the Chester, and at 3:00 p.m., Gálvez had the grenadiers present to parade so that Dickson could inspect them and convey their appearance and quality to Campbell. Given what had been exchanged in the letters that day it can hardly be surprising when at around 9:00 p.m., the dark coast around the fort on the Barrancas became illuminated by the orange light of burning buildings, being destroyed by the garrison to prevent their being occupied by the enemy.

There was no firelight at the mouth of the Perdido. Ezpeleta's troops had marched in close order and in complete silence along the beach to the crossing point so as to avoid detection. There they were met by 12 armed galleys and launches. At midnight the troops clambered into the boats with as much stealth as possible, covered by the guns of the brig *San Pio*. The crossing was completed successfully by 10.00 a.m. the next day, and after a short rest they were back on the march.

---

37   TNA: PRO 30/55/89: Campbell to Gálvez, 21 March 1781.
38   Cusachs, 'Diary of the Operations', p.56.

Thursday 22 March

As yet unaware that Ezpeleta was hours from joining his forces, Gálvez was occupied with the apparent chicanery of the enemy. He voiced his outrage at the apparent arson he had witnessed the night before in a letter dispatched in the early morning to British headquarters, outright accusing Campbell of being a two-faced liar that deserved all that was coming to him. A similar occurrence had happened during the siege of Mobile, and to the mind of Gálvez, this:

> … plainly points out the bad faith with which you act and write, and your Conduct with regard to the Inhabitants of Mobile, a great part of whom were Victims to the most horrible Cruelties under your Sanction, [all proves] upon the whole that the word humanity, so often repeated upon paper, is little known in your heart – and that your intentions are to gain time to complete the Destruction of West Florida and I (who cannot forgive my own Credulity and the ignoble method attempted to deceive me) neither will nor ought to attend to any other propositions than a surrender; assuring you at the same Time, that be it as it will, as the blame is not mine, I shall look on the burning of Pensacola with as much indifference as to see afterward its Cruel Incendiaries perish on its Ashes.[39]

As was invariably the case, the letter ended with the hope that God would preserve the recipient many years. Gálvez then wrote to Chester, informing him that until the matter of the arson was settled with Campbell, he was unable to speak further on the matter of the prisoners and civilians. Campbell was more than prepared to give as good as he got however and had perfect deniability.

> The imperious tone that runs through your Excellency's Letter of this Date Instead of producing the evident intention to intimidate will, you may rest assured only serve to convince me more strongly in opposing the ambitious enterprise of Spain that you Command by every possible obstruction in my Power; Whereby I shall fulfil my Duty to my King and Country, more powerful Motives with me than the fear of your Displeasure. The officer entrusted with the Command of the Redoubt at the Red Cliffs has orders to defend that Post to the last Extremity; if he has deprived an Invading force of any Shelter, Cover or aid to his approaches, he had only done his Duty, but there was no Interference of Women, Children or Private property in this case. I again repeat that if you shall make use of the Town of Pensacola to serve you in your approaches to Fort George, or for shelter or accommodation to your Troops I will and am determined to fulfil the Resolution I have already communicated to your Excellency – The Reflections that more immediately refer to myself, as I feel them unwarranted, so I despise them.[40]

---

39 TNA: PRO 30/55/89: Gálvez to Campbell, 22 March 1781.
40 TNA: PRO 30/55/89: Campbell to Gálvez, 22 March 1781.

Meanwhile, Deans knew his ship would be taken and was dispersing his crew amongst the garrison, as well as continuing to strip the *Mentor* and *Port Royal* of anything useful – sails for tents, and water casks were taken ashore. Two parties were sent into the earthworks on Gage Hill, a lieutenant of the *Mentor* and 40 men were sent into the advanced redoubt, and an unspecified officer and 35 men marched up to the middle redoubt from the *Port Royal*. Farmar observed that some of the Louisiana flotilla had taken up position to cover Tartar Point. The reason being that Ezpeleta and the Mobile contingent, Miró possibly still with them, had arrived, their presence being announced by an agreed triple discharge of musketry. Gálvez at once dispatched the grenadiers and *cazadores* to reinforce them, as they were extremely fatigued from the march and from being harassed by a party of warriors that had hung upon their rear since the Perdido. 'These followers, [though] pursued by our *Cazadores*, remained very active.'[41]

The weary troops and the embattled *cazadores* and grenadiers arrived at Punta de Aguëro or Tatar Point at 5:00 p.m. and were met by Gálvez. A camp was set up under the protection and supply of the ships. However, at 7:00 p.m. 'some Indians came to fire on the troops that were around the fires, killing three and wounding four of our soldiers, not leaving us at peace until morning.'[42]

Friday 23 March – Sunday 25 March

A great commotion was caused on Friday morning when Spanish lookouts spotted sails cresting the horizon to the east, which as they took on a firmer shape through the haze could be seen standing to the west to take advantage of the south-westerly breeze that would carry them towards Santa Rosa. By the afternoon it was clear that this was the reinforcements from New Orleans, which at 4:00 p.m. brought their bows to the channel and pressed through the shallows, slipping over the bar to the impotent roar of the 32-pounders at Barancas Coloradas, and the scream of heavy iron in the rigging. That a second armament of between 16 to 18 vessels could escape without loss, save for some spars and cordage, really went to show how badly the British fort at the cliffs had been sited. For unexplained reasons the Spanish seemed to reject the idea of trying to take the fort at the Barrancas, though it had been Ezpeleta's intention to do so for months, however it is likely that by now they knew it would be a waste of time and lives to silence it and left it alone.

At Campbell's headquarters in Pensacola there seemed no reason not to continue transferring troops and supplies to the forts above the town. In the late afternoon the 16th and 60th Foot left their barracks and marched up the shallow incline from the harbour and into the defences of Fort George. The 16th occupied the defences of the forward redoubt and the 60th that of the centre.

---

41   Baker, 'Combat Diary', p.181.
42   Baker, 'Combat Diary', p.181.

Delighted with the appearance of 2,300 more men over the course of the last two days, many of them seasoned veterans of his operations on the Mississippi and against Mobile, Gálvez prepared for a mass movement of troops from the bay and Santa Rosa to the mainland the next day. Meanwhile Ezpeleta, who had been made *Mayor General del Ejército expedicionario* – a local staff position something akin to an adjutant general in the British army – and the quartermaster made a survey of the outer harbour and the surrounding area, so that a camp could be found closer to the town.

Deans confirmed the course of events in his log, adding that 'One of the fleet, the two-decked ship, that lay outside of Rose Island, got under way and stood to the eastward.'[43] Although it is commonly assumed that Calvo had left in a stew, this ship could refer to the *San Ramon*, however the Spanish sources assure us it cannot have been so. On Saturday, Chester sent Mr Stevenson down to discuss the safety of the women and children. Meanwhile all was movement and industry in the Spanish part of the bay and the camp on Santa Rosa, with Gálvez ordering the troops from New Orleans and those encamped to make their way to the mainland. By nightfall the troops from the island had embarked. Work in victualling the redoubts also continued, with the water casks from the sloops being rolled into the works, as time was now running out to prepare.

Proof that things were changing appeared in both camps during the course of Sunday, 25 March. Farmar noted that at 9:00 a.m., 'The Indians brought in horses belonging to the enemy and 2 scalps.'[44] This was the result of an ambush early in the morning. 'Indians … ambushed … the soldiers who had gone beyond the lines of the outposts, killed and wounded a few, committing their usual cruelty of scalping the bodies of their victims, and others besides.' A sure sign that operations had formally begun was the appearance of Lieutenant Colonel Dickson and a few other prisoners of war, who were obliged to surrender themselves and wait on Gálvez to assure him of their adherence to their parole.[45]

Monday 26 March

Campbell, Deans and Farmar were all witness to the sight of 26 Spanish ships anchoring off Sutton's Lagoon, the closest of the gash like inlets that cut into the shoreline near to the town. The Spanish called it Bayou Chico, as it was smaller than the inlet to the south near the Barrancas called Moor's Lagoon by the British and Bayou Grande, due to its larger size, by the Spanish. Here they could land troops equipment and supplies and also assist in getting the troops to the other side. Gálvez, now having concentrated his forces planned to march his army to the mouth of Bayou Grande, cross it and move to the camp surveyed by Ezpaleta south of Bayou Chico. Campbell determined that a major landing was about to happen and dispatched about 100 men under Captain Thomas Taylor Byrd, 60th Foot, who were joined by 250 warriors

---

43   Servies (ed.), *Log of the Mentor*, p.169.
44   Padgett, 'Farmar's Journal', p.317.
45   Cusachs, 'Diary of the Operations', p.59.

under Cameron.[46] This party disappeared into the forest and went in search of the enemy. Deans recorded hearing the musketry rattle in the distance sometime later in the day. Gálvez reported that, his troops' march through 'five leagues of impenetrable woods, sown with Indians, was very difficult, and in the obscurity and thickness two parties of soldiers had the misfortune of reciprocally mistaking themselves for enemies and firing on one another with the result that several were killed and wounded.'[47]

Tuesday 27 March

From the temporary camp south of Bayou Chico, Gálvez had boats reconnoitre the proposed ground that Ezpaleta had found but reports that the Spanish were landing troops at the mouth of Sutton's Lagoon/Bayou Chico, brought the entire might of the warbands into the woods. The bulk of them moved down to the house of a prominent citizen called Mr Neil, situated on the Pensacola side of the lagoon, about a mile and a quarter from the works on Gage Hill, and close to the mouth of the inlet. There they found some boats being landed, but the Spanish retreated upon being attacked.[48]

This, according to Gálvez had been an exploratory foray, most likely to discover if the Bayou could be used to supply his troops and, according to him, it was successful enough for him to order that all the supplies necessary for the creation of a camp be landed that evening. That night the Spanish gathered around the fires of their marching camps, the noise of the night creatures blending with the crackle of the flames. Then at 10:00 p.m., this was joined by the crack and flash of muskets being fired from the darkness of the woods, and in a minute, war-whoops filled the air. The warriors, having discovered the position of a large camp had crept close, and taken careful aim at the soldiers silhouetted against the firelight, killing, or wounding, several unsuspecting soldiers before anyone could fire back. Gálvez took the vulnerability of his camp seriously, he ordered that battalion guns be loaded with canister and kept in readiness to spray the treeline, and further ordered that work begin on entrenching the camp.

Wednesday 28 March

An encouraging piece of news arrived from the Barrancas Coloradas informing Campbell that the garrison had finally done some actual damage to enemy shipping by hulling a schooner badly enough that it had to ground on Santa Rosa. However, Deans had to record in his log that one of his men had blown off his left thumb and wounded himself in the arm when his musket went off by accident.[49]

---

46   Padgett, 'Farmar's Journal', p.317.
47   Cusachs, 'Diary of the Operations', p.59.
48   Padgett, 'Farmar's Journal', p.317.
49   Servies (ed.), *Log of Mentor*, p.170.

Another dispatch from Alexander Cameron, written at the camp near the redoubt, summarised the damage that had been done to the Spanish since they arrived, but that morale was low.

> I am sorry to acquaint you that the Indians seem much dispirited particularly since the Spanish Fleet have forced their way over the Barr – as they now look upon Pensacola to be lost to the English ... Yesterday afternoon a good many of them Deserted, but having sent after them the Chiefs returned and when I upbraided them today with their unbecoming behaviour as Warriors they replied that if they remained here any longer they were afraid that they would be a lost people; that they had not a pound of powder to defend themselves with in case the Spaniards should become masters of Pensacola – As we had lately refused to send their nation the ammunition which we had formerly promised them – That the Goods which we had promised them as presents were shut up in the Fort, where they were afraid their friends the English would be shut up with them, and by all appearances must fall into the hands of the Spaniards – They therefore desire that we will ensure to them the Presents that were promised them; and that we may depend upon it unless the Goods are lodged in some remote place of safety, that they cannot prevail with their young men to remain or fight any longer.
>
> And if this is not done and that the place should fall, the goods instead of being given to them would be distributed among the Spanish Red Men, and they would return to their nation ashamed and to be laughed at – and I am afraid Sir this will be the opinion of all our Red friends as well as the Chactaws unless the Goods are lodged up the Escambia or some-where they can receive them should Pensacola fall.
>
> The few Creeks who are here I have kept with much difficulty the[y] complaining [t]here was no person in Pensacola to take the least notice of them. That they left women and children near the town who they were afraid would be in great want of provision, and what was worse they were apprehensive they might fall into the hands of the enemy. Sixteen of them go off towards the Perdido with Mr. Macintosh and seven of them in spite of all my Rhetoric deserted to Pensacola – making the same observations as before mentioned.[50]

Meanwhile, after the night attack, the Spanish light troops and the *Pardo* and *Moreno* militia companies of New Orleans were stood too for most of the day while the camp was entrenched and six field artillery pieces were placed at the angles.[51] Gálvez was still negotiating with Chester about the safety of the town and the inhabitants when, at 3:00 p.m., the warriors struck again. It was incredibly difficult for troops under attack by masters of irregular warfare to really gauge numbers, and Gálvez thought that over 400 warriors were involved. Bearing in mind that in other instances of skirmish and ambush on the frontier Europeans tended to double the actual number of enemies they faced, simply because the warriors were so adept at concealment and movement, we can assume the number was not in fact over 200. Immediately the New Orleans militiamen hurried to engage. Most were already veterans

---

50   TNA: CO 82/31: Cameron to Campbell, 28 April 1781.
51   Baker, 'Combat Diary', p.182.

of vanguard work, though they had not until now been in a bush-fight with this many warriors. They fought bravely enough to hold the enemy at a distance until some of the field guns could open fire on the treeline, at which time the warriors withdrew.

It was only a temporary victory, for at midnight, the bone chilling sound of war-whoops pierced the night, followed by the flash and pop of musketry from different quarters, killing or wounding more men, and dissipating by the time the Spaniards could determine where they had been struck from.

Thursday 29 March

At around 9:00 a.m., some of the Choctaws reported their version of the engagements of the last 24 hours,

> they had a brush yesterday afternoon the other side of Suttons Lagoon with the enemy and drove in the picket three times upon which their grenadiers turned out and fired twice at them and retired. 4 of the Indians were wounded one which is wounded in the neck with small shot. The Indians report that they killed and wounded a number of the enemy but could not get their hair on account of the enemy's troops turning out with a number of dragoons.[52]

The mention of cavalry is singular, and undoubtedly refers to the militia cavalry present from New Orleans. Their description of being attacked by grenadiers would fit with the usual practice of responding to a dangerous situation with the most reliable troops. Gálvez was content enough to progress closer to Pensacola and ordered his quartermaster, deputy chief engineer of Havana Don Francisco Xavier de Nava, to begin driving the cattle, while all the artillery and equipment was to be reembarked. A strong force composed of the grenadiers, *cazadores*, other light troops and the New Orleans emancipated Militia marched around the east of Bayou Chico, where it splayed into a sort of pickaxe shape of two channels, and once the landing beach had been secured by these crack troops, the navy could land the rest from the water.[53]

Friday 30 March

Daybreak revealed the entire Spanish army under arms and in marching order. The field states were reported to Gálvez as totalling a force of 3,350 men. As per the plan, Gálvez took 1,100 of the most reliable and hardened troops on a circuitous march around the bayou to the beach, and Ezpeleta would embark the rest and take them ashore in launches once the position

---

52 Padgett, 'Farmar's Journal', pp.317–318.
53 Baker, 'Combat Diary', p.182.

was secured. The log of the *Mentor* described a moderate, southerly breeze and hazy weather.[54]

Miró's entry in the Governor's journal detailed the march:

> We continued advancing in single file with the cannons toward the second pathway [it is never explained what this means]. We were distant from the plaza about a short cannon shot, or a league and a half from our second encampment. After marching a short time, a large group of Indians emerged from their hideouts in the woods, firing rapidly, upon which the general ordered up the cannons of the Militia of Orleans and light troops, which made them flee to the Plaza where they stopped firing entirely. We continued to the aforementioned beach where Espeleta would disembark in the launches with the rest of the army. Accordingly, when the Indians remaining at the rear of the bastion [probably Fort George] began firing on the troops, they assumed battle formation; and the companies of grenadiers, *cazadores*, and the Militia from New Orleans advanced, laying down a heavy fire. The English marched in column from the fort with a cannon to protect the Indians and to incite them to strike at [our] troops, which they considered fatigued.[55]

Just prior to the emergence of this serious attack, Gálvez had ordered Ezpeleta to begin landing his men. The ground in question was quite open, and indeed is referred to as Neils Meadows. Farmar saw things similarly from the opposite side,

> About 8 o'clock an advanced picquet under the command of Captain Kennedy of the Maryland Loyalists was obliged to retreat as the enemy was marching down upon them and began to fire their field pieces. 10 o'clock. Capt. Kennedy party marched down to Neils Meadows about a mile and a quarter from our works. About 2 o'clock the Indians went there also and attacked the main body of the enemy and kept up, a very heavy fire until 5 o'clock at which time they were supported by Captain Johnstone with two field pieces and 1 howitzer, also by 50 negroes. Lieutenant Meggs went with 25 men of the 60th to cover the field pieces. On account of the heavy fire they received from Captain Johnstone, [and] The Indians and Negroes, they [the Spanish] retired under cover of their shipping & galleys. ½ after 5 o'clock Capt. Johnstone & Lieut. Meggs returned. The Indians came in and brought with them 4 of the enemy's drums, 1 head and a number of scalps. The inhabitants of the Town say that they saw a shell from the howitzer fall in the midst of 13 boats full of men coming on shore, which made them return again to their ships. We have one Indian killed and 2 slightly wounded and one negro wounded in the foot.[56]

Deans supports this account: 'The out pickets retreated nearer the fort. A party of Indians was sent out to support the pickets with field pieces; stopped

---

54   Servies (ed.), *Log of the Mentor*, p.172.
55   Baker, 'Combat Diary', pp.182–183.
56   Padgett, 'Farmar's Journal', p.318.

the enemy's advancing and drove them back to their boats.'[57] When the British seemed to be pressing their advantage, Ezpeleta had suggested to Gálvez that the flanks of their growing force should be extended so as to threaten their rear. But Gálvez discerned that this push was only to support the warriors and to open on the Spanish launches with shot and shell. In his report, writing in the third person, he stated, 'the General arrived, and seeing that the troops engaged were surrounded on all sides by a class of enemies whose real advantage consists in never coming out from the cover of the woods, adopted the plan to attack them with a few companies of light infantry.'[58] Two companies of light infantry and two guns were ordered to drive back the Choctaws and Muskogee warriors, and they were apparently successful.

Miró finished up his account of the action:

> But after maintaining fire for four hours, with the intention of blooding them, the [enemy] withdrew, leaving us to take possession of the house of [Neil], named after a Pensacola villager, which is one mile from the fort. Because of this, three of our men were killed and twenty-eight were wounded. I include in the last group the Colonel of the King [Regimiento Inmemorial del Rey] Don Louis Rebolo, the Lieutenant from [Regimiento de] Soria Juan Antonio Figueroa and a Second Lieutenant of the Dragoons; and the stack of arms and some of the munitions were also lost [amongst which must have been the drums]. During the night a large entrenchment was constructed capable of providing cover for the troops, with the two companies of the Navarra in the aforementioned house that was on the right. [59]

In reporting the various movements of the Spanish to Clinton, Campbell voiced his unreasonable dissatisfaction with his auxiliaries, and his disappointment in the action.

> during these several movements of the enemy no Indians could be got to oppose them on their march, and the Troops under my Command were neither numerous enough nor properly adapted to justify my attempting to attack them – The Indians indeed made an attack on their camp between the lagoons on the 28th but with more noise than advantage, and on the afternoon of the 30th they were (without intending it themselves) brought to make a ... attack upon the enemy by the Countenance of some Troops, a Howitzer and two Brass three pounders to support them but without making any impression.[60]

Cameron came to the defence of Franchimastabé, 'The Indians in general as well as their officers behaved with great spirit and attachment; and had we

---

57 Servies (ed.), *Log of the Mentor*, p.172.
58 Cusachs, 'Diary of the Operations', p.61.
59 Baker, 'Combat Diary', pp.182–183. The *Gazeta de Madrid*, no.8, 15 June 1781, p.9, gives the dragoon regiment as the Dragones de Mexico, which though certainly in existence, is not mentioned in any orders of battle, though the Dragones de America is.
60 TNA: PRO 30/55/89: Campbell to Clinton, 9 April 1781.

but as many more of them, particularly on the 30th March, we would have driven the whole Spanish army into the sea. No men could behave better than they did that day. They drove part of the enemy out of their lines, took 4 drums, muskets, scalps etc.'[61]

Cameron's opinion melds well with the summaries given by Deans and Farmar, with the small party of regulars and artillery withdrawing after half an hour, leaving the warriors to continue the fight and face the Spanish counterattack.

By 7:00 p.m. the sandy soil was already being turned up to form an entrenchment. The right flank of the camp, described by Deans and Farmar as covering an elevated plot on the meadow, was anchored on Neil's House and slightly to its rear, and their left rested on the bayou, which Gálvez had a confusing habit of calling the inner harbour. As this was considered the weakest point six guns were placed on this side and two on the right. With the coming of night, work ceased, which was just as well, as the southerly breeze now strengthened into fitful squalls, driving a hard rain across the camps and forts surrounding Pensacola.

Saturday 31 March

By all accounts it was a poor day to die. The rain on the gulf coast is merciless to those caught without proper shelter. The large, heavy raindrops falling in great torrents soak both the soil and anyone on it in a matter of minutes. It would have been an uncomfortable night in the Spanish camp, for not only was everything drenched or leaking but by dawn the squalls had strengthened to a gale and thunder was rumbling mysteriously across the lightening sky above the dark points of the pines. Mortally wounded in the action of the previous day, *Coronel* Don Louis Rebolo became the highest ranking casualty to die in the operation so far.[62]

Doubtless swathed in a cloak, Gálvez splashed through the camp and headed for the house. Tents had been landed, and the men were struggling to erect them in the downpour and high wind, while others continued shovelling the wet soil to construct the parapet on the edge of the camp. When the governor reached the shelter of the house, he perhaps looked back at the mass of exhausted, miserable soldiers. They were men from all over the empire, struggling not only against the enemy but their old foe, nature, and he gave an order that a ration of *aguardiente* be issued to warm them up. From the windows of the upper floor, Gálvez peered at the town, visible through the murk, across the meadow to the high ground where the low shapes of the enemy redoubts were, only a mile and a quarter from where he stood.

Concerned about the threat of artillery fire, and understanding from prisoners he had questioned while at the camp that Campbell intended another sortie, Gálvez ordered Nava to scout for a campground further away from the sight of Fort George.

---

61 Davies (ed.), *Documents of the American Revolution*, Cameron to Germain, 27 May 1781, p.149.
62 *Courier du Bas-Rhin*, no.36, 4 May 1776, p.287.

Sunday 1 April – Wednesday 4 April

No sortie disturbed the Spanish camp, but in the cloudy morning some of the Loyalist dragoons were seen scouting around the neighbouring high ground that Nava had staked out the previous day, prompting him to head out with a guard of 300 men to prepare the area. Deans wrote that his men had been occupied 'preparing guns for an attack, which was laid aside.'[63] Things were no better in the Choctaw Camp, indeed after fighting for the better part of a month, it was becoming clear that Campbell was risking the warrior's lives in bad faith, much as Cameron had already pointed out.

Franchimastabé met with Cameron, Bethune, McIntosh and the Chickasaw deputy, Colbert, in the presence of his assembled warriors at his camp at Six Mile Creek.

> I want to Talk to you – I am sorry to see you in the Woods. I never imagined I should be obliged to talk to you here.
>
> Since our arrival here and the landing of the Spaniards the Indians have behaved well, they have done all that has been done with without being supported as was promised them by the Troops – had they advanced the day before yesterday we would have drove the Enemy off but when they began to run the Troops retreated, – could we manage the Great Guns ourselves we would have drove the Spaniards – But without any Support we find ourselves overpowered, and the Spaniards are so numerous that [though] we do not miss those we kill, … it looks as if they came [to life] again – We have done every thing in our power, we find in vain to make any further attempt; and I now put you in mind of your promise at the Saw Mill, you promised me large presents and it is time you should perform your promise – You also told me that you expected a Reinforcement, but in that you was deceived, I supposed as well as me, as the Talks must have been made here and never could come from the Great King.[64]

Cameron added to Germain that, 'Frenchumastabie [*sic*] seemed in a passion for not being supported with some of the troops, but after General Campbell promised that they should be supported in the future the chiefs promised me for themselves that they would never leave Pensacola before its fate was determined, in which they were as good as their words.'[65]

Although the Spanish were still landing supplies at 2:00 p.m. on Monday, more deserters revealed that the British were intending to target the camp with artillery, and so Gálvez determined to prepare to remove it to a safer position. The artillery and equipment were therefore put back on the ships and the troops were instructed that the tents, food, and larger supplies would be readied to move but kept as they were until dark, and a garrison of just over a hundred men was to be left at the house. Deans reported, 'A strong

63   Servies (ed.), *Log of the Mentor*, p.172
64   TNA: CO5 82/31: Talk by Frenchumastabe Great Medal Chief of the Chactaw Nation to Alexander Cameron Esqr, his Majesty's Superintendant at Six Mile Creek the 1st of April 1781.
65   Davies (ed.), *Documents of the American Revolution*, Cameron to Germain, 27 May 1781, p.149.

reconnoitring party of the enemy on the heights to the southward of Fort George. In the night they moved their encampment from Neil's house.'[66]

Ezpeleta had suggested a camp at the new position a few days before and was now proved correct in his instincts. It stood on the high ground overlooking the Bayou and blocking the road to Mobile, out of range of cannon-fire but close enough to the enemy to be a threat and near enough the water for supply. In the late morning of the 3rd there was a skirmish between the Choctaws and the Spanish advance guard. The noise of the musketry alarmed Deans, but for him it was more pressing to note that the Spanish navy was finally moving against the remaining vessels in the harbour; the *Port Royal* which was essentially a prison ship now for at least 60 Spaniards, two transports and a merchant vessel were taken and brought to the Spanish fleet. The *Gálvezton* went on a cruise up the Escambia Bay to search for others. Deans and his carpenters, armourers and sailmakers had been ashore for days now, occupied in the fortifications, while the sailors made wadding for the guns. Similarly, the Spanish were toiling to fortify their camp from the allied war-bands, with the majority of the troops at work on a glacis. The garrison of Neil's house was relieved by two companies of light infantry. Gálvez was still uneasy about the camp, now worrying it was not big enough, and he sent Ezpeleta and Nava out to examine the possibilities of enlarging it but also to examine the nearby high ground which looked to be from where they would have to attack Fort George.

Thursday 5 April.

The Spanish met daylight, tired and jumpy, as Campbell's Choctaw and Muskogee allies, doubtless joined by some of the Indian agents, had tested the effectiveness of the Spanish camp's defences through the night. Work to clear the trees and brush therefore continued with renewed vigour in the morning.

After meeting with a delegation of Tallapoosas who offered to supply the camp with food and seeing Mr Stevenson (who made sure to get a good look around while he was amongst the Spaniards), Gálvez and Nava inspected the new sights for entrenchments along the creek they intended to use for supplies, it was even suggested that the line from the camp to Neil's house be fortified. Miró seemed to be in a low mood, as he noted that they had suffered 20 dead and 13 wounded since the commencement of operations, 'without yet having even offended the enemy'.[67]

His temper was likely not improved when the flanks of the camp came under fire again that night, wounding two men in their tents, one of whom Gálvez said was an officer. Deans heard four volleys before the shooting died away.

Across the sea at Havana, the king's commissioner, Saavedra, was surprised to learn that the flagship of the expedition, *San Ramon*, had returned to the port of Matanzas on Cuba. Only vague rumours circulated

---

66 Servies (ed.), *Log of the Mentor*, p.173
67 Baker, 'Combat Diary', p.185

of the real drama that had occurred between the Spanish commanders. Calvo was writing furious letters to the minister of the navy, but for now he merely stated accurately that as the ship was too large to cross the bar, and as Ezpeleta and the New Orleans troops had joined Gálvez, he had thought it prudent to return.[68] Francisco de Miranda, was not quite so accepting calling the excuse for not entering the bay specious, 'As we are ignorant of her [the *San Ramon*'s] secret instructions, we are unable to decide as to her conduct, which is publicly denounced with infamy!'[69]

Friday 6 April

As the wounded were receiving their care from the night's alarm, Gálvez now had an intention forming in his head. By being physically present before the enemy works, and seeing the terrain, he could visualise what needed done. But much work needed to be accomplished. The redoubts that needed built to protect the supply route up from Bayou Chico, would require heavy toil in digging and the clearing of the woods and underbrush, and the creation of hundreds of fascines that would hold up the sandy soil. The long low rise from the bayou stretched out to meet the high ground occupied by the British, he decided that this was where they needed to create covered ways and batteries, and that the creek from the bayou would allow them to get the guns up without being exposed to the enemy. It became clear to him that the new camp was no good, as though it was convenient due to being open at the rear to the bayou, it was too easily approachable. An hour or so after first light, as ammunition started to come ashore, Gálvez, Nava, and the engineers rode out to the hill to scout out a line of attack and another new camp. That same day in Havana, Saavedra, who had begun to insist that reinforcements be sent to Pensacola and had succeeded in getting a hundred men on their way in two ships.

Saturday 7 April

During the night Rousseau and the *Gálvezton* netted a pretty catch of inhabitants attempting to flee by water via Escambia Bay, one of which was a parolee from Mobile who some of the Tallapoosas said had been assigned by one of the British Commissaries of Indian Affairs to approach them with gifts. Another prisoner brought in for questioning was an officer of the loyalists – accounts differ if he was from Maryland or Pennsylvania – who was presented to Gálvez as he had been discharged from the British service due to a disagreement with another officer and had been on his way to Georgia when he heard that Pensacola was under attack and had returned to join the Spanish. As there was a cadre of volunteers in Gálvez's force, he was

---

68 Topping (ed.), *Journal of Saavedra*, pp.141–143.
69 Donald E. Worcester, 'Miranda's Diary of the Siege of Pensacola, 1781', *The Florida Historical Quarterly*, vol.29, no.3 (1951), p.165.

allowed to join them.[70] The individual in question was never named, but his rank was given as lieutenant, and it seemed to Christopher New in his book on the Provincial Corps that it was probably William Augustus Bowles, who elsewhere was derided by commentators for some mysterious past villainy. It could be that the timeline given by Baynton is wrong for Bowles' desertion and wandering, or he had absconded again. Either way the possibility of him exploring his options cannot easily be dismissed. However, what is also fairly certain is that he eventually did return to the British side.

> Through this officer and several deserters, the General learned that the Indians were retiring; that they busied themselves in robbing the houses of the inhabitants and in burning all those they could in the country; that several terrified families had asked permission to embark in the brig *Gálvez town*, and that Mr. Deans, Captain of the British Royal Navy's frigate Mentor, had burned his ship to avoid its capture by the Spaniards. On this same morning the General dispatched the Talapuz [*sic*] Chiefs on a mission to the Indians of the English faction, to persuade them not to take part either on one side or the other during this war, and to bring all the cattle they could.[71]

The Tallapoosas, it will be remembered were what the British called the Lower Creeks, and so the principal branch of the Muskogee nation in alliance with the British. The coming of these men to Gálvez might have been a symptom of dissatisfaction, as Campbell wrote,

> The Indians now with us are Chiefly Chactaws and may consist of nearly four hundred Warriors they have with the greatest difficulty by Presents etc been prevailed upon to stay Five Days longer, but I am informed that a considerable body of Upper Creeks and about 200 more Chactaws may be expected to arrive within that time, should that happen the greater part of those now here will probably remain with us longer, what renders those present of very little use, is that they cannot be prevailed upon to Encamp nearer to Fort George than at the Distance of between four and five miles on the Path leading directly to their Nation, in order to be in readiness to push off in Case of accident or misfortune, I fear much they are secretly and underhand instigated and encouraged to this conduct, in short there is no Dependence on the Present set of our Savage Auxiliaries.[72]

Franchimastabé was certainly displeased with how he was being treated, and the demand of Campbell that his warriors should be doing the bulk of the work without commensurate reward. He was by this time seen by the British as the highest rank of chief they recognised. The war-chiefs had their own political priorities. When the siege was over the Spanish would remember who had come to 'talk to them with powder and ball,' as the Chickasaw leader, Opaymataha had once put it. If they fought to the death with the British for

---

70 Baker, 'Combat Diary', p.185.
71 Cusachs, 'Diary of the Operations', p.63.
72 TNA: PRO 30/55/89: Campbell to Clinton, 9 April 1781.

such paltry reward, what in the end would it do but see them starve when the Spaniards withheld gifts and trade?

In Havana Saavedra had convened an emergency meeting of the *Junta*. A British squadron of eight ships of the line and one frigate had been sighted near Cape San Antonio. It was thought they must be going to Pensacola as Jamaica was probably aware of the expedition from the *Childers*, which had slipped away from Pensacola on 10 March.[73]

Present at this meeting were *Mariscal de Campo* Cagigal and *Chef d'Escadre* de Monteil. The Frenchman quite sensibly advised caution, but the Spanish were too worried that the threat to Gálvez was real, and it was decided that they must send help to Pensacola. Monteil was asked to join the operation, but he had all but made up his mind to return to St Domingue after a joint cruise in response to a reported British naval relief force had resulted in no more than a good opportunity to practice manoeuvres. There was no reason for him to stay at Havana if there was not going to be a combined operation. His threat to leave was a contributing factor to the *Junta* deciding to send men and ships to Pensacola. Monteil would have preferred to have attacked Jamaica and was somewhat resentful about being kept around for what he deemed something that did not require his ships, but he was persuaded that the risk could not be taken and agreed to sail with Solano's squadron.[74]

Sunday 8 April

A dreary day of rain and work lay ahead for the troops in both camps. At Spanish headquarters, Gálvez wrote to Mobile asking that they send a few delegates from the nations friendly to Spain that could speak with the British allies, still painfully present at Pensacola, regarding their neutrality.

At Havana, the detachment consisted of staff, artillery, ammunition, and supplies, numbering 1,627 from nine regiments in two brigades, commanded by *Brigadier* Don Geronimo Girón and Don Manuel de Pineda.[75]

Monday 9 April

Every morning, one of the 24-pounders in Fort George was loaded with a blank charge and fired to start the day, thereafter the various reveilles began to be tapped out in the battalion camps by the drummers, and the routines of military life took over. On this day the report was lounder than usual, and those hurrying to the scene discovered the shocked gun crew examining a burst barrel with some consternation. Although no one was hurt it had been a lucky escape as by some accident the cannon had been over-loaded, and it was a miracle it had not so much as scorched anyone. There was a rattle of

---

73   Topping (ed.), *Journal of Saavedra*, p.144.
74   Quatrefages, 'La Collaboration Franco-Espagnole', p.53.
75   Topping (ed.), *Journal of Saavedra*, p.144.

musketry from the allied camp that afternoon as some Indian Department officers came in with 60–70 Muskogee warriors.

It was on the 9th that Campbell's long summary of the siege so far, replete with florid allusions and a strange mix of confidence and despondency, was dispatched to British headquarters.

> He [Gálvez] shows no Intention as yet of approaching nearer except to reconnoitre and to us it appears mysterious whether he actually means to take us by force or Blockade – we conceive he is not at all pleased with the appearance of our Defences … two Forty Gun Ships and two Frigates would destroy their whole expedition and would reflect Glory and Honor of his Majesty's Arms – The very Force that we understand detached from Jamaica to Curacao upon Intelligence of the Dutch War in Expectation of Rich Prizes would be sufficient to preserve a Province to the British Empire, to demolish a formidable armament of the Haughty Spaniard, and to thwart the … ambition of a Frenchman and implacable Foe; greater and more noble Objects than the amassing of Private Fortunes and the enriching of individuals. The Seamen of the Mentor and Port Royal have joined us, we have Plenty of Provisions, our Fortifications all in good order, we desire our Enemy but not so far as to forget our Duty, and were it not for Desertion, every circumstance would be in our favour – But notwithstanding every – attention to prevent it, 18 have gone off within these few Days – We must undoubtedly fall unless we are relieved.[76]

Campbell was quite obviously dispirited at the prospect of what was to come and seemed to be setting the scene to lay blame upon his Muskogee and Choctaw allies, even though other journals quite clearly contradict his claim that they did nothing, indeed so far, the majority of the Spanish casualties had been caused by the warriors.

Meanwhile, Cagigal's reinforcements had set sail from Cuba. Of course, this was unbeknownst to Gálvez, who had yet to make a final decision upon where to begin his siege-works. He received councillor Stevenson again who wished to explain why a small party of British soldiers were still in the town, the excuse for which Gálvez reluctantly accepted. He continued to take a great interest in the reports of deserters, but he would have been wise to treat their information lightly, as the information imparted was that 300 Muskogee warriors had come into the camp that afternoon, bringing the number encamped north of Fort George, close to 1,200.[77] It had been a month since the operation had begun, and it cannot have been far from the Governor's mind that Superintendent of the Army Urriza had promised a basic supply for an army of 4,000 men for three months. Perhaps he and Ezpeleta were able to joke ruefully about what Ezpeleta had quipped whilst enduring the interminable months waiting for action in Mobile, 'If you do not bring enough forces to take Pensacola, we could enjoy ourselves by camping out within its sight.'[78]

---

76   TNA: PRO 30/55/89: Campbell to Clinton, 9 April 1781.
77   Baker, 'Combat Diary', pp.185–186.
78   Rojas, *Ezpeleta at Pensacola*, p.118.

9

A Greater Challenge than Expected (10 April–21 April)

Tuesday 10 April – Thursday 12 April

The Spanish were not the only ones to entertain deserters. Both Farmar and Deans mentioned the singular occurrence of a Spanish deserter from the Regimiento Fijo de Luisiana, appearing on the 10th, but who turned out to be one of the Waldeckers that had been captured at Baton Rouge in 1779 and elected to serve the Spanish rather than be sent as a prisoner to Vera Cruz or Havana. The soldier was returned to his regiment after offering his impression of the Spanish camp and reporting that, 'the enemy are bad off for provisions & men only get 1 pound of meat per day.'[1]

The search for a new Spanish encampment continued, with a new ground being rejected as it was deemed to have no significant advantage. Nava continued to scout for a position that could still be supported by the navy but was close enough to the high ground selected for the siege-works to facilitate the reduction of the enemy defences, which he staked out in the course of the next few days. The Spanish redoubts on the creek were reported to be completed, and four naval guns were placed in each.

In the opinion of Farmar, Wednesday occasioned nothing worthy of note. Deans had had little to report over the last few days except that the carpenters, armourers and men were busily employed, but his log now recorded that some warriors had opened fire on a flag of truce and that the next day a gun had exploded at the Barrancas Coloradas, killing a sailor of the *Port Royal*.[2] Substantially it was the same in the Spanish camp on the edge of Bayou Chico, the labour being the monotonous landing of heavy artillery, ammunition and food. On the 11th, Gálvez had the diversion of speaking with another deserter, who reported what was known about the Spanish in the enemy camp, namely that they were 3,000 strong. Additionally, Gálvez

---

1   Padgett, 'Farmar's Journal', p.318.
2   Servies (ed.), *Log of the Mentor*, p.174.

heard the often-repeated rumour from prisoners, that reinforcements were on their way from the Muskogee nation and Jamaica.

Campbell agreed with Farmar and Deans,

> Nothing Material happened from the 9th of April until the 12th When the Enemy was discovered to have made a movement in advancing and to have taken possession of a Hill about one mile and three quarters distant from Fort George, whereupon an attempt with our Provincial Troops and Indians as made to dislodge them but they were found to be in force with cannon and the dislodgment of them impractical; The Enemy however lost several men in this affair and General Gálvez himself was slightly wounded.[3]

The Spanish had been changing ground since 5:30 a.m., but lookouts on duty at Fort George had belatedly spotted Spanish troops moving north in the afternoon through the woods on the opposing high ground to the west. The journal of Sergeant James A. Matthews, recorded, as part of a general summary, that the movement was discovered by 'our mounted scouts and Indians' who 'discovered the enemies advance, and drove them back until they opened on us with two field pieces, when we fell back to our first redoubts.'[4]

This would seem to have been a strong screen of skirmishers sent forward to mask the movement of the army to its new encampment. Shortly thereafter, the north facing guns of the fort and redoubts opened fire on them. According to Gálvez this occurred at 1:00 p.m.

When the smoke had cleared the Spaniards had withdrawn out of sight, but about four hours later Gálvez was informed that a sizeable enemy contingent was moving out to attack them. This was composed of a party of warriors supported by the Royal Foresters. Firing soon became pretty general, and the Spanish spotted two guns. The British and their allies moved out in three columns, one to fix the enemy in place, apparently made up of the loyalists, while the warriors took the flanks.[5] Unluckily, one of the loyalist lieutenants was shot in the head as he left the defences. A sharp skirmish developed in which the British forces were supported by the guns of the forts firing canister. The officer was carried back inside, alive but insensible, and doomed to die in a few hours. Meanwhile, the tragedy of war was compounded as one of the Waldeck sentries was killed outright by fire from the fort, which also wounded a sergeant.[6] Being informed that the enemy was moving in three groups in an attempt to encircle them, Gálvez himself rode forwards to find the likeliest spot that his might happen.

---

3   TNA: PRO 30/55/89: Campbell to Clinton, 12 May 1781.

4   John Francis Claiborne, *Mississippi, as a Province, Territory, and State: With biographical notices of eminent Citizens* (Jackson: Power and Barkdale, 1880), vol.I, footnote, p.126. Matthew's corps has yet to be identified and he is only stated to have been a long-time resident of Natchez, who died at an advanced age. Presumably he belonged to 16th, 60th, or the Loyalist Provincials.

5   Baker, 'Combat Diary', p.187.

6   Padgett, 'Farmar's Journal', pp.318–319.

Our light infantry replied to the fire of the Indians and English troops that supported them with the greatest firmness; but seeming to the General that a continuation of this would compel him to fight too long, he ordered the companies to retire to the protection of the nearest battery and that the enemy be fired upon with grape shot whenever he approached.[7]

Gálvez now rode towards the shelter of one of the newly completed redoubts or one of the small, entrenched artillery positions that covered the angles of the camp, but one of the outflanking parties of the enemy were already enfilading the withdrawing Spaniards,[8]

at one of the advanced batteries a bullet struck him [Gálvez] which went through one of the fingers of his left hand and furrowed his abdomen, and having retired to his tent to allow the surgeons to bind his wounds, he ordered Major-General Ezpeleta to take command … and to order whatever necessary, until his wounds permitted him to again supervise all things. Those of our batteries that had begun firing continued to do so against the Indians until these were obliged to retire, then it ceased on both sides without further loss to us than one killed and nine wounded.[9]

This firing only died away with the coming of night.

Friday 13 April

From the lines of Fort George, which composed the Advanced, or Queen's Redoubt, the Centre redoubt, and the main fort above Pensacola, it was just possible to discern large Spanish working parties with possibly as many as 1,000 men spread across the countryside. They were building breastworks along the line of supply and further back around the encampment, while also clearing the forest around the camp. More difficult to observe at a mile's distance was the movement of heavy guns and ammunition from the ships in creek of the Bayou up to the new base of operations. Sergeant Matthews reported that, during the night work began on extending the advanced redoubt.[10]

Saturday 14 April

Deans received information that the three men left in charge of the *Mentor* up at the mouth of the Black River had set fire to her and gone into the country on the approach of the Spaniards. Gálvez had actually heard of this on the 8th, and as Deans (whose account occasionally strays from the others

---

7   Cusachs, 'Diary of the Operations', p.64.
8   Servies (ed.), *Log of Mentor*, p.176
9   Cusachs, 'Diary of the Operations', p.64.
10   Claiborne, *Mississippi*, vol.1, p.126.

by about 24 hours, due to the practise in the Royal Navy of calculating a day as starting from noon rather than midnight) does not specify when the event took place, only when he received the information, it is hard to determine when it sank.[11]

Work on the Spanish breastworks and trenches continued from dawn until dusk, with 600 troops now being detailed to make fascines for shoring up entrenchments and digging out a deep pit for the powder magazine. Indications show that Gálvez had not been feeling well since 21 March and the shock of the gunshot wound that must surely have broken or shot off one of his fingers and bruised his abdomen can only have weakened his system more. Therefore, bad weather was not to be welcomed. However, at 8:00 p.m. the sky darkened to the west, and a fresh breeze began to whisper a warning through the tree branches and the dangling moss. The first drops of heavy rain began to pepper the ground shortly thereafter, accompanied by deafening peals of thunder. The wind rose and the rain began to hammer mercilessly into the sandy soil. All work in both camps had to cease, and the Spanish infantry were ordered to rely on the bayonet if the British attempted a sortie, as their powder was entirely soaked. The heavy gusts of wind were so strong and at times so sustained that most of the tents, including Gálvez's and the hospital tent, were blown down, and 'the surgeons prognosticated that many of the wounded would die of convulsions and the fears that this might happen to our General greatly worried everyone.'[12]

Sunday 15 April

The rain lessened at dawn, though Sergeant Matthews diarised that wind and incessant rain continued for four days. Every man and the entrenchments were drenched. A fine drizzle then proceeded from 4:30 a.m. for six hours, after which the storm could be seen as a black patch of sky to the southeast. A party of 90–100 Choctaws arrived in the British lines, led by Benjamin James, a Virginian born trader and agent in that nation, and another named Alexander Frazer, both of whom were, like McGillivray, mixed race. It is hard to say whether they were encouraged or not by what they found, as the rain had 'washed in a great quantity of sand from the barme and ditch of the fort and the redoubts.'[13] Deans went so far as to describe the ground works of the fort and redoubts under water during the worst of the storm. Coincidentally the Spanish also received a delegation of what Miró called 69 Chataes from Mobile, who encamped outside the lines, near one of the redoubts. All work had been suspended and remained so when the rain ceased, as the forest and ground began to steam under the glare of the sun, the order went out for the troops to take the opportunity to dry their clothes and equipment.

11 Servies (ed.), *Log of Mentor*, p.176.
12 Cusachs, 'Diary of the Operations', p.65. Convulsions being a term thought to mean chills and fevers, which Gálvez was familiar with as it is thought he might have contracted Malaria.
13 Padgett, 'Farmar's Journal', p.319.

Monday 16 April

It was another day, as Farmar liked to put it, of little consequence. Typified by the passage of deserters and small parties between the forts. Three soldiers from the 16th and 60th and one Waldecker came into the Spanish camp. Which rather seemed to confirm the statement of one of the Royal Foresters, who had come in the day before, reporting that most of the garrison was prepared to desert, and that the storm had done some damage. Though not as often, Campbell also received deserters and at around 8:00 p.m. a soldier of the Regimiento de Flandes reached the British. A small group of sailors managed to get to Fort George from the Barrancas Coloradas but if they had anything of interest to say, Deans did not mention it.

Tuesday 17 April

Whatever information came into headquarters, it was usually common knowledge a few hours later. Farmar was able to note in his journal that the Spanish deserter, who he said was a sergeant – which would explain why Miró thought he would have information to impart – told Campbell that the Spanish were very badly off for provisions, and it was from him that it was learned that Gálvez had been wounded. Not only that but an express arrived from St Augustine, accompanied by a guard of Muskogee warriors, which delivered some copies of dispatches the garrison had already received, but also informing them of the British victory at Camden.

Deans received confirmation that the *Mentor* had indeed been burned. After the siege he would face a court martial of seven officers, convened at Deans insistence to investigate his actions at Pensacola, and he was completely exonerated. One of the members of the court was Captain Horatio Nelson.

No matter what the sailors who had come in from the Navy Redoubt at the Barrancas the day before had told Campbell, he probably sent one back with a reply, as a sailor was taken prisoner on his way there when he tried to cross the picquet line of the light infantry of the Regimiento de Navarra. He carried food and some letters.

> In one of these General Campbell assured that Admiral Rowley would send him considerable help, that his troops would defend themselves to the last extremity, and that whilst there was some desertion, far from this causing him any anxiety it augmented his confidence, for those [who were] truly soldiers remained, and that besides the arrival of the Creek Indians, he expected considerable reinforcements from other friendly nations.[14]

---

14   Cusachs, 'Diary of the Operations', p.65.

The period of rest at the Spanish camp had ended, and the troops were once again at work digging trenches, breastworks, gun emplacements and hauling up supplies.

Wednesday 18 April

A small ship bearing news of the recapture of Nicaragua by Matias de Gálvez was cause for a special parade in the Spanish camp that afternoon. Farmar clearly heard the *feu de joie* from the British fortifications. Busy as he was occupied assigning his men to the guns in Fort George and overseeing the construction of a mortar battery inside the abattis of the advanced redoubt, Deans also noted the general salute of cannon from all the ships in the harbour, which actually included all the artillery then mounted in the Spanish redoubts as well. Each gun firing three rounds in celebration of the victory. During the day the Spanish engineers 'went to explore the crescent battery of the salient of Fort George without the enemy noticing it.'[15]

Thursday 19 April

The firing of the 19th was in earnest rather than salute. The Choctaws, who had lain in wait during the night, opened fire on the Spanish camp early in the morning, producing another brisk skirmish. The allied warriors returned with a wounded man bleeding from a ball to the thigh, and one scalp. This must have made the appearance of a party of Tallapoosas quite disturbing for the Spanish outposts, however these brought with them 42 cattle and peacefully encamped not far from the Chataes near the Spanish lines. When all was tranquil the engineers went back out to survey the Queen's Redoubt, often also called the crescent battery or the demi-lune, 'and measurements taken of the distance from it to the place best suited to reduce it, and this new exploration was indispensable as we had no exact plans, and the country was wooded and each step was a risk and a clash with the Indians.'[16]

It was at 2:00 p.m. that the patrolling frigates signalled that sails had been sighted, causing no little alarm given constant references by enemy deserters of a relief force. Gálvez was told 14 sail were in sight. The newcomers were closely monitored. Two hours later they were reported as being over 20, and apparently Spanish from their signals. Gálvez, however, had not been informed that the armament was on its way, and he had read nothing about them in the dispatches from Havana he had received the previous day. A ship was immediately dispatched to ascertain whose ships were coming in. Deans's opinion on the matter was a simple and disappointed '5 sail in sight, supposed to be the enemy's.'[17]

15 Cusachs, 'Diary of the Operations', p.66.
16 Cusachs, 'Diary of the Operations', p.66.
17 Servies (ed.), *Log of the Mentor*, p.178.

Campbell feared the worst as well: 'on this Day a Fleet appearing in the offing … we conceived them to be French or Enemies. The next day being hazy we could make no discoveries in regard to the Fleet; The weather being still thick on the 20th though not so much as the Day before, we could only discern a Brig at anchor without the Bar of the Harbour.'[18]

As was standard practice, Solano and Monteil had their signal numbers hoisted, and frigates out in advance. At 9:00 p.m. their identity was confirmed by the besiegers. The fleet had sighted land at about noon and their worry had been that Gálvez might already have been defeated or not be in control of the harbour. But the ships in the harbour signalled Spanish ownership of the port, and Saavedra was able to be told that preparations to attack were under way and even that Gálvez had been slightly wounded.[19]

Friday 20 April

The voyage from Cuba had been largely uneventful but Solano had taken no chances of running blindly into a British squadron unprepared. The Franco-Spanish fleet sailed either in three compact columns, or in a large block if any suspicious vessel was spotted, with frigates out in advance as scouts. One of these, the French *Andromache*, grounded on the bar and only floated free during the night with the help of boats and launches after throwing 14 guns overboard and emptying water casks over the side. Solano and Monteil came ashore during the morning to have a conference with Gálvez. They placed the artillery, the sailors, and naturally Cagigal's troops, at the service of Don Bernardo, which he gratefully accepted and gave orders that the camp was to be extended some 2,400 feet to accommodate the reinforcements.[20] However, the fleet could not yet enter the bay as they could not find a pilot to show them the way over the bar.

> … we resolved to take the step of using the frigate *Andromache* to enter the port, but … The wind having become very light we were not able to make the port. About 8 we found ourselves caught on the coast of the island of Santa Rosa without knowledge of the passage, for which reason we anchor immediately, consequently we remained on board, receiving the best treatment from the naval lieutenant, M. La Lonne, commander of the said vessel, whose character was amiable and generous; he was distinguished generally. During the night we fired several cannonades and rockets, with the idea that these signals might be heard or seen by our detachment on the island of Santa Rosa or by the frigates which were in the port, and that they might send us a pilot. But as it turned out we were too far distant and they did not hear them.[21]

---

18   TNA: PRO 30/55/89: Campbell to Clinton, 12 May 1781.
19   Topping (ed.), *Journal of Saavedra*, pp.151–152.
20   Baker, 'Combat Diary', p.187.
21   Worcester, 'Miranda's Diary', pp.174–175.

The king's commissioner was in the French cutter, *Serpent* which being one of the lightest ships was being used as a tender. It had been hoped that they could pick up a pilot from the *Andromache*. Also aboard was *Mariscal de Campo* Manuel Cagigal, his son, and his aides de camp, one of which was probably Francisco de Miranda.

It would seem that the arrival of Spanish reinforcements prompted Campbell to accede to the demands of his allies and to secure the ammunition and provisions which were 'deposited in two small vessels … for the maintenance and use of the Indians.'[22]

These were the armed sloop *Christiana* and the galley *Pontchartrain*, and they were guarded by a small force of unidentified African American sailors or armed inhabitants. Their masters, Henry Smith, and Donald McPherson, were instructed to bring aboard enough materials to burn them in case of imminent capture and to then take them high up the Escambia river.[23]

Saturday 21 April

'More ships for the enemy,' wrote Sergeant Matthews 'and the rumour is they bring a number of French troops.'[24] The rumour was of course correct, founded on the discovery of several gun carriages which washed ashore, marked as belonging to *Andromache*, which had been required to throw some of her guns overboard after grounding on the bar. 'At seven o'clock in the morning' wrote Francisco de Saavedra,

> we sailed in search of Sigueza point on Santa Rosa Island … and at two thirty o'clock in the afternoon we were off another point, at the very entrance of the port and opposite the Barrancas Coloradas, where the English had their battery called the red cliffs battery. Naval Lieutenant Villavicencio came alongside in a boat, and he guided us into the entrance of the port, although he had protested that he did not know it very well.[25]

Since being in contact with the shore, Saavedra had obviously heard about the anomaly of such an apparently formidable battery which was unable to do any more than moderate damage, even to ships which went aground. When he came under fire, he seems to have taken the opportunity to probe the reason why:

> When we passed in front of the battery, the enemy fired at us eighteen cannon shots of heavy calibre; they fell near us but none struck our vessel, although we ran aground on the bar within their range, but M. Lalone, commandant of the *Serpent*, an officer of much ingenuity and intelligence, ordered all the men and artillery moved to the bow and the vessel floated free without giving the English

---

22   TNA: PRO 30/55/88: Campbell to Galvez, 24 May 1781.
23   TNA: PRO 30/55/89: Campbell to Smith and McPherson, 20 April 1781.
24   Claiborne, *Mississippi*, vol.1, p.126.
25   Topping (ed.), *Journal of Saavedra*, p.153.

time to secure their aim. At first glance it seemed strange that this battery had not done notable damage to as many vessels as passed within range of its guns daily, but there were two reasons for this: first, the distance from the battery to the opposite extreme of the channel is greater than it appears; … second, because the battery is on an elevated site, the firing was aimed without variation and therefore was very inaccurate.[26]

The party were met by *Capitános de Fregata* Miguel Alderete and Don José Serrato in longboats which conveyed them from Pensacola harbour to the Bayou Chico and inland via the channel, passing as they did all the apparatus and industry of an army engaged in siege operations. They landed at the redoubt, garrisoned by the navy, and were taken up through the earthworks to the camp.

> Gálvez received us with a vivid display of joy. That evening when he and I were alone, he related to me the entire sequence of his operations and described his distress at finding himself obliged to lay formal siege to three forts garrisoned by soldiers almost as numerous as those he had brought. Moreover, the English had on their side many Indian nations, warlike, cruel, excellent marksmen skilful in the handling of muskets, who had harassed his small army sorely in the march it had to make in a country full of dense forests and with many obstructions, the most appropriate land in the world for ambushes. Seven times he had been obliged to move the encampment before being able to take post in a location advantageous for launching the attack. [27]

It was decided that Cagigal's troops would be landed on Santa Rosa. A sensible precaution as it would not only allow the troops to enjoy their first night ashore in days to recover but would lighten the ships that would need to cross the bar, and they could be picked up from the north shore in Santa Rosa channel to be transported to the camp. All possible information was afforded to Solano, and Saavedra lodged in a 'comfortable sort of barrack' which belonged to the vicar of the troops from Louisiana, the Capuchin Father Cirilo of Barcelona. Cirilo had sung the *Te Deum* after the victory at Manchac in 1779, and had already been appointed by Bishop of Havana, Echevarría, to serve as the vicar over the Floridas.

The British officers on the parapets of Fort George could, with a telescope, watch the enemy boats and row-galleys cross and recross the bar, continually harassed but never stopped by the Red Cliffs Battery. The seriousness of the situation now confronting the British can easily be observed by the summary given by *Capitán* Miranda:

> All the army welcomed us with infinite joy, for not only were they fatigued with the endless and not well-combined marches they had made in the 42 days since they had disembarked at the island of Santa Rosa, but by the various camps which they had occupied, the entrenchments and so forth (seven counting this one),

---

26 Topping (ed.), *Journal of Saavedra*, p.153.
27 Topping (ed.), *Journal of Saavedra*, p.153.

the construction of revetments, fascines, and other defences, besides this they considered all their work useless, and were in despair of the enterprise. The army numbered, including militia and Negroes, 3,701 men. Of these 500 were out of action, and so, they were able to count on only 2,000 regulars for the attack … With the consolidation of our detachment, 1,504 troops of our navy, and 725 French, the army amounted to 7,803 effectives.[28]

De Monteil reported to the minister of the navy that, 'The announced [British] squadron did not appear, but the fortress seems more difficult to reduce than had been believed with the landing of the troops, that of the squadron which I provided about 800 soldiers under the orders of M. Boiderut, comprising more than 7,000 men, I hope the siege will make great progress.'[29]

It should be noted that from the time of Gálvez's wound to his recovery, which began to occur from around this time, though he was never so incapacitated as to need to be superseded, the commanders of the army were effectively Jose de Ezpeleta and Manuel de Cagigal who were congratulated by Gálvez for the capable handling of the operation while he was sick. There is a distinct vagueness about Gálvez's activities in this period into mid-April, and he only begins to be seen taking physical control of events again, rather than planning and strategy, towards the end of the month.

---

28 Worcester, 'Miranda's Diary', p.176.
29 Quatrefages, 'La Collaboration Franco-Espagnole', p.54.

10

Brisk & Bloody Skirmishing (22 April–28 April)

Campbell wrote of this period: 'From this to the night of the 28th the enemy [were] employed in Reconnoitring, which occasioned frequent skirmishes, that however could not be improved as I wished from the Backwardness of the Indians and their encamping at the great Distance I formerly Reported, whereby nothing could be affected by Ambush or Surprise.'[1]

Sunday 22 April

After accepting the hospitality of the Vicar of Florida, and doubtless attending terce, Francisco de Saavedra was assigned a billet with the Regimiento Immemorial del Rey. About half an hour later he saw Cagigal ride out of the camp accompanied by a large suite consisting of his three aides de camp, the chief of artillery *Teniente Coronel* Vincente Risel, Nava and Ezpeleta, escorted by a party of *cazadores*. They quickly overtook the column of troops assigned to the work detail that day and headed northeast.[2]

Some diversion was afforded as well by the appearance of two companies of French *chasseurs* and a company of the French marine artillery, who marched into camp and were guided to their ground, signalling the beginning of the disembarkation of the reinforcements. Gálvez may well have not quite recovered from his bout of sickness, but indications suggest he kept himself busy drawing up an order of battle which reflected the updated nature of his command. Saavedra meanwhile made himself familiar with the newly enlarged Spanish camp, which according to the map drawn by Campbell's acting chief engineer, *Kapitänleutnant* Henry Heldrig of the 3rd Waldeck, lay directly over the trail from Mobile to Pensacola.[3] Saavedra wrote:

---

1   TNA: PRO 30/55/89: Campbell to Clinton, 12 May 1781.

2   Saravia, *Gálvez*, p.375.

3   'Plan of the siege of Fort George and works adjacent at Pensacola in West Florida, 1781, by Henry Heldring capt. lieut: in the 3th Regmt of Waldeck, & acting engineer at Pensacola',

The camp was well located. On the right it was protected by the inlet or estuary by which supplies were brought in from the port; it faced the forts of the enemy, about 1,500 *toises* distant; a part of the back was protected by the bayou; and the centre was surrounded by the forest, which had been cleared somewhat by the cutting of the trees and branches used in raising the parapet. These trees were rather tall pines, and the forest, though dense, was not as rank and tangled as those in the tropics, where the vegetation is more luxuriant than in the temperate zones. Redoubts crowned with heavy and small calibre Artillery were constructed in the corners of the camp and in places most exposed to attack.[4]

The parapet itself was made of 'earth and logs, the height of a man and 7 feet thick with its moat and banquette against the sudden violent attacks of the Indians, who, even despite this precaution used to kill our men inside their own tents at night by climbing into the dense foliage of the trees that overhung the parapet.'[5] Miranda described the camp fortifications similarly, 'The troops continued their labours on the trenches, which were almost completed, The said entrenchment was formed of heavy pines and stakes filled with a sandy clay of a thickness of about 7 feet, and its corresponding foss,[6] which has to be pounded by heavy artillery in order to attack [break] it.'[7]

The building of this type of earthwork had not changed since the days when there had been an old timber fort at Pensacola in 1698. An engineer would hammer an outline with pine stakes joined by string or rope if it was available, creating two parallel lines about six yards apart. On these marks were piled logs to the required height, which would appear to be somewhere around five feet in this case, to create a wide, deep trough into which soil, excavated from what would become the ditch, was packed, as Miranda outlined. Once this was completed, fascines would be used as a sort of roof and padding, and, along with gabions, could also be used in enough quantity as part of the retaining wall. More earth was banked against the outward side to create a slope which hopefully would deflect or absorb artillery. The ditch was often protected by a low scarp, and in front of that felled trees were placed with their branches facing outwards, and sometimes sharpened, to form an abattis. Though it does not appear that the Spanish deployed an abattis, the British certainly did, and when reading through the construction of the siege works, it is this construction that should be kept in mind. Trenches were substantially the same principle only the timber and fascines here were placed to keep the soil out rather than in.

Saavedra, being a curious man, also had a look at the neighbouring camps: 'Outside our camps, by the front right-hand corner [northeast] and a short distance away was located the camp of the Indians of our alliance,

William L. Clements Library, University of Michigan Library Digital Collections, <https://quod.lib.umich.edu/w/wcl1ic/x-581/wcl000685>, accessed 17 July 2023.
4   Topping (ed.), *Journal of Saavedra*, pp.155–156.
5   Topping (ed.), *Journal of Saavedra*, pp.155–156.
6   Miranda is probably abbreviating fausse-braye, a low outer rampart.
7   Worcester, 'Miranda's Diary', p.178.

which comprised of several small nations ... For their protection they had huts made of tree bark which, although small and uncomfortable, withstood inclement weather very well.'[8]

Cagigal and his entourage arrived at the edge of the shelf opposite Gage Hill as midday approached and selected a spot for the first trench either 300 or 656 yards from Fort George, depending which side is telling the story. The sight of the Spanish amongst the pines caused a violent and rapid reaction from the British.

> About 12 o'clock we observed about 5 or 600 of the enemy on a hill within the distance of 300 yards from the advanced Redoubt and fired five guns at them. They then retreated [and] there was immediately some cracks and Indians pursued them also a detachment from the 60th & Provincials Reg't [under] the command of Capt. Byrd who when they got upon the ground found that the enemy had retired to their camp.[9]

Deans, while not quite so colourful also recorded the scramble,

> ... a body of the enemy appeared in the valley to the NW of the advanced redoubt. The redoubt fired several shot amongst them which put them to the rout. The Indians, with some of the light troops, pursued them and fired several vollies upon them. Took the engineer's plan of the [south] works & supposed the engineer to have been wounded as a good deal of blood was seen where the plan was found.[10]

The Spanish noted several warriors lying dead or wounded but the number was never confirmed. The ground in question was described by Miranda as being 'about 600 meters from the enemy fortification, covered by some scattered inclines which there are intervening.'[11] The terrain itself being found to be devoid of rocks 'it is noteworthy that for many leagues around not one stone of any size is to be found.'[12]

Campbell's aide de camp, Hugh Mackay Gordon was the one who, picking his way through the felled and shot-shattered trees, discovered the map, and putting it together with the blood assumed that the engineer had likely been killed by a ball ricocheting off one of the pines. Although probably correct in deducing the manner of death, the victim was actually an unlucky soldier from the Regimiento de Soria.[13]

From the captured map it was clear that Gálvez did not intend to blockade the fort but to attack it, and not only that but it showed the British where he wished to do it from.

---

8   Topping (ed.), *Journal of Saavedra*, pp.155–156.
9   Padgett, 'Farmar's Journal', p.321. A possible early use of the derogatory slang for poor white southerners, 'cracker', which possibly derives from the Gaelic, *Craic*, and by the eighteenth century referred to Celtic immigrants. Farmar is probably referring to the Royal Foresters or Royal Volunteers, an unusual early instance of this phrase being used if so.
10   Servies (ed.), *Log of the Mentor*, p.179.
11   Worcester, 'Miranda's Diary', p.176.
12   Topping (ed.), *Journal of Saavedra*, pp.157–158.
13   Baker, 'Combat Diary', p.188.

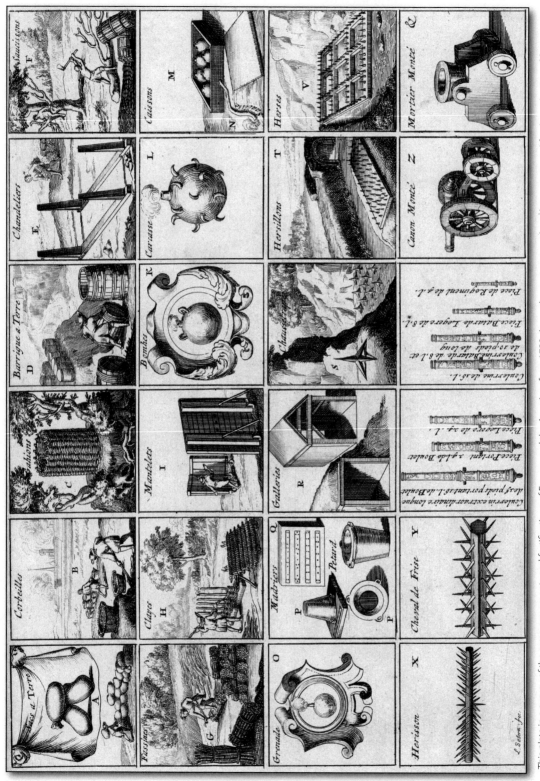

This plate in a survey of the arms, armaments and fortifications of Europe and the Americas from 1720 shows the common tools and weapons used for the reduction of fortresses during the eighteenth century. (British Library Flikr)

Monday 23 April

With the last of the reinforcements landed it was ordered that the breastworks be extended around the new section of the camp. The reorganisation of the army, now numbering some 7,600 soldiers and sailors was completed, with five brigades having been created and with all being in readiness to begin working on reducing Fort George. At 10:00 a.m., Nava led out a detachment of *cazadores* to finalise the placement and begin work on the parallels. However, once again they were spotted and fired upon, though no skirmish seems to have developed this time, Campbell was gaining confidence to attack any working parties that presented themselves. News from a deserter suggested the British intended on extending their own works on one side of the advanced redoubt, and would launch a sortie that night, so the Spanish slept on their arms.

Tuesday 24 April

Though there was no attack in the night, evidence of Campbell's determination to oppose the Spanish was shown as they now attempted to open their trenches. At dawn, *Brigadier* Girón and *Coronel* Nava headed out with a strong guard to continue staking out the trenches. They were spotted at between 7:00 and 8:00 a.m., carrying fascines to a location behind the hill, and may have been work parties constructing the new defences of the camp, which were completed that day. A party of warriors which formed part of the picquet guard responded. That day they were facing Girón, who resolutely ordered his *cazadores* to advance, 'and their fire made the Indians retire.'[14] However, Captain Byrd was in support, this time and as the Spanish pursued into the shallow valley that separated the two sides, his detachment of the 60th Foot gave them a volley at 70 yards at which they in turn withdrew, though the firing did not cease, and one of the British was wounded in the leg.

Gálvez relates more details from the Spanish perspective,

the light infantry returned the fire that was made on it with a great deal of firmness, now advancing now retiring, according to the circumstances; but as the firing continued for quite a time, the General ordered two more companies to go out of the Camp in support of the others. This lasted for more than one hour.[15]

Half an hour later, Byrd was supported by 50 or so Provincials accompanied by two howitzers and two guns, which, when they opened fire, caused Girón to break off the fight. Miró recorded that an officer of the Regimiento de Hibernia, *Teniente* Don Phillipe O'Reilly was wounded along with nine men

---

14   Padgett, 'Farmar's Journal', p.322.
15   Cusachs, 'Diary of the Operations', p.68.

whose regiments were not identified.[16] A second skirmish occurred later in the afternoon, but without much of a result other than one of the Irish being captured. He was confirmed missing by Miranda, who did not know if he was dead or a prisoner.

Exploring continued, as at 8:00 a.m. Cagigal and his staff plus several naval officers, accompanied by Saavedra, embarked on a brig to see if Fort George could be attacked from the sea. Cagigal had a shrewd eye for position and did not see why the immense power of the warships was not being used to attack the British. His calculation was that if howitzers or mortars could be rigged on one of the warships, it could be brought close inshore, guarded by a frigate, and fire on Fort George from the sea with shells.

The vessel had two 24-pounder bow chasers and these were fired, with the elevation set, estimated Saavedra, at 12 degrees. At a range of under a mile, one shot went high but reached the centre redoubt, and the other struck the esplanade of Fort George. Deans recorded the response. 'At 2, the howitzers went down to the beach abreast of the brigg, covered by a party of the Waldecks. Fired several shot at her and sent her off.'[17] Summing up the day, Sergeant Matthews wrote, 'Enemy came out of their works and a skirmish ensued. They retreated after losing several of their number. During this skirmish a brigantine anchored near the lower end of the town and opened fire on Fort George, which was returned, but the distance was too great to be effective on either side.'[18]

Cagigal, took soundings and decided that shallow draught vessels with large artillery could demolish or harass the fort by entering the port. He returned in the afternoon.[19] Gálvez took no action on this, either due to a disinclination to share the limelight with another officer of similar rank, or because he did not want to risk losing ships due to the British ability to bring down counter-fire. This last consideration brings up the accord with Governor Chester, the spirit of which was to safeguard the town and its inhabitants. Although naval fire would have allowed the bombardment to commence much earlier, this would mean shooting over the rooftops of Pensacola, and the British would be firing back, not only from the forts but from the beach, the consequence of which would be to draw counter-fire onto shore.

In the evening an express arrived reporting that 'Lord Cornwallis had totally defeated the Rebels at Guildford Killed 2000 of them, and taken a number of cannon stores, [and] prisoners upon the news of which at 8 O'clock we fired a *feu de joy*.'[20] Much as when the Spanish guns saluted Matias de Gálvez's success in Nicaragua, the sudden discharge was alarming at first, not least because the British uncharitably let off a few live shots. Miranda wrote:

After dusk we saw that the enemy had made a general discharge of his artillery on all sides of Fort George, and following this another volley of musketry which

16   Baker, 'Combat Diary', p.188.
17   Servies (ed.), *Log of Mentor*, p.179.
18   Claiborne, *Mississippi*, vol.1, p.126.
19   Topping (ed.), *Journal of Saavedra*, pp.157–158.
20   Padgett, 'Farmar's Journal', p.322

surprised us to the point that afterwards we supposed that it was a salute in celebration of the triumph which the royal troops under the command of Lord Cornwallis had achieved against the Anglo-Americans commanded by General Grune [Greene]. Three of the cannon facing our camp were loaded with balls which entered the camping place.[21]

Wednesday 25 April

With the laying out of the Spanish trenches now having been delayed by aggressive enemy skirmishing, the largest action of the siege yet took place when Nava, Risel, and some French officers once more went out about an hour after daylight, supported by two companies of *piquetes*, from the Immemrorial del Rey and Princesa regiments, with another five companies waiting in readiness. On this ride the French artillery commandant saw enough to report to Monteil that the *Demi Lune*, or the Advanced Redoubt, was the key to the British position.[22] The first shots were fired at about 7:00 a.m. as the British advanced picquet raised the alarm.[23] In the words of Sergeant Matthews, 'a brisk engagement ensued.'[24] Miró's as usual more leavened account added artillery to the mix, 'The enemies who were on guard began to fire with a field artillery cannon and the [small] arms of the Indians.'[25]

According to Miranda, the Spanish had 'encountered two companies of enemy infantry which were formed upon the same terrain marked out by us the previous days. At their sides were two parties of savages who fired in good order and more regularly than they were accustomed to do.'[26]

Francisco de Saavedra recorded that 'When they drew near to Fort Half Moon they met two enemy infantry companies drawn up on the very terrain they had surveyed on the previous day and alongside the English companies, hordes of savages who were firing with more order and regularity than usual. A bloody skirmish ensued which lasted until seven-thirty o'clock when both sides retired.'[27]

Six Spaniards were wounded, while only one Provincial was seriously injured on the British side, plus one deserter from the Royal Foresters escaped. He was apparently French and found to be suspicious when being

---

21 Worcester, 'Miranda's Diary', p.178. The Spanish only learned of Cornwallis's victory the next day.
22 Quatrefages, 'La Collaboration Franco-Espagnole', p.56.
23 Padgett, 'Farmar's Journal', p.322.
24 Claiborne, *Mississippi*, vol.1, p.126.
25 Baker, 'Combat Diary', p.188.
26 Worcester, 'Miranda's Diary', p.178.
27 Topping (ed.), *Journal of Saavedra*, p.158. It is at times like these when one cannot help but look with a concerned eye at the strong similarity between Miranda's and Saavedra's diaries. Even in English some passages look identical in phraseology and information. There are differences, but as Miranda also wrote a prequel diary of events that occurred before he even arrived at Pensacola, and a copy of Farmar's Journal was found in his papers, a comparison between Miranda's diary and Saavedra's (preserved in the Casa-Residencia of the Jesuit Fathers of Grenada) in Spanish may well be necessary in the future.

questioned, as such he was confined aboard ship. When the shooting had died away and the Spanish had retired the surreal dual nature of the siege revealed itself in the form of Councillor Stephenson appearing under a flag of truce once again to dine with Gálvez and object in the politest way possible to the Spanish navy shooting over the town, which Chester deemed close to a breach of their agreement.

In their usual uncanny way Saavedra and Miranda observed the same result. Gálvez once more assured Governor Chester that 'neither his troops nor his Indian allies would molest the citizens or cause them the least damage. On this basis a solemn agreement was made between the generals of both nations, and many families who had fled toward Georgia returned to Pensacola.'[28] Stephenson withdrew in the afternoon apparently satisfied, having imparted also the news of Guilford Courthouse as the meaning of the *feu de joi* the previous night.[29] Gálvez therefore chose to reject Cagigal's plan to fire on the forts from the water not out of vanity, but certainly to maintain his honour.

Thursday 26 April

Gálvez 's willingness to entertain Stephenson was partly his devotion to the notions of 'civilised warfare', in which soldiers and gentlemen did not wage war out of anything but a devotion to their government, and much like lawyers, took little personal interest in the politics of the struggle, thus the citizens of Pensacola were able to go about their business, to some extent, uninterrupted and the siege was less that of the town but the forts that protected it, leaving the inhabitants as almost spectators to the violence. However, it was also partly a tactical decision as Gálvez cannot have been ignorant of the fact that Stephenson reported all he saw in the increasingly large and well defended Spanish camp to Chester, who passed it on to Campbell. The latest visit for instance brought in a fresh count of the enemy ships resting in the harbour. The councillor had counted 11 Spanish and four French ships of the line and a few frigates, all drying their sails after a rain-shower. Gálvez was more than content under the circumstances to let the British know exactly what they were up against.

In the pre-dawn the British advanced picquet, then possibly still occupying the ground the Spanish wished to entrench, was changed from Byrd and Kearny's loyalists to a 50-man detachment of the 16th and 60th, led by Lieutenants Richard Carrigue (16th) and Charles Ward (60th). Work was progressing on the British side, by enlarging the fortifications of the advanced redoubt with the objective to extend it to the left and right and to dig a mortar bed. The left wing, Deans said, being completed by the end of the day, though the Spanish emphasise only the right wing, due to the map indicating this flank being that which Gálvez wanted to approach from.[30]

---

28 Topping (ed.), *Journal of Saavedra*, pp.158–159.
29 Topping (ed.), *Journal of Saavedra*, pp.158–159.
30 Servies (ed.), *Log of the Mentor*, p.180.

Gálvez knew well enough that the British were making progress in extending their defences. If he did not gain the ground he needed soon, it would become useless to him, or prove very costly to sustain. The chief problem was that it was proving difficult to do much more than stake out lines before being pounced on by the British picquets and their Choctaw and Muskogee allies, who, despite what Campbell said, clearly sent warriors up to the fortifications and quite regularly, so as to always be present by the morning when the Spanish tended to make their presence known. With this impediment in mind, it was determined to send out the engineers again and while the infantry kept the British back, they were to complete their survey and the marking out of the trenches. The work on which would be carried out by a large detachment that night.

Five companies of *cazadores* and grenadiers commanded by *Capitán* de Bouligni, of the Regimiento Fijo de Luisiana headed out just after 3:00 p.m. Though Campbell never mentioned this specifically he, or someone else, had certainly posted the advance picquet near enough to where the captured Spanish engineer's map had indicated they wished to site their trenches that they could more or less deny it to them. Though Gálvez had the men to simply take it by force, it was never his way to flagrantly waste lives. To expose a couple of battalions to the fire of every gun in the forts would have been an unnecessary sacrifice. But has been seen, the irregular tactics being used by the British and especially their allied war-bands were proving exceptionally effective at preventing Spanish progress, so long as Gálvez restrained himself the British could hold.

In the mid-afternoon, one of the Spanish companies became overextended, and with accompanying whoops and war-cries, the warriors struck, 'more than 200 English soldiers and a large number of Indians ... penetrated the forest to their right, apparently with the object of cutting off one company which was far advanced.'[31] The Spanish saw the attack unfolding and pushed up two field guns which kept the warriors at bay and forced them to fall back toward the English soldiers who, 'losing ground little by little, were pushed back against Fort Half Moon.'[32]

Gálvez's diary of operations reported that this elicited a violent response from the British artillery, '... this battery began to fire with heavy artillery and several howitzers preventing for the time being the conclusion of the exploration.'[33] Unable to answer such weight of fire there was only one option for the Spanish, and in the words of Saavedra, 'Seeing that their task was frustrated and that it was growing dark, our men retired; they had however marked the place where the trench must be opened.'[34] Unusually, despite the dynamic nature of the action, no source on either side makes mention of casualties.

Miro's combat diary records that, 'At 9:00, p.m., was ordered the departure for this purpose [opening the trench] of 700 workers and 800 armed men

---

31   Topping (ed.), *Journal of Saavedra*, p.159.
32   Topping (ed.), *Journal of Saavedra*, p.159.
33   Cusachs, 'Diary of the Operations', p.69.
34   Topping (ed.), *Journal of Saavedra*, p.159.

[grenadiers and light infantry] to protect them. But although we had the good fortune not to be heard the night was filled with such a strong rain that it wasn't possible to find the markers locating the entrenchment.'[35] Gálvez's opinion of the affair was that 'to arrive there it was necessary to traverse a thick wood, and the way was made more difficult on account of the great number of trees that had been cut and pits that had been dug from place to place, for which reason, and also because strict silence had to be observed, the march was taken up at a slow pace.'[36]

Saavedra was told that indeed progress had been too slow, 'As it happened 1:30 came, and the Quartermaster, aware that it was not possible for the troops to remain until dawn, was instructed by Brigadier Don Geronimo Girón to withdraw the workers and following them, the troops.'[37] Heavy rain and thunder added to the decision to pull most of the troops back, though two companies of grenadiers were posted to keep the area under observation.

Friday 27 April

Just after daybreak two companies of *cazadores* left the Spanish camp and headed into the woods to relieve the grenadiers with orders to prevent the British from probing any further or removing the markers for the earthworks. In aid of which work parties were sent out to clear a road to the build-site, and once again the engineers were out collecting data. At 8:00 p.m., Campbell's forward picquet was relieved by 50 men of the Provincials under the Irish born former surgeon from Baltimore, Captain Patrick Kennedy of the Maryland regiment.[38] Interestingly, Sergeant Matthews's account states that there were 'The volunteers, with a few regulars and Indians.'[39] Perhaps indicating an additional element of the Florida Royal Volunteers.

At almost exactly the same time, Gálvez was questioning two deserters, which Deans indicates were Marylanders, and was being told that Campbell and his officers continued to prepare to defend themselves to the last extremity.

One hour later a flurry of shots was heard from the direction whence the *cazadores* had gone, and almost at the same time a report reached Gálvez that the British were felling trees for use in extending the advanced redoubt. This was exactly what he did not want and could not allow. Four companies of *cazadores* and two field guns were stood to arms and within the hour were hurrying towards the scene of the week's fighting. 'The troop proceeded to the place where the trees were being felled,' wrote Saavedra in his journal, 'and the advance parties discovered the beginnings of a parapet that was on a line with the terrain where our parallels had been drawn. Some cannons had

35   Baker, 'Combat Diary', p.190.
36   Cusachs, 'Diary of the Operations', p.69.
37   Baker, 'Combat Diary', p.190.
38   New, *Maryland Loyalists*, pp.48–49.
39   Claiborne, *Mississippi*, vol.1, p.126.

already been mounted there, and more than 200 men and some Indians were in position to defend this post.'[40]

It was about 10:00 p.m. when the Spanish came in sight, at which time the two field pieces in the new earthwork opened fire. This was returned by the Spanish pieces, and the shooting soon became general and continued for about an hour and a half. It is indicated that whoever was in command, and no one is specifically named, now lost sight of his objective to cover the work of the engineers and to harass the enemy and instead pressed to storm the works then under construction. As usual the British allied warriors were quick off the mark and with unerring precision swiftly found a flank to attack. Men began to fall as they pushed ahead, and despite casualties, the Spanish might well have secured their objective except that as soon as they presented a clear target, the guns of the Advanced Redoubt were able to target them, as where the field howitzers. 'One of the interpreters says' noted Farmar, 'that 3 shells from the howitzer[s] burst in the centre of a column and that the enemy had a party of men to carry off the dead & wounded.'[41]

The advance faltered under a hail of grape and musketry. After two hours of fighting a senior officer, who Miranda called 'General del Caso', was informed that they were suffering casualties and rode out to see for himself. The only staff officer to be found with a name even approaching this is one, *Coronel* Baron du Kassel, who was one of Gálvez 's senior aides de camp and was attached to the Regimiento de Flandes.[42] However, the only other Spanish general present was Cagigal. Whoever it was, the troops were recalled upon an evaluation of the engagement, and the effect of the British artillery. Miranda's diary includes a summary of the results:

> At 6 in the afternoon the said companies retired and the enemy remained in the woods, apparently constructing a redoubt which enfiladed jointly the parallel line marked out by our engineers, I do not know if it was because of this event or that two Germans of our foreign troops having deserted in the afternoon, but when the troops and officer of the previous day were already formed for going out after dusk to repeat the operation of the previous day an order came for everyone to retire, and nothing was done that night. Others pretended that this change was the result of the engineer-in-chief having explained that his plan of attack was imperfect, revoked it, and would not be responsible for the success of an attack in that direction.[43]

How accurate Miranda was can be gauged from Miró's entry in the Headquarters journal, where he reported that grapeshot had killed four men and wounded 12, including, specifically a French officer in the Regimiento de Guadalajara named *Teniente* Don Francisco Casteron. 'This fire continued until 12:30. At dark it was decided to begin the entrenchment but due to

---

40   Topping (ed.), *Journal of Saavedra*, pp.160–161.

41   Padgett, 'Farmar's Journal', p.323

42   Robert Churchill, *S.A.R. Spanish Records, Spanish-English War, 1779-1783: Men under Gen. Don Bernardo de Gálvez and other records from the Archives of the Indies, Seville, Spain* (Washington: Daughters of the American Revolution Library, 1926), vol.II, p.416.

43   Worcester, 'Miranda's Diary', p.181.

the desertion of a soldier from Luciana [Louisiana] it was suspended. It was observed at dark that there were Indians in the trees, perhaps to observe the activities of the camp.'[44]

In the British camp more warriors arrived during the afternoon, this time from the Chickasaw nation, 54 men came in with, John Colbert. The newcomers arrived just in time to witness the return of the war parties involved in the days skirmish. 'The Indians came about 2 o'clock and brought a great number of scalps, firelocks and bayonets.'[45]

The great number alluded to is of course difficult to ascertain beyond what the Spanish admitted to, Farmar heard that two deserters from the Irish brigade had come in and reported 100 killed and wounded, whereas Deans reported that three scalps were brought in, and that three bodies were discovered on the field. Eager to be useful, the newly arrived Colbert took his Chickasaws out to the Barrancas Coloradas with ammunition for the garrison, and as none of the Spaniards mention killing or capturing them, it must be presumed they were successful.

Saturday 28 April

Dean said that the 28th was taken up with routine work that seemed to keep the navy carpenters and armourers constantly occupied, but Farmar added, 'About ½ after 11 o'clock three deserters came from the enemy – one of them belonged to the 16th & one to the Provincials who inform the General that great number of them would desert [the Spanish] if the General would forgive and agree upon a signal which was to fire three guns at 12 o'clock which was complied with.'[46]

The Spanish mention no more desertions than three through the whole day.

Even at daybreak Gálvez, Miranda and Saavedra could see the freshly constructed redoubt built on the site of the skirmish the previous day. Campbell's willingness to contest the entrenching ground and Gálvez 's wish to reduce casualties, whether due to illness, humanity, or both, was certainly working for the British. So, Gálvez ordered the engineers to seek out a position from which their own artillery could suppress that of the British, and cover the position selected for the intended attack. He even allowed Cagigal to make a plan to bombard the works from the sea if necessary. Meanwhile a party of 200 workers and three companies of *cazadores* were dispatched to find or drive an alternate road to the one they had been using to reach the principal ground.

> Effectively they found a road, sufficiently clear and suitable for the purpose, which the hauling of wood and other uses had formed previously. They made their reconnaissance without being molested by the enemy who, believing undoubtedly that our attack would be by the upper part, in which we had previously made

---

44   Baker, 'Combat Diary', p.190.
45   Padgett, 'Farmar's Journal', p.323.
46   Padgett, 'Farmar's Journal', p.323.

repeated observations and so forth, waited for us in the woods toward where the port could be seen. They had been hauling artillery [there] since morning.[47]

Both the engineers and the workers did their tasks swiftly, so that by the late afternoon, two companies of grenadiers could be posted at the site of the new battery. Once again it was thought best for the construction to be undertaken during the night. At this time the work being carried out was a one-to-two-mile stretch of trench and a covered way, marked on Heldring's map as following the natural line of the ridge opposite Fort George.

> At 10:15 the work began without being observed despite the clarity of the moon and the natural noise of the shovels with no misfortune other than one or more soldiers being injured by shovels while hurriedly digging. The distance of the entrenchment from the camp is something like 500 *toises* and to the enemy forts, something like 400. There are 555 men working tonight.[48]

The Regulations of 1768 were very firm on how working parties were to conduct themselves: 'The Workers appointed to open a Trench, will always conduct themselves with order and silence, they will march United to where the Engineer leads them, and from the moment they are posted, their Officers will watch with incessant attention to the importance of advancing the work, and covering themselves promptly.'[49] The instructions as to the method of guarding and defending a covered way, were also followed to the letter.

> The Trench Guard will be assembled at the time set by the General of the Army: The incoming Troops will march in order, and without any noise: when they have relieved their post, the Soldiers will sit on the firing step. They will have their muskets straight in front of them with the butt resting on the ground, and the sentinels will carefully observe the movements of the besieged … The Trench Officers will take care that it is kept clean by forcing the Soldiers to go to the common places. All the fascines, gabions, baskets … and stakes, will be made similar to the models that have been given; and when they are not, the Major of the Trench, or the engineer commissioned for their receipt, will reuse them: the regiments that have taken them, will be obliged to make others, without payment, and the officer in charge of that work will be punished for his lack of care. The time of Peace will be part of the instruction of the Infantry to carry out the aforementioned works, and earthworks with perfection, and brevity.[50]

Gálvez had the satisfaction of hearing from Nava, about an hour later that the work had been completed with the laying of 350 fascines in the works, without being discovered. Girón was duly sent to take command and soon a report came back that the troops were in place and under cover of the new works.

---

47   Worcester, 'Miranda's Diary', p.182.
48   Baker, 'Combat Diary', p.190. About 800 men were detailed as a guard.
49   Anon, *Ordenanzas de 1768*, Tomo I, pp.221–222.
50   Anon, *Ordenazas de 1768*, Tomo I, pp.222–223.

A 1781, 'Plan of the Port of Pensacola and the marches, encampments and attacks of the Spanish Troops Commanded by Mariscal de Camp Bernardo de Gálvez . . .' Note the prominent route of the *Gálveston*.

Key: 1: Town & Old Fort of Pensacola. 2: Fort George and its two advanced batteries. 3: Freshwater stream called San Miguel. 4: The Second Bayou (Bayou Chico). 5: The Mores Estuary (Bayou Grande). 7: Encampments of the Spanish Troops. 8: Marches dotted in black. 9: Attacks. 10: Outer Redoubts of the Encampments. 11: Two cannons that drove away the British Frigates. 12: Fort Barrancas Coloradas. (Courtesy, William L. Clements Library, University of Michigan Library Digital Collections)

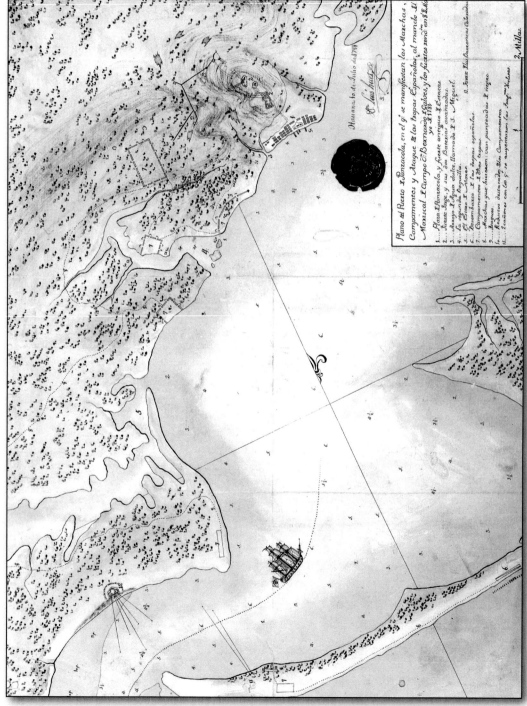

11

The Last Extremity
(29 April–8 May)

Sunday 29 April

'On the night of the 28th the enemy were discovered at work on a Hill bearing nearly due West of the advanced Redoubt,' reported Campbell to New York,

> distant therefrom about three quarters of a mile, and on being reconnoitred were found to be in Force; next morning proved a little foggy, but on it is Clearing off, it was perceived the Enemy had in the Course of the night made an Intrenchment of about one mile in Length, and already Sufficiently deep to cover them from our cannon – a heavy Fire – from our Artillery however obliged them to desist from their work during the day, But which they resumed toward Evening.[1]

Farmar recorded the implications for this deft bit of misdirection, 'About 1 o'clock p.m. our advanced picquet was obliged to retire near the advanced redoubt as the enemy had got some 9 and 12 pounders upon their flanks, fired from the fort and the two redoubts several shot and shells during the day & night at the enemy's works.'[2] Ominously for the British, Deans observed the enemy using their new found impetus throughout the day in, 'throwing up works in two places in front of the advanced redoubt. Brought the heavy guns to bear upon them. Kept annoying them from the fort & redoubts.'[3]

Miranda believed the achievement to be nothing short of miraculous and thought this was due to the sandy soil being soft and devoid of large rocks. Miró, ever more concerned with getting to the point, made an efficient summary.

> When the enemy became aware of the work that had been done in the night, they began to fire cannon, following with mortar fire and grenades from the circular

---

1   TNA: PRO 30/55/89: Campbell to Clinton, 12 May 1781.
2   Padgett, 'Farmar's Journal', p.323.
3   Servies (ed.), *Log of the Mentor*, p.181.

fort and [there was] some [fire] from the opposite side with 22-pounder cannon that we defended with four small cannon placed to the left of the entrenchment. They made mortar, grenade and cannon fire until 7:30 in the morning with the object of disturbing the work of the battery. It commenced with four mortars and six 24-pounder cannons, resulting all day in not more than three wounded and one killed.[4]

The Spanish, of course did more than just shelter and beam proudly at their earth and timber marvel, as Gálvez said in his report to Madrid,

> On the 29th at four o'clock in the morning the laborers were relieved to perfect the trench and continue the opening of the covered road. At six o'clock the enemy observed the work that had been done and began to fire cannons and mortars to annoy us; and several parties of them who approached to explore the trench with two field pieces were vigorously repulsed with two others that were placed at the head and tail of it. At half past eleven the fire of the enemy stopped, probably to cool their artillery. At eight o'clock at night 800 men-[under]-arms left the Camp to relieve those in the trench, and 600 to begin the construction of a battery of 6 cannons of 24 and several mortars, that it was proposed to make on a height suitable for the purpose of diverting the enemies' fire, whilst another was being constructed closer. 600 men were also destined to continue the trench and to construct two redoubts to the right and left of it for its defence.[5]

At midday the general staff had come to inspect the works, and were allowed to do so unmolested, Saavedra was amongst them, and he recorded everything he saw.

> The trench was about 1,000 *toises* distant from our camp. It must have been about 350 *toises* in length, and it comprised two galleries. The troop was sheltered perfectly, and the work demonstrated the diligence of those who had done it. It would have been unattainable even with a force of twice as many sappers if sandy soil had not spared them many difficulties. I also examined where the first battery was to be placed. Some people there said that it was little more than 300 *toises* distant from Fort Half Moon and 500 *toises* from fort George. It appeared to me that the distance from both was much greater and that it was at least 500 *toises* from the former and 700 form the latter. The terrain was deceptive because there was a ravine midway between the trench and the forts, and experience proved later that it had indeed misled the calculations of the experts.[6]

As the day ended, the British batteries growled to life in a slow and measured bombardment of shot and shell until 1:00 a.m.

---

4   Baker, 'Combat Diary', pp.190–191. Grenades in this context refers to explosive artillery shells.
5   Cusachs, 'Diary of the Operations', p.70.
6   Topping (ed.), *Journal of Saavedra*, pp.162–163. A *toise* is 1.95 metres.

Monday 30 April

Campbell was of the opinion that the days between 28 April and 1 May were decisive ones.

> Next morning it appeared they had carried on throughout the night with redoubled Vigour, for at Break of Day a Battery was to be seen on the Right of their Intrenchment in great Forewardness [*sic*] both for mortars and cannon – and the Right of the whole again protected by a Square Redoubt. Our Fire this morning cause[d] them for some Time to give over working but after a little cessation they again resumed their work under cover, and unremittingly continued at labour the reminder of the Day and the ensuing night so that their Battery Appeared next morning the 1st of May Complete.[7]

According to Farmar the Spanish advanced picquet was driven in that morning and a prisoner was taken by some of the allies. It was with great difficulty that the warriors were persuaded to give him up. The firing of shot and shells into the Spanish work continued through the morning, and later in the day, a ration of tobacco was given out to the company of the *Mentor*. Matthews also recalled, 'This morning our field pieces were advanced beyond the upper redoubt, and for three hours from the fort and our batteries we kept up a heavy cannonade, which was replied to. The Choctaws brought in a prisoner, who was ransomed by Gen. Campbell.'[8] On the Spanish side, the third officer to command the trenches, *Coronel* Ezpeleta took his post, and was present through the bombardment and the fire of the war-parties who engaged the new positions.

> Some parties of savages came through the nearby woods toward our camp and covered by them they fired on our advanced positions. The latter answered them immediately with field pieces and [muskets] and they retreated after having mortally wounded a soldier in our camp who was resting in his tent. From here they retreated under cover of the woods to the shores of the bay where our launches come through to unload whatever they have on board. And surprising 6 sailors who negligently were fishing on the opposite side of the swamp, they killed them or carried them away as prisoners.[9]

In the headquarters journal the usually restrained Miró was positively loquacious, recording that the bombardment had wounded a *teniente* of the Regimiento de Luisiana, and that enemy warriors had killed a soldier of the 2ª Cataluña that day, but the most interesting thing he recorded related to the early skirmish in which the British had gained possession of a map,

7   TNA: PRO 30/55/89: Campbell to Clinton, 12 May 1781.
8   Claiborne, *Mississippi*, vol.1, p.126.
9   Worcester, 'Miranda's Diary', p.183.

At 11 they ceased firing and the Battery began the construction of esplanades and a platform completing the interior of the same. A soldier deserter of the enemy has come and says that they believed that the reason for the entrenchment activity was to persuade them that the attack would come from the other side [of the defences], as [was] indicated in a document [that they] found at the foot of a tree, which described in rough draft the direction of one part of the assaults, lost deliberately by the Volunteer Engineer Don Gilberto Gilman with some sketches of the location of the *Pino Gordo*, which was situated exactly where the last redoubt was constructed.[10]

When this entry was cleaned up to be send to Madrid there was no mention of the place called Pino Gordo as being the spot where the fighting had taken place earlier in April, nor of the subterfuge of leaving a map for the British to find. However, the pine tree in question was notable enough to attract notice, and so might be what the Spanish were calling the site of the intended redoubt. As to the map, if this was done, then volunteer engineer Gilman's attempted misdirection was never brought to the attention of Gálvez, or anyone else as the days of struggle to complete groundwork, and daily casualties amply testify. Saavedra reported that the British allied warriors had attacked the camp at 10:00 a.m.:

… some parties of savages approached within half a musket shot of our camp, and under cover of the thickets of the forest they opened fire on the advanced posts. The latter responded at once with artillery, and the savages retired, after having mortally wounded a soldier inside his one tent. From there the savages, concealed by the forest, went to the banks of the creek by which launches came into the camp. They surprised four sailors who were loitering carelessly and killed and scalped them.[11]

Now that the Spanish fortifications were finally started, the sappers were constantly at work improving the defences, the French Cannoniers de Brest and the Spanish artillery were soon to become extremely busy, and it was no longer a case of occupying or denying the ground but a race as to who could fortify faster.

Tuesday 1 May

From the late morning the rumble of artillery fire, delivered steadily and with care, was now the backdrop to the working parties of both sides. The British noted with concern that the enemy works had been considerably enlarged by the sappers. Farmar counted three guns mounted, and seven embrasures cut, with more being worked on, they would not have fire superiority for much longer. Throughout the day the Spanish continued to work, trying to ignore the shriek of iron overhead, quite aware that every few hours or so

---

10   Baker, 'Combat Diary', p.191. *'Pino gordo'* means fat, or large, pine.
11   Topping (ed.), *Journal of Saavedra*, p.163.

some poor soul was struck down by shell fragments. At some point in the morning, British allied warriors approached the camp through the forest, and 'the mulattoes and negroes of Louisiana, who are famous marksmen, went out against them and frightened them away; nonetheless, they killed a sailor who was bathing in the creek.'[12] At 3:00 p.m., Gálvez visited the trenches and was escorted by a naval officer, as Francisco de Longoria who was meant to have been in command that day was mortally ill, but then 'the fire quickened as never before, killing a French artilleryman and wounding two,' which prompted the general to order a cessation of work until dark. However, the firing 'continued immoderately all night, killing a soldier and wounding seven.'[13]

Saavedra reported that on this day, 'The *banquette* of the trench was completed, as well as the parapet and esplanades of the battery, in which six bronze 24-caliber cannons and four mortars were placed that night.'[14] To which were added two 8-pounders and two 12-pounders.

Wednesday 2 May

The monotonous thump of the British artillery continued through the night and beyond the hours of dawn but despite the sprays of sandy soil tossed by the solid shot and the crash of the shells exploding in the trees, Gálvez and his staff rode out and took up a position to the right of the encampment where a house belonging to a Mr Ucell stood, midway between the town and the finished battery. *Mariscal de campo* Cagigal continued to the bay in a frigate to observe from the water. Dismounting at a convenient grove of trees, and covered by a company of light infantry, Gálvez could watch the play of the guns.

In the new battery the big 24-pounder barrels were softy gleaming under the overcast sky, the artillerymen waited in their positions, slow-matches smouldering on the linstocks as British iron intermittently howled overhead. At 9:00 a.m., Gálvez gave the signal, the colours of Spain were raised above the parapet, the crimson ragged cross of burgundy plain to be seen in the south westerly breeze, and the command was given to fire the first shots. It was a fine start, and it was common to commence a bombardment with some pomp, but the effect was not terribly dramatic, nor was the damage, save for the one man of the 16th killed and five men wounded (three of whom were sailors), in return for three Spaniards wounded and one dead. Campbell and the garrison noted that the solid shot was directed towards the advanced redoubt, and that mortars occasionally lobbed shells against Fort George and the middle or Prince of Wales's redoubt.

---

12 Topping (ed.), *Journal of Saavedra*, p.164. These will be the *Pardos* and *Morenos*, whose companies of grenadiers and *cazadores* from Havana and New Orleans might possibly have been grouped together during the siege.
13 Baker, 'Combat Diary', p.191.
14 Topping (ed.), *Journal of Saavedra*, p.164.

Saavedra's gloomy presentiments about the distance to the British works would seem to have been accurate and it was noted that the new battery could be targeted from two sides, by the half-moon battery and Fort George. In the afternoon the quartermaster and engineers went to trace out the continuation of the trench and extend it to Pino Gordo, and up to a point '250 *toises* from the half-moon'. Here a much stronger battery was envisaged. As night settled 1,600 soldiers and labourers went out to begin work. By midnight, working parties and guards were in position and performing their duties, while the British were occupied rebuilding their parapet.[15]

In addition to the new battery, the communications from the camp to both could not be ignored either,

> At night they [the British] have suspended fire doubtlessly with the object of repairing their merlons since we are sure that they have some damage to their parapets from our recent heavy fire. One [company] left to continue [digging] a connecting road to the entrenchment toward the defences of Fort George so as to establish a battery. The sound of the working parties could be heard through the night in the British lines.[16]

Thursday 3 May

Campbell was now faced with rapidly expanding enemy works, being progressed by a level of manpower he was unable to match, and though for now his artillery had the range, they would soon be outgunned. He therefore determined to launch an attack:

> On the night between the 2d and 3d the Enemy being discovered to have advanced their approaches as far as the hill in Front of the advanced Redoubt, I had projected a joint attack of the few regular troops we could spare and of the Indians. The Regulars (after a heavy Fire from our Artillery) to attack in flank while the Indians attacked the Enemy's Rear; But the Regulars and Indians in making the necessary Detour having lost one another, the attack was obliged to be recalled on the 3rd and the ensuing night the enemy used such diligence in forwarding their works notwithstanding the interruption from our Shot and Shell that by Day Light of the 4th their Line of intrenchments was Completed and a regular Redoubt finished on their left flank at the Distance of Merely six hundred yards from the advanced Redoubt on which there were no cannon as yet mounted. [17]

Though they did not yet have the range, the Spanish and French gunners fired 534 shot and 186 shells during the day, 'they killed one man of the 16th & wounded one of the seamen belonging to the Port Royal, and one

---

15 Topping (ed.), *Journal of Saavedra*, pp.164–165.
16 Baker, 'Combat Diary', pp.191–192.
17 TNA: PRO 30/55/89: Campbell to Clinton, 12 May 1781.

man of the 16th, but did very little damage otherwise. At night we repaired the work at the advanced Redoubt and worked at the counter battery on the right wing.'[18] Deans observed that: 'At 11 the enemy advanced in a large body towards our outer works and took possession of a rising ground in front of the advanced redoubt. AM, the enemy throwing up works on ditto. The advanced redoubt and SW battery continually cannonading each other. Several shells thrown from the enemy's bomb battery into the lines of Fort George.'[19]

Gálvez was now in the habit of visiting the trenches in the afternoon, where he would speak with the officer of the day, inspect progress, and see what needed his personal attention. He was a popular officer, who believed in letting the men see him and sharing their dangers in so much as was possible for a commander-in-chief. Ezpeleta too made a great impression, and *Sargento* Manuel Ozcoydi of the Regimiento de Navarra recalled that 'the only general on the scene during the siege was Ezpeleta.' Though it is not represented elsewhere, and Ozcoydi may well have been flattering a superior officer. He also suggested that Ezpeleta took the lead in progressing the siege after 30 April.[20]

Gálvez had received exaggerated news from the daily trickle of deserters that the mortar shells were doing damage in the fort. In Miró's tally of the day, it was clear that the artillery duel was becoming serious.

> There was fire all last night and it was observed that they had done some work on their fortifications and also the repair of their merlons that had been damaged. Our entrenchment was built with a branch … toward the left in order to establish the battery. Firing began with shot and bombs by the enemy which they continued all day, resulting in eight wounded and one dead. Our battery of cannons and mortars have fired and according to information from deserters it was concluded that we had done some damage [21]

Deans's log was grim 'One of the Port Royal's men got his leg shot off and a soldier of the 16th Regiment wounded in the arm. The enemy still continuing the approaches in front of the advanced redoubt and a heavy cannonade from their battery. The man belonging to the Port Royal who was wounded is since dead.'[22]

As usual work continued during the night, and in the morning, Campbell having been unable to launch an attack to impede the extensions of the Spaniards the previous day, and concerned his own fresh works would soon be made redundant, organised another attempt to bring the fight to the enemy.

18   Padgett, 'Farmar's Journal', p.324.
19   Servies (ed.), *Log of the Mentor*, p,183.
20   Rojas, *Ezpeleta at Pensacola*, p.121.
21   Baker, 'Combat Diary', p.192.
22   Servies (ed.), *Log of the Mentor*, p.183.

Friday 4 May

At dawn the British cannons were warming up for the day as part of their usual routine where they would bombard the enemy works until the barrels started to become hot, and they were then forced to reduce the rate of fire. It was also quite common for either side to send out parties to collect shot and unexploded shells to fire back. In the dim light of dawn, which given the lack of any noted change in the log of the *Mentor*, must have once again been overcast, the second in command of the trenches, *Capitán* Don Andrés Tacón of the navy thought he caught a blur of movement from the enemy fortifications which he interpreted to be groups of soldiers moving into the woods. Having decided he had seen an enemy movement he reported this to the officer of the day, Don Pablo de Figuerola, who did not assign any importance to it.

At 10:00 a.m., the guns of the British batteries began to slow, perhaps in anticipation of midday, which would heat the pieces faster, and then ceased firing. Then, curiously, an hour and a half later, the bombardment resumed. Miranda recorded:

> At 12:30 the enemy began a lively fire of mortars, cannons, and howitzers over the Queen's redoubt and works to the left of our parallel, which attracted the attention of as many of us as heard it in the camp, but not so the commanders and chiefs of the trenches, who had started to eat. They believed themselves as safe and out of risk as in the *plaza mayor* of Madrid. The rapidity and good accuracy of the enemy fire forced our unwise and inexperienced troops to remain under cover of their entrenchment, not taking any more risks than those which could come from the artillery, and under this concept only two sentinels remained exposed on the left side observing the enemy movements toward the Queen's redoubt, facing the place from which the enemy fire was coming.[23]

The result of this was that, in the words of Saavedra: '200 chosen men were assembled in that spot [to the left of the works], where they remained hidden until noon, when the troop was eating, when the sun was very powerful in that climate, the hour they judged most opportune for a surprise attack.'[24] Campbell's troops had done well and had also been lucky that Figuerola had been so complacent as to order his troops to stack their weapons, and that according to Saavedra, no one had noticed the British had not been firing shot after the first discharge. Campbell told Clinton that he 'sent out 120 men of the Pennsylvania Loyalists Maryland Loyalists and dismounted Dragoons under the Command of Major [John] MacDonald to make the attack and about 80 men of the 3d Regiment of Waldeck under the Command of Lieutenant Colonel de Horn of that corps to surprise them [the Spanish].'[25]

Among the Loyalists and Germans was William Augustus Bowles, who must have elected to serve with his regiment after being reinstated.

23   Worcester, 'Miranda's Diary', p.185.
24   Topping (ed.), *Journal of Saavedra*, p.166.
25   TNA: PRO 30/55/89: Campbell to Clinton, 12 May 1781.

Interestingly there is no mention of any warriors being present in the sortie, which may well represent the results of an exodus from the allied camp making fewer allies available, and so it would be the work of the bayonet rather than the hatchet and knife. Preoccupied with keeping their heads down was the grenadier company of the Regimeinto de Mallorca, and half a company of the Regimiento de Hibernia. Despite having two sentinels up, their attention was drawn to the enemy forts as MacDonald and Von Horn led their raiders out of the trees and began doubling towards the flank of the earthwork. When the Loyalists and Germans were 40 yards away the Majorcans, who were closest to the enemy, awoke to their danger. Shouts of alarm and musket shots spurred the attackers into a run and in a moment, they were over the parapet.

What followed was a blur of violence. The calls of their officers and NCOs were quickly cut short, as the Majorcans, unable to react quickly enough, had no choice but to run or surrender. Most of the officers and sergeants fell to multiple stab wounds, while dozens of men, caught in the press and left behind, called for quarter, which the British officers found very difficult to get their men to honour as their blood was up. The Majorcan grenadiers were driven through the works, pursued by Waldeck and Loyalist bayonets, and ran into the Hibernians, screaming 'We are lost! We are bayonetted.'[26]

Sergeant Matthews gave a brief summary of the attack with evident satisfaction.

A detachment of Pennsylvania and Maryland loyalists, with the light horse and the Waldekers and some volunteers, marched out to storm the enemy's entrenchments. Under cover of a heavy fire from our upper redoubt, we were almost upon them before they discovered us. A panic ensued. We dashed at them with the bayonet, drove them out of their works, spiked their cannon, burnt their fascines and cotton sacks, and killed forty or fifty. We had one ensign killed, and a corporal and fifteen men wounded.[27]

'All the troops on guard were terror-stricken,' wrote Saavedra. 'The enemy overran the trench up to the redoubt at the angle of the two galleries, where they spiked four cannons and burned the couplings and fascines, then retired, carrying off as prisoners three officers, all gravely wounded.'[28]

The panic spread down the line to the companies of marine infantry, but by this point the Loyalists and Waldeckers had relented in their pursuit, and were setting about spiking guns, burning carriages and fascines, and looting the dead and wounded.

Upon hearing of the attack, Gálvez ordered Ezpeleta to take four or five companies of *cazadores* and secure the position, but it is likely Ezpeleta had already set off. Though he wasted no time there was little else to do but put out the fires and clear away the bodies, as the enemy had withdrawn with their spoils to the cheers of their comrades in the works. It had been an

---

26 Worcester, 'Miranda's Diary', p.187.
27 Claiborne, *Mississippi*, vol.1, p.126.
28 Topping (ed.), *Journal of Saavedra*, p.166.

audacious sortie and well conducted, unusually for the period the Loyalists and Waldeckers seemed only too eager to make use of their bayonets. Saavedra reported 20 dead and 'as many wounded' which roughly tallied with Miranda's estimation of 35–40 casualties.[29]

The British lost two men; a subaltern of the Waldeck Regiment was killed by a cannon ball, presumably as they were retreating, and a sergeant of the Provincials was killed as he entered the battery. One Royal Forrester was wounded and one Waldeck NCO similarly.[30] Most of the captured officers and NCOs did not survive their wounds, doubtless being the men who were best armed when the enemy struck, they were left abandoned by their men and run through until they fell. Miranda heard that *Teniente* O'Daly of the Hibernia had his arm amputated at Fort George but died an hour later.

Gálvez's response to this was to instruct Cagigal to form a flying column and to ensure that there were never less than three companies on duty at the advanced post at any time. Gálvez had the dead buried solemnly at a spot which faced the British entrenchments, and after speaking a few words, returned to the business at hand.

Thousands of 1752 and 1757 Model muskets were sold to the Americans and shipped to western depots via New Orleans. This 1757 pattern was in use by the Spanish regular army at Pensacola, and many of the Southern Nations as well. (Plate from Morla's *Tratado de Artillería*, 1784)

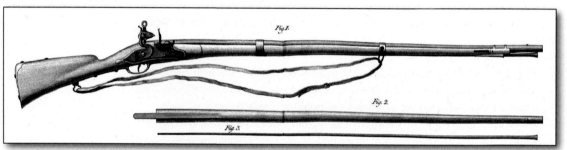

Saturday 5 May

At 9:30 a.m., the commander of the trenches, Don Pablo Figuerola was placed under arrest pending a court of enquiry into his apparent negligence, which Girón would prosecute. Meanwhile repairs had to be made to the redoubt at Pine Hill, and the Spanish artillery had to keep up the bombardment. However, 'The enemy fire has been lively and well-directed. We had 9 dead and 11 wounded … A wall was constructed of cotton bales and sand bags over the left wing of our parallel to cover the workers and to shelter the construction of the battery and cannons laid out before.'[31]

That night the wind rose, and a storm blew which flooded the camp and the trench, putting a stop to the work. Deans reported 'heavy rain which continued till ½ past 4, a.m., during which time it swept great quantity of sand from the covered way into the ditch and undermined the fort in several

29   Topping (ed.), *Journal of Saavedra*, p.167.
30   Padgett, 'Farmar's Journal', pp.324–325.
31   Worcester, 'Miranda's Diary', p.186.

places sweeping away the bricks from under the foundations.'[32] Most of the ships of the Franco Spanish fleet had to cut their anchors and avoid running aground. Solano had been planning to send two ships of the line into the bay which would threaten a seaborn bombardment, but the storm forced him to abandon the plan and head out to sea. He sent word ashore that he would be back as soon as the wind permitted.

Sunday 6 May

When the Spanish finally found the range of the fortifications it told. Farmar recorded that at 'about ½ after 9 o'clock the enemy began to fire from two mortars [elsewhere identified as howitzers] they had in their work in the front of advanced redoubt the shot and shell fired from the enemy during the day amount to 563 shot and 206 shells.'[33] Three men were incapacitated by one and 'as one of the seamen belonging to the Port Royal was picking up the shot fired from the enemy a 24lb ball struck him in the britch and buried itself in his flesh – he lived after it about five hours.'[34] This destructive fire was very damaging to the advanced redoubt and dismounted three field pieces, all of which had to be repaired during the night. Amid this heavy fire, some warriors brought in a deserter from the Pennsylvania Loyalists to Fort George. According to Farmar the man was convicted very swiftly and sentenced to 500 lashes which were inflicted that day. Neither Deans nor Campbell mention the deserter or the trial.

Campbell was mostly concerned with laying down effective counter fire where it was of most use 'on the night of the 6th two Embrasures were shut up in the Body of the advanced Redoubt that pointed towards the enemy's first Battery, both on account of the Security of our own men, and because we found our Cannon against that Battery of little Prejudice to the Enemy – Any material Damage done within the Day was completely repaired during the night.'[35]

Deans spotted a new piece of artillery at play which helped cause the damage. 'The enemy mounted a mortar on their advanced work and threw several shells into our advanced redoubt. Two seamen at the advanced redoubt wounded by the bursting of a shell.'[36]

At 5:00 a.m., the Spanish had inspected the damage to their camp done by the storm. 'There was not a single bed that was not made into soup because all the tents were rotten.' The troops worked up to their waists in water repairing the trenches. A scouting party from the Chataes went out to investigate a rumour that the Barrancas Coloradas had been abandoned, but it proved false. Saavedra wrote in his journal, 'I have never in my life heard such terrifying claps of thunder. The rain penetrated my tent even

---

32 Servies (ed.), *Log of the Mentor*, p.185.
33 Padgett, 'Farmar's Journal', p.325.
34 Padgett, 'Farmar's Journal', p.325.
35 TNA: PRO 30/55/89: Campbell to Clinton, 12 May 1781.
36 Servies (ed.), *Log of the Mentor*, p.184.

though the fabric was double, and all night long, I was soaked in water and stiff with cold.'[37]

Once again, accurate fire from the British batteries was proving a credible deterrent to the prosecution of the siege, as four grenadier officers were killed that afternoon. Saavedra had a long talk with the commander in chief, and

> the general told me of the great difficulty in which he found himself and the enterprise he had planned. In Havana he had been given a very scant supply of cannonballs, and already there were so few remaining of the 24-caliber balls, which were the ones he needed most, that there were not enough to supply the batteries for two consecutive days. Almost all the cannon-balls fired by the enemy were gathered up; the soldiers were paid two *reales* for each brought in, but this did not make up the shortage.[38]

With the fleet at sea, he could not draw on their more ample stores as he had hitherto. Gálvez was therefore determined to try and storm the half-moon battery that very night. The chiefs of the departments and senior officers met at midnight, and between 12:30 and 1:00 a.m., the assault force moved out towards Pino Gordo.

Monday 7 May

Miró, though not noting Gálvez's anxiety to shorten the siege did record that the assault did not go to plan.

> Don Geronimo Girón went out with 800 men under orders to assault the fort called the Half Moon with everything needed to take it and burn it. This operation did not take place for contrary orders were given very close to the instant for the beginning of the action. There commenced work in the entrenchment to carry out cotton [bales] and bags for dirt to construct a shelter for the battery that would fire on this fort, which is considered the principal one, to force surrender by the remainder.[39]

More specifically, this aborted attack was to consist of Girón's 800 men, including 100 French *chasseurs* commanded by *monsieur* Amarithon, equipped with axes, ladders and other equipment, led by a deserter who had offered his services earlier in the siege, and divided into three groups. However, Girón found the moon to be very bright, and Miranda said that the time of the attack had not been fixed properly, so the spearhead was still under cover at 3:00 a.m., when Ezpeleta arrived with the reserve. Both officers then reported to Gálvez that as it was almost daylight, the chances of attacking undiscovered were now too low to progress and the attack was called off.

---

37 Topping (ed.), *Journal of Saavedra*, p.168.
38 Topping (ed.), *Journal of Saavedra*, pp.168–169.
39 Baker, 'Combat Diary', p.193.

Two hours after dawn, unaware of how close they had come to a storm of Bourbon bayonets, the artillerymen in the Queen's Redoubt were making fuses. Both sides' artillery was engaged, with the British especially aiming for the new works. It was dangerous, for not only were the materials vulnerable to being hit generally, but it happened that there were a number of loaded shells lying around alongside a quantity of loose powder. Deans wrote that these were contained in an artillery cart, and Farmar that it was a box, but in either event the Spanish had begun firing, and one of their shells found it, which blew the ammunition up and ignited one of the discarded British ones which burst on the ground. One of the Waldeck Regiment was killed and another wounded. Unknown to all at that moment, it was an ominous precursor.

News came from deserters that the Spanish were running out of supplies. A noon the Pennsylvania Loyalist deserter who had been flogged was drummed out of his regiment with his hands tied behind him and large sign pinned to his breast with his crime. The man was taken close to the Spanish works and left there, but apparently soon returned to the British camp. 'The whole of the Indians went out about ½ past 12 o'clock to endeavour to get upon the rear of the enemy's encampment, they would not suffer a white man to go with them, they returned in a short time with ten scalps.'[40] The enemy fire was as pestering and destructive as the previous day. 'About 2 o'clock p.m. a shell from the enemy's flank battery came in at a window of one of the barrack rooms of the advanced redoubt which killed Lieut. Carroll & wounded Capt'n Forster of the 16th Reg't.'[41]

Though the Spanish batteries were becoming more effective, the counter fire was as well. The Spanish and French sappers, engineers, and artillerymen won the admiration of the army for their perseverance under fire to progress the battery opposing the Advanced Redoubt. 'Work was continued all night with great courage and perseverance.'[42] Four or five men were killed and 16 wounded in the course of the day, including those who fell in an attack by the British allied warriors, which Miró described:

At 11:30 the Indians came to fire on the encampment, from which the Militia of Orleans went out in response. They withstood the attack, but three were wounded and two were killed, with the usual cruelty of scalping them and cutting off their ears. Their fire on the entrenchment wounded an officer of the Regiment of the King Don Francisco Conget and 4 soldiers of the same regiment.[43]

According to Miranda, the initial fusillade from the warriors killed one of the soldiers and wounded another, at which time the militia rushed to pursue, 'and killed two (whose scalps they took) and wounded 4.'[44] Miranda likewise reported that the warriors managed to take a prisoner who they intended

40 Padgett, 'Farmar's Journal', pp.325–326.
41 Padgett, 'Farmar's Journal', pp.325–326.
42 Topping (ed.), *Journal of Saavedra*, p.170.
43 Baker, 'Combat Diary', p.193.
44 Worcester, 'Miranda's Diary', pp.190–191.

to torture in revenge for a relative they lost at Mobile, but who was saved by Campbell who paid them off with 200 *pesos* and some rum. We will recall Farmar mentioning briefly that a prisoner was extracted from some warriors on 30 April, and Saavedra mentioning an attack on the camp on 1 May being seen off by the Militia of New Orleans. While that does not mean Miranda, who seems to have compiled his account with the aid of others, has confused this event, Campbell never once mentioning having to ransom a Spanish captive in his complaints about his auxiliaries. Instead, it represents some of the confusions and uncertainties inherent with piecing together six different perspectives.

That evening 60 men of the Provincials under Captain Kearny took charge of the Queen's Redoubt, and the 16th Foot relieved the guard of the camp.

12

All the Banners of America

Fresh breezes from the north had typified the previous day, and it was much the same as the sky began to brighten over the town of Pensacola on 8 May. First through a series of blues and greys, until finally the sun emerged over the far shore and its light strengthened over Deer Point and Santa Rosa.

The British fire was as usual sluggish through the night and with the coming of dawn, accelerated. The Spanish guns returned the compliment. Bourbon troops in the trenches knew well enough they would have three or four hours of serious bombardment to sit through.

At the left-hand battery near Pine Hill, Francisco de Nava; standing with his staff of artificers – Gilabert, and Joaquin de Peramas – was all satisfaction. No military engineer could be insensible to the feeling of accomplishment when finishing a new battery. It reinforced the teachings of Vauban, that in essence the shovel was mightier than the sword. This one, especially, seemed to prove that, as it had been progressed so swiftly and courageously at no little cost in lives, and must have given the chief engineer much to be pleased about when he reported that the platforms had been laid. All that was now needed was the glacis and the mounting of the guns. He expected the eight 24-pounders being prepared for mounting would be able to open fire by noon. When they did so they would be firing from a distance no greater than 530 yards.

Campbell grudgingly agreed that it was impressive work and counted six embrasures so far. He had known for days that this was a most dangerous battery to leave to its own devices. Doubtless he was contemplating his options bearing in mind that, like Gálvez, he was running low on ammunition, and contemplating perhaps another sortie, maybe this time involving the allied warriors. Out at the Advanced Redoubt, the finite resource of gunpowder would have been being doled out to the troops for cartridges. As this would have been a regular duty given the amount of skirmishing occurring every day, no one seems to have thought twice about it, even remembering the explosion of the previous day, as such the door to the powder magazine was opened for the apportioned grains to be issued.

Francisco de Saavedra was anticipating a violent and exciting day, and had asked *Capitán* Don Benito Pardo de Figuerola of the Regimiento de la Corona, a friend of Gálvez, to go out to an advantageous spot from where

The most popular and accomplished contemporary engraving of the Siege of Pensacola showing the devastating explosion of the advanced magazine, note also Gálvez being represented with a sling to show his wound. (Library of Congress)

they could observe the firing of all the batteries. This spot could have been that which Gálvez had chosen previously on the day the first battery opened, or perhaps it was the knoll at Pine Hill.

As to what the other diarists we have been keeping company with were doing is unknown for anything of the normal routines they might have included were blotted out by the explosion.

Gálvez's report to Madrid said it occurred at 8:00 a.m. Campbell and Miró thought it was 8:30. Deans and Farmar reckoned it to be 9:00, with Saavedra vaguely writing that it was a little after that while Miranda thought it closer to 9.30. If we gauge it by the most commonly agreed times, the end of the siege of Fort George came between 8:30 and just after 9:00 a.m. Saavedra and Benito Pardo had just reached their ground. The fire of the two sides seemed to be at its height, with many shells exploding over at the new Spanish battery, in which there were only two howitzers that as yet could return fire. All agree that it was from one of these pieces that the fatal shell was fired, the results of which are best left to the participants.

The three British eyewitnesses viewed the calamity from Fort George. Campbell wrote in his report to Clinton five days later that,

a six inch shell having just skimmed over the Bomb Proof Roof burst directly opposite and close to the Door of the Magazine, and Communicated the Flames to the Powder within; The Explosion whereof in an instant reduced the body of the Redoubt to a heap of Rubbish, whereby 48 Military, 27 Seamen and one

Negro were deprived of life and 24 soldiers and seamen wounded: Two Flank works that had been added since the Commencement of the Siege to the Defence of the Redoubt (Wherein were placed 2 ten and 2 eight inch Mortars 3 eight and 3 five and a half inch Howitzers and four Brass Field Pieces 3 Pounders) still remained entire.[1]

Farmar reported much the same in that,

a shell from the enemys front battery was thrown in at the door of the Magazine at the advanced redoubt, (as the men were receiving powder) which blew it up and killed forty seamen belonging to H.M. ships the Mentor & Port Royal & forty-five men of the Pennsylvania Loyalists were killed by the same explosion there were a number of men wounded besides.[2]

Deans, who it must be admitted might have been closer than the others due to the amount of his men in the forward redoubt, though it is not specified, was struck by progress of the explosion, and he felt that the number of men who were instantly killed, horribly burned, or buried by their own fortifications was much higher.

… the magazine was blown up by a shell from the enemy advanced works. The magazine adjoining the barracks carried the conflagration through the whole redoubt. Near a hundred seamen & soldiers were either blown up or buried in the ruins, amongst whom were a midshipman & 16 seamen killed and 1 wounded belonging to His Majesty's Ship *Mentor*… 13 killed & 8 wounded in the advanced redoubt belonging to His Majesty's Sloop *Port Royal*.[3]

In the Spanish camp, Miranda and de Gálvez heard the explosion clearly, and a sudden flow of officers hurrying to the trenches must have occurred, while the troops peered through the woods from the breastworks of the camp. 'We heard from the camp a great explosion which alarmed us generally without our being able to ascertain the danger,' Miranda wrote. 'The major general [Ezpeleta] went immediately to the section of the trench from which the noise was heard, and we saw a great column of smoke rising toward the clouds.'[4] Saavedra and Benito Pardo had just enough time to register what had happened before haring away to spread the news, 'We ran back to the camp from which the general and the other officers were already emerging because of this remarkable event. They hastily headed for the trench at a quick march, with all the companies of grenadiers and *chasseurs* [*cazadores*].'[5]

---

1   TNA: PRO 30/55/89: Campbell to Clinton, 12 May 1781.
2   Padgett, 'Farmar's Journal', p.325.
3   Servies (ed.), *Log of the Mentor*, p.185.
4   Worcester, 'Miranda's Diary', p.191.
5   Topping (ed.), *Journal of Saavedra*, pp.170–171.

By the time the officers arrived at the trenches, the redoubt was engulfed in flames and continuing to emit explosions. Miró's headquarters journal provides the most detailed description of the sight.

> … it happened that one of the shells from the howitzers in our redoubt set fire to the gunpowder magazine of the Half Moon Fort spreading to the other munitions. Flame was seen to cover it and the planking closest to it, scattering firebrands along the parapet and the stockade, whose ruin from loaded bombs, grenades and barrels of gunpowder killed 105 Englishmen including two exhausted officials who sought refuge in the place.[6]

As soon as it was clear what had happened, Gálvez summoned Girón, Ezpeleta, and Nava, to his side. His orders were clear simple, they were to take all the grenadiers and *cazadores* available, and attack. There was a brief pause while officers raced to bring up as many men as could be found, and there is circumstantial evidence to suggest the Girón's brigade supplied the bulk of the troops, but the columns were swiftly formed. As soon as all was ready, screened by 100 men equipped with tools to break through the ruins and extinguish the fire, the Spanish went forwards at the double. Indeed, they moved so fast that Saavedra used the word impetuous to describe it. Girón and Ezpeleta were Gálvez's lions, his fighting officers, and they did not hesitate in the attack. The king's regulations indeed demanded silence, speed, and audacity. The *Ordenanza de 1768* states that, 'The Officers in charge of attacking a covered way, do not allow their Troops to fire until they are close to the Stockade; and given their discharge, they will jump inside with fearlessness to drive out the enemy: During the attack of the covered way, the batteries must shoot (without ceasing) on the works, which defend them.'[7]

Reeling from the shock, the British nevertheless responded swiftly. In Farmar's account the immediate concern was to get as many guns out or spiked as possible, doubtless to prevent their being instantly turned on the remaining forts, 'Capt. Byrd with seventy men of the 60th regiment immediately went up to the advanced redoubt & brought off 2 field pieces & one howitzer & a number of the wounded men, but was obliged to retire as a great quantity of shell was lying about filled.'[8] Deans substantiated this, and expanded on the sudden passage of troops towards the danger area.

> Immediately after the explosion, the enemy advanced which obliged the few remaining to retreat after spiking up the cannon & bringing off two field pieces. The enemy appeared in a large body on the right of the advanced redoubt but soon withdrew under cover of the ruins, the middle redoubt firing upon them. The enemy kept up a brisk fire from their musquetry & two field pieces upon the middle redoubt which was reinforced from Fort George with an officer & 12 seamen.[9]

---

6   Baker, 'Combat Diary', p.193.
7   Anon, *Ordenanza de 1768*, Tomo I, pp.222–223.
8   Padgett, 'Farmar's Journal', pp.325–326.
9   Servies (ed.), *Log of the Mentor*, p.185.

The breeze, blowing from the north would have blown the smoke from the burning and musketry, along with ash and airborne debris away from the scene of the action, and so both sides would have had a periodically unobstructed view. It was clear that the Franco-Spanish had reacted faster, otherwise Campbell would surely have attempted to hold the ruins, and indeed the Spanish accounts speak of encountering enemy fire as they approached. 'There [was a] lively fire through gunports from those who defended the fort, succeeding in wounding and killing many of us.'[10]

Nava and his sappers rushed the burning wreckage and, negotiating the abatis, cut a way through the stockade, and moving to their right, used the ditch as a means to move around under cover of the ruins where they began constructing a shelter where a battery could be emplaced. Girón led his column smartly around to the left, and Ezpeleta's men clambered into the ruins, where (it is implied) an officer of the Immermorial del Rey planted the Royal standard atop the rubble.[11] By the time the grenadiers and light infantry came up, the remaining British forts were firing rapidly with musketry and cannon, which compelled the Spanish to retire behind the ruins and possibly to the treeline to the British right. Miró added that, 'These operations were supported by our fire from the cover of the merlons of the flank Battery until it [the new battery] could stop [the fire of the enemy] cannon and reduce the [fort's] gunfire.'[12] Amongst the blue coated artillerymen and sailors under Deans and Johnstone, working the guns in Fort George was likely a distinctive figure, wearing skirts and stays, her hair beneath her bonnet astray and her face smeared and shining from sweat and powder. Elizabeth Woodward was 40 years old and married Private Samuel Woodward of the Marylanders, the story of how she got to West Florida is worth deviating to for a moment. In her memorial to Lord Palmerston, she stated that,

That in the year 1776, being with her first husband (John Jasper,) a serjeant of marines, on board the brig *Stanley*, tender to the *Roebuck*, she was wounded in her left leg, in an engagement with three French vessels, when she was actually working at the guns. That the marines having been landed at Cape May, in America, her husband was taken prisoner by a Captain Planket, of the rebel army, near Mud Fort … and sentenced to suffer death; That by her means he was enabled to escape, with 22 American deserters, to whom she served arms and ammunition; and on their way to join the army their party was attacked by the enemy's light horse; she was fired at, and wounded in her left arm; but, undismayed, took a loaded firelock, shot the rebel, and brought his horse to Philadelphia (the head-quarters of the army),which she was permitted to sell to one of General Sir William Howe's Aide-de-Camps.[13]

10   Baker, 'Combat Diary', pp.193–194.
11   Mario de Soto Serafin, Conde de Clonard, *Historia orgánica de las armas de Infantería y Caballería españolas desde la creacion del ejercito permanente hasta el dia* (Madrid: Francisco del Castillo, 1856), vol.V, pp.58–59.
12   Baker, 'Combat Diary', pp.193–194.
13   Memorial of Elizabeth Hopkins, in Anon., *The Soldier's Companion, or Martial Recorder, Consisting of Biography, Anecdotes, Poetry and Miscellaneous Information* (London: Edward Cock, 1824), vol.I, p.73.

What at first seems to be a story too good to be true, becomes replete with verifiable events, for whereas it may be hard to confirm Mrs Woodward's service and injury, the *Stanley* was indeed one of two tenders to HMS *Roebuck* in the summer of 1777 during the operations around Cape May and Fort Mifflin which included fortifications on Mud Island.[14] The fight with the French would seem more difficult to prove, however the *Roebuck* did fight on the Delaware in late 1777, and then removed to Rhode Island the next year to help face down the French fleet. Her memorial continued, 'After many fatigues and campaigns, her first husband died, and she married (Samuel Woodward,) a soldier in Colonel Chambers' corps; was with the troops under the command of General Campbell.'[15] Chambers of course being the commander of the Maryland Regiment, and as such we can guess that widowed Elizabeth, by now a mother of one daughter, remarried sometime between the summer of 1778 and December 1779 and followed her husband to Florida. As someone who was apparently used to the workings of artillery, she seems to have made herself useful in the batteries of Fort George. During the siege, Mrs Woodward 'served at the guns, and tore her very clothes for wadding.'[16] With only fragmentary references to women, both military and civilian during the siege, the testimony of Elizabeth Woodward, seeking an allowance as 'during the course of her life, from her zeal and attachment to her king and country, she has encountered more hardships than commonly fall to the lot of her sex is remarkable.'[17] Later, in the War of 1812, Elizabeth was married to sergeant Jeremiah Hopkins of the 104th Foot and went by the name Mammy Hopkins.[18]

Sergeant Matthews's diary offered a sparce summary of the action, 'a shell from the enemy fell on our magazine, exploded and blew it up, killing upwards of one hundred of our men, and destroyed the upper redoubt. The enemy advanced in force and took possession of it. The guns in Port George and from the middle redoubt kept up a heavy fire, but the enemy, from their new position, killed a number of our men with small arms.'[19]

Campbell's report deviates significantly from the others by suggesting that one Spanish attempt was repulsed and gives this as the reason as to how some of the guns could be withdrawn. As the mortar beds on either flank were still in some state of repair,

> ... the Fire from which (owing to the intrepid coolness of the Artillery particularly of Captain Johnstone who Commanded them) repulsed the Enemy in their first attempt to advance to the Storm, and gave Time to Carry the wounded, two 5½ Inch Howitzers & three Field Pieces But the Enemy having by this Time brought up their whole army, there was a necessity of abandoning these works after first Spiking up the Artillery remaining in them – Besides which one twenty

---

14   William J. Morgan (ed.), *Naval Documents of the American Revolution* (Washington: United States Printing Office, 1986), vol.9, p.338.

15   Anon., *The Soldier's Companion*, vol.I, p.73.

16   Anon., *The Soldier's Companion*, vol.I, p.73.

17   Anon., *The Soldier's Companion*, vol.I, p.73.

18   Anon., *The Soldier's Companion*, vol.I, p.74.

19   Claiborne, *Mississippi*, vol.1, p.126.

four pounder, 6 twelve pounders and one 9 pounder were lost in the Redoubt: The Enemy at this Time assumed a Countenance as if they intended to storm our remaining Works; However on finding us prepared for their attack, and in readiness to receive them, they dropped their Design.[20]

The Spanish accounts mention the operation as a single relatively fluid event, but it is possible that some of the references to the audacity and speed of the attack leave something out, or it is simply that Campbell, having to put some sort of positive patina on a disastrous situation, mistook the mustering of troops as hesitation, during which time the very adept Captain Johnstone of the Royal Artillery, who had supported the skirmishing through April and the first week of May, bravely continued to hold his very perilous position, truly to the verge of the last extremity. A feat which in later times would doubtless have earned him a high gallantry medal.

In any event the Spanish and French had successfully taken the ruins of the advanced redoubt by about 10:00 a.m., and over the course of the rest of the morning began to make it safe, from both further explosions and enemy fire. Two howitzers and two other long guns, presumably some of the field pieces, were hurried up and directed to the site Nava had found to entrench.

A lull now occurred, which the Spanish put down to their fire being too well directed, though this is not mentioned by the British, rather, Saavedra thought, Campbell was already preparing to surrender; paying off the Muskogees, Chickasaws and Choctaws who had remained, whilst sending off a detachment of 300 men to Georgia.

At some time between 2:00 and 3:00 p.m., a white flag appeared over Fort George, which came as a surprise to many of the Bourbon officers, who likely expected a few more days hard and dangerous graft to prove they could get their guns into position before Campbell would be forced to surrender. Indeed, though slightly lower on the hill and therefore extremely vulnerable to shelling, Fort George was by far the largest of the British fortifications on the high ground above the town. However, Campbell, made a humane decision, perhaps prompted by the ghastly nature of the accident that morning, to not prolong the inevitable longer than he already had.

> At this time an officer on horseback appeared accompanied by a servant carrying a white flag. He advanced to be met on the left of the fort by the Major General [Ezpeleta] and Major Decois, Officer of the French Navy, assistant to the artillery, and from the right by the Quarter Master with his aide Don Franco del Rey, who were in the works just described. Upon meeting our men the English officer presented an open letter that General Cambel [sic] had sent. Because it was written in English the General ordered that it be translated to French. The letter asked for 24 hours suspension of hostilities to deal with the capitulation, but the General answered Senor Cambel that only three hours would be considered in which to arrange the suspension of hostilities. The English officer returned to the fort with assurance that all hostility and work would cease. A group of our

---

20   TNA: PRO 30/55/89: Campbell to Clinton, 12 May 1781.

men formed and advanced to the tree that the English indicated as the boundary. The General waited there for the results of the first letter, [which was] followed by three [more] letters written by each general. Our general remained at this spot, sending to the Plaza as hostage the Lieutenant of Iberria [Hibernia] Don Cornalio, bringing another English officer to the camp.[21]

Ezpeleta may have played a greater part in this event, as another version of the story has the fiery *Navareno* receiving a verbal request for a day's preparation, refusing the 24-hour deadline, and curtly countering with three, at which point the British officer – the Fort Adjutant and Barrack-Master, Andrew Rainsford – asked to see 'the General'. Ezpeleta is supposed to have levelled the fellow by responding that he was the general, and he had three hours before he stormed the next earthwork with fire and sword.[22] There is no easy way to decide which is the more accurate. The 'Major General' in Miró's diary is certainly Ezpeleta, but he usually means Gálvez when using the phrase, 'the General' unless it is specific to the case, which it partially is here. It is clear that 'our General' is Gálvez and so this might be a rather strategic way of being vague. As far as Saavedra is concerned, Gálvez was involved, and Miranda implied the same. But it is said to have been Ezpeleta by the editor of Saavedra's journal, whose statement was based on the biography of Ezpeleta written by Rojas in 1980 and the paper written in 1982. Both of which were based heavily on Ezpeleta's own correspondence, and the colourful testimony of a *Sargento* Ozcoydi of the Regimiento de Navarra, who witnessed Ezpeleta's ire in the ruins.[23] It is certainly possible that Ezpeleta did issue the three hour deadline, which was confirmed by Gálvez who took charge when the British returned with the acceptance and some preliminary terms.

By the end of the day, an outline of the terms to be discussed had been agreed, with Gálvez watering down much of Ezpeleta's more stringent suggestions, as his old friend thought he had been too easy on the British in the past. The sum of it all was that West Florida was to be ceded, in return for the honours of war and repatriation to a friendly port.[24]

All the next day was taken up with finalising the negotiations and preparing the documents, though Campbell also hurriedly wrote instructions to detached forces informing them of what had occurred. That day he sent a dispatch to Smith and McPherson on the Escambia River, 'come immediately here with the Negroes that were on board the Vessels under your command and you are to take care that no damage is done to the Vessels. Your Persons and Properties are Fecund by the Capitulation.'[25] This order was complicated by the appearance of McGillivray and some Muskogee's, and perhaps others, making good their escape who proceeded to help themselves to the goods. Though they stopped short of burning the vessels, neither commander was

---

21   Baker, 'Combat Diary', pp.193–194.
22   Rojas, *Ezpeleta at Pensacola*, pp.118–119.
23   Topping (ed.), *Journal of Saavedra*, p.171; see, Francisco Medina Rojas De Borja, *José de Ezpeleta, gobernador de la Mobila, 1780-1781* (Seville: Escuela de Estudios Hispano-Americanos, 1980); Rojas, *Ezpeleta at Pensacola*, p.119.
24   Topping (ed.), *Journal of Saavedra*, p.172.
25   TNA: PRO 30/55/89: Campbell to Smith and McPherson, 10 May 1781

able to stop them and Gálvez later blamed Campbell for allowing it to happen in defiance of the articles of capitulation.

The bureaucracy of war could not detract from the realities. As Deans noted, one of the sailors who had been caught in the explosion succumbed to his wounds while the negotiations continued, which, given the possible injuries sustained from such a powerful explosion and such a hot fire, might well have been a blessing. The articles being signed by the commanders that day, all was now in readiness for the formal handover of the defences and town to the Spanish. This took place on the following afternoon with the combined Franco-Spanish army drawn up behind its trenches, ranged along the low hill of Pino Gordo, across the blackened ruins of the British advanced redoubt, and either side of the road to Mobile. A vivid display of faded but impressive uniforms of Bourbon white, the reds of the Hibernia and *Morenos*, blues of the artillery, engineers, the Havana and marine regiments and the French *chasseurs*. Miró paints the picture best.

> From very early [the troops] have been getting together a great deal of their equipment and continued [to do] so all day. At 3:30 four companies of grenadiers and one of French chasseurs departed for the ceremony of delivering the zone. At 5:45 the ceremony took place as planned. General Cambel left Fort George at the head of his troops accompanied by five aides-de-camp, and one person dressed in black. Following were detachments from the 16th regiment. Another two detachments from several regiments followed them. The captain of the frigate, Mr. Duis [Deans?], with his sailors and a 3-pounder cannon on which was displayed the flag of the frigate. The political governor [of Pensacola] Piter Chestre [Peter Chester] with a town council then followed the Commander of Artillery, Mr. Thomson [Johnston] with all of his troops: another two detachments followed, supplying a rearguard for two covered carts and the Regiment of Waldeck with its two flags and two artillery pieces, all this troop turning to align with the breastworks of Fort George from which it emerged, with the 10 Companies of [Spanish] Grenadiers in battle formation before this. The generals advanced and after greeting each other, ours went with the first [commanding officer] of the King's Regiment [Immemorial del Rey] to where the flags of Cambel were surrendered, and the captains of the Navy Don Felipe Lopez de Carrisola and Mr. Bolderic of the French Navy conducted them to our troops. Then the General remained with the same group [while] the Commander of the Navy [Presumably Deans] surrendered the frigate to the General, who in turn gave it to the Baron de Quesel [Kessel] to add it to [the] others. Concluding the ceremony, the English Major ordered his troop to lay down their arms and giving a half turn to the right passed by a Cordon of Sentinels of our troops which took over the guard in the forts and raised the colours of Spain.[26]

Though a detailed description, it is not always clear what is going on. Some accounts claim six companies of Spanish grenadiers were at the ceremony and that two companies occupied the works of Fort George, whilst the light

---

26 Baker, 'Combat Diary', p.195. Three other sources report the ceremony occurring between 3:00 and 3:30 p.m.

infantry of the French brigade occupied the middle redoubt. The sources disagree if Gálvez led his grenadiers into the fort, and though none implicitly state he did not, he remained at his headquarters that night. The remainder of the garrison left for cantonments at dawn the next day, while the Spanish sang a *Te Deum* organised and led by Father Cirilo. The Royal Navy Redoubt at the Barrancas Coloradas surrendered on 11 May and was occupied by 139 men of the *Régiment du Cap*. The Siege of Pensacola was over and the business of accounting to superiors began.

In his report to Madrid, Gálvez gave a tally of his prisoners, as 1,113 men, 101 women and 123 children. He took the liberty of noting that 300 men had absconded to Georgia during negotiations, while 105 had been blown up in the half-moon battery, (though it is difficult to ascertain how many of these were killed in the fight for the ruins), and 53 had deserted, which meant, Campbell had about 1,600 regular troops in the defences.[27]

Francisco de Saavedra recorded in his journal that in total the garrison must have numbered 1,621 men, which did not include a large number of African Americans who were of an unspecified legal status, many of whom had taken an active part in building the entrenchments and fighting. The Convention devoted several articles to this point, which determined that freemen who had taken up arms were required to surrender them and go home, slaves were to be returned if the owner could be identified and, if not, then their value would be given. No one mentioned the Muskogees and Choctaws, who amounted to about 500 warriors, which means that from the middle of May Campbell had at least between 2,100 and 2,200 fighting men. There was additionally, 143 guns, one mortar, six howitzers, 40 swivel guns, 2,150 muskets, and a healthy amount of ammunition captured.[28] Campbell gave a detailed breakdown of his losses on the day of the official surrender, which showed that a high proportion of fatalities came from the Royal Navy and the Provincials; 222 killed wounded and missing. Casualties for the allied warriors is unknown, though it would seem they were light.[29] It is certain that Campbell had misjudged both the Provincials and his allies as by far it was these troops that bore the brunt of the active fighting during the siege.

The Spanish admitted to 272 killed and wounded, and it is noticeable that the British sustained at least 90 dead to the Spanish 74, largely due to the number of men lost in the explosion of the magazine. Losses due to sickness for either side are not mentioned.

In his excellent biography of Gálvez, Saravia included a graph showing that the majority of the Spanish casualties up to 24 April had been lost to Choctaw or Muskogee fire, and it was only after Cagigal's reinforcements arrived that he began pressing his advantage, with corresponding casualties.[30]

In his report of 12 May, Campbell blamed the loss on overwhelming numbers of the enemy and a lack of materials and troops with which to fight

---

27   Cusachs, 'Diary of the Operations', p.75.
28   Topping (ed.), *Journal of Saavedra*, pp.172–173.
29   TNA: PRO 30/55/89/47: Return of the Killed and Wounded and Deserted of His Majesty's Land and Sea Forces during the Siege of Fort George in West Florida, 10 May 1781.
30   Saravia, *Gálvez*, p.226.

them, 'It has been my great misfortune to have been employed in this ill-fated corner of His Majesty's Dominion; But I trust that the Calamities that have befallen West Florida shall not be imputed to me.'[31] While many felt that on the contrary the losses between 1779–1780 could indeed by blamed on Campbell, and estimates of between 9–11,000 enemy troops aside, it should be acknowledged that Campbell, though certainly dependant on relief or intervention to save him, likely would have forced Gálvez to make a costly assault to take the Advanced Redoubt, and possibly make a movement closer to the camp of the Muskogees as Choctaws. If Campbell blamed any party specifically it was of course his allies, who as has been seen he called auxiliaries, and who, he felt, had not done enough. The lack of a man like John Stuart who was known and respected by the southern nations during the siege was an important factor in the reluctance of the Choctaws and Muskogees to commit themselves totally. Few seemed to trust Campbell very much and given his curious stance of demanding they shed their blood, but do so on his terms, it is not too surprising Campbell's largest single active contingent slowly lost faith in the British struggle. The British commander did his best to downplay the loss to Britain, and he hoped the cost to Spain would prove its own wound. Gálvez was assuring Madrid of the great loss in men, money, and munitions to the British, while amply praising as many of his officers and allies he could fit into the report to his uncle.

Ironically a few weeks after the fall of the province, there was a debate in Parliament regarding funds for the building of a new fort at Pensacola. Some in London feeling that, since (so far as they knew) the Spanish had tried to take it twice already; it would be well to fortify the place so as to cause an enemy considerable damage if they were to try a third time. Germain opined at the time that Pensacola was naturally very important but quite safe but learned of the reality of the situation in August.

Rewards and praise were doled out to the victorious commander and his men with gusto, both in Spain and France. Monteil conveyed the news of the victory directly to France, declaring that Gálvez, now the second youngest man to be made *teniente general* in Spanish history, had overcome every hazard and fatigue with courage and determination. In addition to money and titles, Gálvez was confirmed as supreme military commander in the Indies, and his opponents in Havana were all either dismissed or strategically promoted back to Spain.

The American Congress was less enthused, finding it hard to believe that the governor of Louisiana, who had always shown a great partiality to the cause of America, could have accepted a treaty which allowed for the repatriation of over 1,000 enemy troops to New York, where they could rejoin the fight as the Convention of Fort George only required Campbell's garrison to never take up arms against Spain. Washington was satisfied enough that Gálvez had no choice, however the offense caused by the terms of the surrender show how naïve many in the United States had been about Spanish war aims.

---

31   TNA: PRO 30/55/89: Campbell to Clinton, 12 May 1781.

Although any reverse for the British could be seen as damaging, and there were hopes of seeing the red crosses of Spain eventually advance against St Augustine and Georgia, undoubtedly the outcome favoured Spain above the United States. The consequences of the Siege of Pensacola were the fulfilment of the directive to secure the Gulf of Mexico and the Bahama Channel, which was a war aim derived from a wish to improve internal security. In so doing, royal monopolies could be re-examined. For the progress of the wider war (which unknown to all was but six months away from effectively ending), it was not as indifferent to Congress's aims either. Although Campbell's troops were to be sent to New York, the Americans did now have a direct and uninterrupted back-channel for supply that reached beyond New Orleans, from St Louis to the markets of Havana and Vera Cruz, which bypassed the British blockade, with a host of friendly ports for privateers to shelter in. In terms of military prestige, the operation was a testament to the flexibility of the Spanish regular infantry, as had been reformed since 1764, as well as the provincials and disciplined militia. All had performed well in the complicated amphibious operations, and in the hard marches, entrenching and constant skirmishing, while the engineers and artillery had surpassed themselves. The navy also did a very creditable job but had met no impediment to their support of the army except Calvo's own reasonable caution in crossing the bar. That being said, there was no mishap in the transportation of the troops or the supply of the land forces. While the Spanish navy was now a lesser creature to its French cousin and likely unable to defeat the British in open water, the operation showed that its presence was still a potent force when given room to operate. The success was significant to the army, which since 1763 had suffered only remarkable defeats, especially the debacle of Algiers. Gálvez was not only leading the largest force he had ever commanded, but the largest force Spain had put in the field since 1776, and the second largest of the present war.

For Gálvez personally it was the final act of his *Reconquista*, having attained the goal he had hoped to achieve in early to mid-1780. Now elevated to supreme commander, he revealed that he had harboured a grander ambition of capturing Jamaica and the Bahamas, which he foresaw as a combined operation between the French and Spanish.

Gálvez stayed at Pensacola for a few months, and then left with the bulk of the army, first returning to New Orleans to quash a loyalist rebellion which had recaptured Natchez, and then arriving back in Havana in August, where he would begin planning his attack on the Bahamas and Jamaica. A scheme that was to form part of a wider three-pronged Franco-Spanish strategy to simultaneously remove the British from the Caribbean and aid the Americans in such a way that a decisive blow could be struck which would convince the British that they had no hope of reclaiming the colonies.

When he arrived, he found that Saavedra had been extremely busy financing what would prove the final victory. After the fall of Pensacola, he had been sent to Cap Françoise (Cap-Haïtien, St Domingue) to discuss strategy with *Lieutenant Général des armées navales* Comte de Grasse in July. Once again, Spain could only lend direct military support to joint Franco-Spanish objectives, as such Jamaica seemed to offer an excellent option, but first, the French would need to press forwards in delivering a victory for Congress. That being said, in a crucial meeting between Saavedra and de Grasse on his flagship, *Ville de Paris*, the 'humiliation of a nation that so openly claimed dominion of the sea,' was thoroughly discussed, and the part Spain would play in ensuring the independence of the United States was significant.[32] De Grasse was already planning to take possession of Chesapeake Bay and to make a junction with Washington, Rochambeau and Lafayette, there to completely cut off Cornwallis from outside aid, where it would be possible to 'totally destroy him or oblige him to surrender.'[33] As at Pensacola, the disconnected nature of British strategy would see an inability of central command to send effective aid to anywhere that was not deemed of the first importance, whilst the allies were becoming frighteningly cohesive. De Grasse had his reservations however and wished to take no more than 25 ships with him. To this Saavedra countered that, based on his intelligence reports, Rear Admiral Thomas Graves had 20 ships at least in New York, and was expecting reinforcements. Saavedra put it to de Grasse that he would be better taking 30 ships, but this would comprise almost his entire force and leave St Domingue undefended. So de Grasse proposed that if the Spanish contributed some ships of the line to the expedition he could leave some ships behind to defend the colony. Saavedra told him that the political situation would make direct military aid to Congress's forces impossible as this might infer a recognition of the United States that Carlos III had yet to give, however, now Pensacola was taken, the Spanish fleet at Havana, recently placed under command of Solano, would be able to guard St Domingue while de Grasse took the fleet to the Chesapeake. 'This expedient pleased the *Comte* enormously, and from that moment I noted on his part a great reliance on everything I proposed to him.'[34] While a plan had been found, financing it was another matter, Saavedra was appraised by de Grasse and French officials in the colony that there was no money, and efforts to raise a sum from the colony had been negligible. Saavedra handed over 100,000 *pesos* from a consignment of 500,000 destined for Puerto Rico and Santo Domingo, and told de Grasse, he must apply to Havana for a loan. The Comte agreed, and Saavedra returned to Havana ahead of the French to prepare the way. A quarter of a million *pesos*, was in fact the number the French needed, and Saavedra's promise was a gamble, as he had no indication when he made it, where the money was to come from at such short notice.

At Havana, Saavedra learned to his great relief that the Council of the Indies had made one million *pesos* available to the French. Just as it had for Havana, the wealth of the Indies had come to the rescue. With considerable foresight, the Spanish government had begun organising colonial revenue for the war effort in August of 1780. The critical line of the King's personal plea for a popular war fund ran: 'I have resolved to ask for a *donativo* of one *peso* from every freeman who is an Indian or of mixed blood, and two pesos from every Spaniard and those of the higher class. These last may also pay for their servants and workers and later discount the amount from their salaries or daily wages.'[35] The timing was finite, and the distances were vast.

---

32   Topping (ed.), *Journal of Saavedra*, p.200.
33   Topping (ed.), *Journal of Saavedra*, p.201.
34   Topping (ed.), *Journal of Saavedra*, p.202.
35   Granville & Hough, *Texas Patriots*, pp.23–24.

The decree only reached *Commmandante General* of the Provincias Internas, 'Caballero' Teodoro de Croix at Arispe in the summer of 1781, but by this time the nearer colonies had produced the bulk of the finance for the Bourbon military operations for the crucial year of the war in America, indeed the money Saavedra had already given to de Grasse had been part of the initial deposit from New Spain. The ingenuity of Saavedra and the immense wealth of Mexico did not seem to have an end as nine million was earmarked for the suggested invasion of Jamaica. As impressive as this was, the catch was that the money was not in Cuba. Saavedra heard that the money he needed for Rochambeau's army had left Vera Cruz but was still at sea, and the treasury at Havana was bare. There was no time to either sail to Mexico and fetch them or wait for their arrival, as the French would soon be at the agreed rendezvous point at Matanzas.

Early on 16 August, an announcement was made, explaining the situation and asking all citizens to contribute whatever sum they could to keep the French fleet at sea. The result, if we are to believe Saavedra, was quite extraordinary, with the desired sum being reached in six hours. A popular and romantic legend has the bulk of the money being raised by the ladies of Havana who contributed their jewels to the defeat of the British. The public fund was delivered to de Grasse as agreed and the admiral would later credit this as vital to the success of the operation.[36] It was the news of the French being at sea that spurred Washington into committing to the Yorktown campaign, which could not have occurred without the money from Havana. Saavedra need not have gone to such lengths, five days later, the million *pesos* from Mexico arrived, and were duly despatched to the Chesapeake. The Spanish, it is true, fired no iron at Yorktown, but it cannot be denied that the ammunition they did send was just as devastating.

Much could be written on the projected next step for the Spanish, while Washington, Rochambeau and de Grasse besieged Yorktown. More still on the brief counter-rebellion at Natchez, the arguments between Gálvez and Campbell about the prisoners, and the wider affairs of the Spanish empire, which were all connected or effected in some way to the war effort but alas it is beyond the scope of this book to do so. After a tedious period in which Campbell and Gálvez accused each other of breaking the terms of the treaty, the British troops were safely conveyed to New York, and one imagines the Waldeckers were secretly pleased to have been captured, as it meant they no longer had to serve in West Florida. As it happened, they would have little opportunity for further service, as by the end of the year another British garrison would have surrendered Yorktown, and with it, the bulk of the southern field army.

The logistical feat of achieving a landing of over 7,000 men and equipment in a place as remote as West Florida was a worthy accomplishment and was promising for the future. However, the plan to take Jamaica never materialised due to the ending of the war, the end of which is often only remembered in a Spanish context due to the failure at Gibraltar. However, Cagigal did take the Bahamas in 1782, while the campaign on the gulf would

---

36   Chavez, *Spain and the Independence of the United States*, pp.202–203.

Washington and Rochambeau at Yorktown by Coudert, 1785. The meeting of the French and American forces in Virginia was made possible by the 1.5 million *pesos* supplied by Havana and Vera Cruz in the late summer of 1781. (Anne S.K. Brown Military Collection)

remain the most successful Spanish operation of the conflict, but one which, due to the complicated politics between Spain and the United States, would remain a neglected topic as the new nation memorialised its great struggle for independence.

History can be many things, and there are fewer more bitter ideological struggles today than that of identity, and who can therefore stake a claim to a significant heritage, and therefore exert a certain superiority, or security over their opponents. The symbol of Bernardo de Gálvez and his polyglot army has rightly become a symbol of Hispanic American pride, allowing people usually dismissed in the story of the United States to claim their part in the founding of the country as well. Native American nations, historically vilified as the enemy of both worlds, and denigrated in the Declaration of Independence, also vie for recognition in the popular retelling of how the United States came to be and what therefore it really represents, given it was an event which was to have such devastating impacts on the people of the continent over the next century.

Much is lost altogether in the collision of two points of view, and if military history can do a service beyond informing a reader how their ancestors chose to slaughter each other, it is that. This is certainly a time in our shared history where we must strive for balance and reason, rather than extremes, and to use history as less of a weapon but more as a bridge.

Appendix I

Spanish Order of Battle[1]

Complete Franco-Spanish force as of 23 April 1781, 7,485 men.[2]
Commander in Chief, *Mariscal de Campo* Don Bernardo de Gálvez.

1st Brigade: *Brigadier* Jerónimo Girón de Moctezuma – 1,592.

    Rgto Immemorial del Rey.
    Rgto de Principe.
    Rgto de Navarra.
    Rgto Fijo de Havana.

2nd Brigade: *Coronel* Manuel Pineda – 1,386.

    Rgto de Soria.
    Rgto de Hibernia.
    Rgto Flandes de Valon.
    Rgto de Mallorca.

3rd Brigade: *Coronel* Francisco Longoria – 1,343.

    Rgto de Guadalajara.
    Rgto de Espana.
    Rgto de Aragon.
    Rgto Fijo de Luisiana.
    Dragoons.[3]

---

1   It is unknown as to which brigades included the Rgto de Mallorca and the Rgto de Toledo, indeed some orders of battle exclude them, but there is no clear reason why. As such their positioning is speculative, the author also has no guidance for the position of the Toledo regiment.

2   Haarman, 'An Order of Battle', pp.194-195. Saravia, *Gálvez*, pp.374-375.

3   The cavalry of the expedition was drawn from small detachments of the Dragones de Luisiana, the Carabineros de Nueva Orleans and either the Dragones de America or Dragones de Mexico, there is uncertainty as to which of the latter was present in force.

4th Brigade: *Capitán de Navío* Felipe Lopez de Carrizosa – 1,323.

Sailors.
Infantería de Marina.

Reserve Division

Campo Volante: *Coronel* Pablo Figuerola – 741.

Rgto Segundo de (Voluntarios) Catalunya.
Compañía de Fusilieros de Habana.
Milicias Libres de Habana.
Milicias Libres de Nuevo Orleans.

French Brigade: *Capitaine de Vaisseau* M. de Boiderut – 509.
(Detachments from the St Domingue Garrison)[4]

Rgt Agenois.
Rgt Gatinois.
Rgt Cambresis.
Rgt Poitou.
Rgt Orleans.
Rgt du Cap.
Regiment-Royale Artillerie.

Artillery: *Teniente Coronel* Vincente Risel – 471.

Rgto Real de Artilleria.
Real Cuerpo de Artilleria de Marina.
Corps royal d'artillerie de la marine.
Régiment Royal-Artillerie.

---

4   No formal list for the French brigade is given, it is only known that officers from these
     regiments were mentioned in the Spanish dispatches, but we must presume that the force
     represented detachments rather than full battalions. It is known for instance that two *chasseur*
     companies were involved in the surrender.

Appendix II

British Order of Battle

Garrison of Fort George, Pensacola as of 1 May 1781. Approximately 2,000 Men.[1]
Commander in Chief, Major General John Campbell.

7 Companies, 16th Regiment of Foot.
1 Company, 3rd Battalion, 60th Regiment of Foot.
Captain Johnstone's Company, 4th Battalion, Royal Artillery.
Pennsylvania Provincial Battalion.
Maryland Provincial Battalion.
Florida Royal Foresters.
Florida Royal Volunteers.
Ships Companies of HMS *Mentor* and *Port Royal*.
Allied War-Bands, from the Choctaw, Muskogee and Chickasaw Nations.

---

1   Haarman, Albert, 'An Order of Battle', p.195.

Select Bibliography

The National Archives (TNA)

PRO 30/55: British Headquarters Correspondence, North America. 30/11: Cornwallis Papers.
CO 700/FLORIDA Maps and Plans: Series I. CO/82: Colonial Office Papers Class 5, America and the West Indies.
MPD 1/194: Plan of the Entrance of Pensacola Harbour, 1771.

Printed and Online Sources

Adams, John A. Jr, *Conflict and Commerce on the Rio Grande* (College Station: A&M University Press, 2008)

Anon. (ed.), *The soldier's Companion, or Martial Recorder, Consisting of Biography, Anecdotes, Poetry and Miscellaneous Information* (London: Edward Cock, 1824)

Archer, Christon J., *The Army in Bourbon Mexico* (Archer: University of New Mexico Press, 1977)

Baer, Friederike, *Hessians: German Soldiers in the American Revolutionary War* (Oxford: Oxford University Press, 2022)

Baker, Maury, 'Bernardo de Galvez's Combat Diary for the Battle of Pensacola, 1781', *Florida Historical Quarterly*, no.2 (1977), pp 176-199

Bartram, John, Francis Harper (ed.), *Diary of a Journey through the Carolinas, Georgia, and Florida, 1765-66* (Philadelphia: The American Philosophical Society, 1942)

Baynton, Benjamin, *Authentic memoirs of William Augustus Bowles, esquire: ambassador from the United Nations of Creeks and Cherokees, to the court of London* (London: R. Faulder, 1791)

Bicheno, Hugo, *Rebels and Redcoats* (London: Harper Collins, 2003)

Boyd, Mark F., 'Spanish Interest in British Florida, and in the Progress of the American Revolution,' *Florida Historical Quarterly*, vol.32, no.2 (1953), pp.92–130

Boyd, Mark F., 'The Fortifications at San Marcos de Apalache,' *Florida Historical Quarterly*, vol.15, no.1 (1936), pp.3–17, 19–34

Braisted, Tod, 'A History of the Provincial Corps of Pennsylvania Loyalists - Part 5 of 7', *The Online Institute for Advanced Loyalist Studies*, <http://www.royalprovincial.com/military/rhist/paloyal/pal5hist.htm#palbunk>, accessed 06/07/23

Buel, Richard Jr, *In Irons: Britain's Naval Supremacy and the American Revolutionary Economy* (New Haven: Yale University Press 1998)

Burgoyne, Bruce E., 'A Diary Kept by Chaplain Waldeck During the Last American War, Part IV', *Journal of the Johannes Schwalm Historical Association*, vol.3, no.2 (1986), pp.25–37

Bushnell, David Ives, 'Myths of the Louisiana Choctaw', *American Anthropologist*, vol.12, no.4 (October–December, 1910), pp.526–535

Bushnell, David Ives, 'The Choctaw of Bayou Lacomb, St. Temmany Parish, Louisiana', *Bureau of American Ethnology*, Bulletin 48 (1909), pp.1–37

Butler, Lewis, *Annals of the King's Royal Rifle Corps: The Royal Americans* (London, Smith, Elder & Co, 1913)

Caughey, John Walton, *Bernardo de Gálvez in Louisiana 1776 1783* (Gretna: Firebird Press, 1998)

Chartand, Rene, *The Spanish Army in North America 1700-1793* (Oxford: Osprey, 2011)

Chartrand, Rene, *Louisbourg 1758: Wolfe's First Siege* (Oxford: Osprey, 2000)

Chartrand, Rene, *The Armies and Wars of the Sun King 1643- 1715: The War of the Spanish Succession* (Warwick: Helion, 2021)

Chavez, Thomas E., *Spain and the Independence of the United States: An intrinsic gift* (Albuquerque: University of New Mexico Press, 2002)

Claiborne, John Francis, *Mississippi, as a Province, Territory, and State: With biographical notices of eminent Citizens* (Jackson: Power and Barkdale, 1880)

Clement, W. E., *Plantation Life on the Mississippi* (Gretna: Firebird Press, 2000)

Cometti, Elizabeth (ed.), *The American Journals of Lt. John Enys* (Syracuse: Syracuse University Press, 1976)

Cusachs, Gaspar, (ed.), Gilbert Pemberton (trans.), 'Bernardo de Galvez's Diary of the Operations. Against Pensacola', *Louisiana Historical Quarterly*, vol.1, no.1 (January1917), pp. 44–85

Dalrymple, William, *Travels Through Spain and Portugal, in 1774, with a Short Account of the Expedition to Algiers* (London: J. Almon, 1777)

Davies, K.G. (ed.), *Documents of the American Revolution, 1770-1783* (Shannon: Irish University Press, 1972)

Descola, Michael Heron (trans.), *Daily Life in Colonial Peru 1710-1820* (New York: The McMillan Company, 1968)

Dornemann, William E., 'A Diary Kept by Chaplain Waldeck During the Last American War, Part III', *Journal of the Johannes Schwalm Historical Association*, vol.3, no.1 (1985), pp.46–63

Duffy, Christopher, *The Military Experience in the Age of Reason* (New York: Athaneaum, 1988)

Eelking, Max, J.G. Rosengarten (trans.), *The German Allied Troops in the American War of Independence, 1776-1783* (Albany: Joel Munsell's Sons, 1893)

Faye, Stanley, 'Spanish Fortifications of Pensacola, 1698-1763', *Florida Historical Quarterly*, vol.20, no.2 (1941), pp.151–168

Fehrenbach, T.R., *Comanches: History of a People* (London: Vintage Books, 2007)

Fernandez-Armesto, Felipe, *Our America: A Hispanic History of the United States* (New York: W.W. Norton & Company, 2014)

Granville W. and N. C. Hough, *Spain's Texas Patriots – Its 1779-1783 War with England During the American Revolution. Part 5 of Spanish Borderlands Studies* (Midway: SHHAR Press, 2000)

Griffith II, Samuel B, *The War for American Independence* (Chicago: University of Illinois Press, 2002)

Gutiérrez, Pedro L., Gene A. Smith (eds), *From Colonies to Countries in the North Caribbean: Military Engineers in the Caribbean and Gulf of Mexico Region* (Newcastle: Cambridge Scholars Publishing, 2016)

Haarman, Albert W., 'The Siege of Pensacola: An Order of Battle', *Florida Historical Quarterly*, vol.3, no.44 (1965) pp.193–200

Hagist, Don, N., *Waging War in America, 1775-1783: Operational Challenges of Five Armies* (Stroud: Helion & Co, 2023)

Hämäläinen, Pekka, *The Comanche Empire* (New Haven: Yale University Press, 2008)

Hangar, Kimberly S., *Bounded Lives, Bounded Places: Free Black Society in Colonial New Orleans* (Durham: Duke University Press, 1997)

Harvey, Robert, *A Few Bloody Noses: The American Revolutionary War* (London: Constable and Robinson, 2001)

Harvey, Robert, *Liberators: Latin America's Savage Wars for Freedom, 1810-1830* (London: Robinson, 2002)

Haynes, Robert V., 'James Willing and the Planters of Natchez: The American Revolution comes to the Southwest', *Journal of Mississippi History*, vol.37 (February 1975), pp.1–40

Heckel, Steven W., *Junípero Serra: California's Founding Father* (New York: McMillan, 2014)

Historical Manuscripts Commission, *Report on American manuscripts in the Royal Institution of Great Britain* (London: HM Stationary Office, 1904-1909)

Holmes, Jack D.L., 'Alabama's Bloodiest Day of the American Revolution: Counterattack at the Village, January 7, 1781', *Alabama Historical Review*, vol.29 (July 1976), pp.208–219

Holmes, Jack D.L., 'Juan de la Villebeuvre: Spain's Commandant of Natchez During the American Revolution', *Journal of Mississippi History*, vol.37, pp.97–126 (1979)

Jackson, George B., 'John Stuart: Superintendent of Indian Affairs for the Southern District', *Tennessee Historical Magazine*, vol.3, no.3 (1917), pp.165–191

Kinnaird, Lawrence (ed.), *Annual Report of the American Historical Association for the Year 1945* (Washington: US Printing Office, 1949)

Klein, Herbert S., 'The Colored Militia of Cuba: 1568-1868', *Caribbean Studies*, vol.6, no.2 (1966), pp.17–27

Krebs, Daniel, *A Generous and Merciful Enemy: Life for German Prisoners of War during the American Revolution* (Norman: University of Oklahoma Press, 2013)

Kuethe, Allan J., 'The Development of the Cuban Military as a Sociopolitical Elite, 1763-83', *The Hispanic American Historical Review*, vol.61, no.4 (1981), pp.695–704

Kup, A.P., 'Sir Charles McCarthy (1768-1824), Soldier and Administrator', *Bulletin of the John Rylands Library*, vol.60, no.1 (1977), pp.52–94

Langkton, George E., *Native American Legends: Southeastern Legends and Tales from the Natchez, Caddo, Biloxi, Chickasaw, and other Nations* (Little Rock: August House, 1987)

Ludlum, David S., *Early American Hurricanes, 1492-1870* (Boston: American Meteorological Society, 1963)

MacNiven, Robbie, *British Light Infantry in the American Revolution* (Oxford: Osprey, 2021)

McAllister, Lyle N., *The Fuero Militar in New Spain, 1764-1800* (Gainsville, University of Florida Press, 1957)

Mahan A.T., *The Influence of Sea Power upon History 1660-1783* (Boston: Little Brown & Company, 1884)

Martin, S. & B. Harris, *Savannah 1779: The British Turn South* (Oxford: Osprey, 2017)

Medina Rojas, Francisco De Borja, *José de Ezpeleta, gobernador de la Mobila, 1780-1781* (Francisco: Escuela de Estudios Hispano-Americanos, 1980)

Morgan, W.J. (ed.), *Naval Documents of the American Revolution* (Washington: United States Printing Office, 1986)

Murphy, W. S., 'The Irish Brigade of Spain at the Capture of Pensacola, 1781', *Florida Historical Quarterly*, vol.38, no.3, (1959), pp.216–225

New, Christopher, *Maryland Loyalists in the American Revolution* (Centreville: Tidewater Publishers, 1996)

O'Brien, Greg, *Choctaws in a Revolutionary Age* (Lincoln: University of Nebraska Press, 2005)

O'Donnell, James H., *Southern Indians in the American Revolution* (Knoxville: University of Tennessee Press, 1975)

Oberg, Barbara B. (ed.), *The Papers of Benjamin Franklin* (New Haven: Yale University Press, 1992)

Oldmixon, John, *The British Empire in America* (London: John Nicholson, 1708)

Osborn, George C., 'Major General John Campbell in West Florida', *The Florida Historical Quarterly*, vol.27, no.4 (April 1949), pp.317–339

Padgett, James A., 'Bernardo de Galvez's Siege of Pensacola in 1781 (As Related in Robert Farmar's Journal)', *Louisiana Historical Quarterly*, vol.26, no.2 (1943), pp.311–329

Pecquet, Louise, *Some Prominent Virginia Families* (Lynchburg: J.P Bell Company, 1907)

Pelayo, Vizuente Picon, *Diccionario Enciclopedico Hispano-Americo* (Barcelona: Montaner Y Simon, 1887)

Quatrefages, Rene, 'La Collaboration Franco-Espagnole dans la Prise de Pensacola', *Revue Historique des Armées*, no.4 (1981), pp. 44–63

Racine, Karen, *Francisco de Miranda, a Transatlantic Life in the Age of Revolution* (Wilmington: Rowman & Littlefield, 2003)

Ramirez, Bibiano Torres, *Alejandro O'Reilly in Las Indias* (Sevilla: Publicaciones De La Escuela de Estudios Hispano-Americanos de Sevilla, 1969)

Rea, Robert R., 'Life, Death and Little Glory: The British Soldier on the Gulf Coast, 1763-1781', in Coker, William S., *The Military Presence on the Gulf Coast* (Pensacola: Gulf Coast History and Humanities Conference, 1978)

Reid, William, *An Attempt to Develop the Law of Storms by means of Facts* (London: John Weale, 1850)

Rézette, Robert, *The Spanish Enclaves in Morrocco* (Paris: Editions Latines, 1975)

Robertson, Spence, *The Life of Miranda by William Spence Robertson* (Chapel Hill: University of North Carolina Press, 1929)

Saavedra, Francisco de, Aileen Moore Topping (ed.), *Journal of Don Francsico de Saavedra de Sangornis 1781-1783* (Gainsville, University of Florida Press, 1989)

Santiago, Mark, *A Bad Peace and a Good War: Spain and the Mescalero Apache Uprising of 1795-1799* (Norman: University of Oklahoma Press, 2018)

Saravia, Gonzalo M. Quintero, *Bernardo de Gálvez: Spanish Hero of the American Revolution* (Chapel Hill: University of North Carolina Press, 2018)

Servies, James A. (ed.), *The Log of H.M.S. Mentor, 1780-1781* (Gainesville: University Presses of Florida, 1982)

Spring, Matthew E., *With Zeal & Bayonets Alone: The British Army on Campaign in North America, 1775-1783* (Norman: University of Oklahoma Press, 2008)

Starr, J. Barton, *Tories Dons and Rebels: The American Revolution in British West Florida* (Gainsville: University of Florida Press, 1976)

Stockdale, John, *The Parliamentary Register: Or History of the Proceedings and Debates of the House of Commons* (London: John Stockdale, 1802)

Thonhoff, Robert H., 'The Vital Contribution of Spain in the Winning of the American Revolution: An Essay on a Forgotten Chapter in the History of the American Revolution', *Granadaros y Damas de Galvez*, <http://granaderos.org/vital.html>, accessed 02/08/23.

Thorning, Joseph F., *Miranda World Citizen* (Gainsville: University of Florida Press, 1952)

Vinson, Ben, *Bearing Arms for His Majesty, The Free Coloured Militia in Colonial Mexico*

Walker, Charles F., *The Tupac Amaru Rebellion* (Cambridge: Belknap Press, 2014)

Wall, Steve (ed.), *Wisdom's Daughters: Conversations with women Elders of Native America* (New York: Harper Collins, 1994)

Weber, David J., *The Spanish Frontier in North America* (New Haven: Yale University Press, 1992)

Wickwire, Franklin & Mary, *Cornwallis and the War of Independence* (Northampton: The History Book Club, 1970)

Wilkie, Everett C., 'New Light on Gálvez's First Attempt to Attack Pensacola', *The Florida Historical Quarterly*, vol.62, no.2 (1983), pp.194–199

Worcester, Donald E., 'Miranda's Diary of the Siege of Pensacola, 1781', *The Florida Historical Quarterly*, vol.29, no.3 (1951), pp.163–196

Wright, James Leich, *William Augustus Bowles, Director General of the Creek nation* (Athens: University of Georgia Press, 1967)

From Reason to Revolution – Warfare 1721-1815

http://www.helion.co.uk/series/from-reason-to-revolution-1721-1815.php

The 'From Reason to Revolution' series covers the period of military history 1721–1815, an era in which fortress-based strategy and linear battles gave way to the nation-in-arms and the beginnings of total war.

This era saw the evolution and growth of light troops of all arms, and of increasingly flexible command systems to cope with the growing armies fielded by nations able to mobilise far greater proportions of their manpower than ever before. Many of these developments were fired by the great political upheavals of the era, with revolutions in America and France bringing about social change which in turn fed back into the military sphere as whole nations readied themselves for war. Only in the closing years of the period, as the reactionary powers began to regain the upper hand, did a military synthesis of the best of the old and the new become possible.

The series will examine the military and naval history of the period in a greater degree of detail than has hitherto been attempted, and has a very wide brief, with the intention of covering all aspects from the battles, campaigns, logistics, and tactics, to the personalities, armies, uniforms, and equipment.

Submissions

The publishers would be pleased to receive submissions for this series. Please contact series editor Andrew Bamford via email (andrewbamford@helion.co.uk), or in writing to Helion & Company Limited, Unit 8 Amherst Business Centre, Budbrooke Road, Warwick, CV34 5WE

Titles

No 1   *Lobositz to Leuthen: Horace St Paul and the Campaigns of the Austrian Army in the Seven Years War 1756-57* (Neil Cogswell)

No 2   *Glories to Useless Heroism: The Seven Years War in North America from the French journals of Comte Maurés de Malartic, 1755-1760* (William Raffle (ed.))

No 3   *Reminiscences 1808-1815 Under Wellington: The Peninsular and Waterloo Memoirs of William Hay* (Andrew Bamford (ed.))

No 4   *Far Distant Ships: The Royal Navy and the Blockade of Brest 1793-1815* (Quintin Barry)

No 5   *Godoy's Army: Spanish Regiments and Uniforms from the Estado Militar of 1800* (Charles Esdaile and Alan Perry)

No 6   *On Gladsmuir Shall the Battle Be! The Battle of Prestonpans 1745* (Arran Johnston)

No 7   *The French Army of the Orient 1798-1801: Napoleon's Beloved 'Egyptians'* (Yves Martin)

No 8   *The Autobiography, or Narrative of a Soldier: The Peninsular War Memoirs of William Brown of the 45th Foot* (Steve Brown (ed.))

No 9   *Recollections from the Ranks: Three Russian Soldiers' Autobiographies from the Napoleonic Wars* (Darrin Boland)

No 10 *By Fire and Bayonet: Grey's West Indies Campaign of 1794* (Steve Brown)

No 11 *Olmütz to Torgau: Horace St Paul and the Campaigns of the Austrian Army in the Seven Years War 1758-60* (Neil Cogswell)

No 12 *Murat's Army: The Army of the Kingdom of Naples 1806-1815* (Digby Smith)

No 13 *The Veteran or 40 Years' Service in the British Army: The Scurrilous Recollections of Paymaster John Harley 47th Foot – 1798-1838* (Gareth Glover (ed.))

No 14 *Narrative of the Eventful Life of Thomas Jackson: Militiaman and Coldstream Sergeant, 1803-15* (Eamonn O'Keeffe (ed.))

No.15 *For Orange and the States: The Army of the Dutch Republic 1713-1772 Part I: Infantry* (Marc Geerdinck-Schaftenaar)

No 16 *Men Who Are Determined to be Free: The American Assault on Stony Point, 15 July 1779* (David C. Bonk)

No 17 *Next to Wellington: General Sir George Murray: The Story of a Scottish Soldier and Statesman, Wellington's Quartermaster General* (John Harding-Edgar)

No 18 *Between Scylla and Charybdis: The Army of Elector Friedrich August of Saxony 1733-1763 Part I: Staff and Cavalry* (Marco Pagan)

No 19 *The Secret Expedition: The Anglo-Russian Invasion of Holland 1799* (Geert van Uythoven)

No 20 *'We Are Accustomed to do our Duty': German Auxiliaries with the British Army 1793-95* (Paul Demet)

No 21 *With the Guards in Flanders: The Diary of Captain Roger Morris 1793-95* (Peter Harington (ed.))